COMMANDER OF THE KARTERIA

COMMANDER OF THE KARTERIA

Honoured in Greece. Unknown at home.

Maurice Abney-Hastings

authorHOUSE®

AuthorHouse™
1663 Liberty Drive
Bloomington, IN 47403
www.authorhouse.com
Phone: 1-800-839-8640

© 2011 by Maurice Abney-Hastings. All rights reserved.

No part of this book may be reproduced, stored in a retrieval system, or transmitted by any means without the written permission of the author.

First published by AuthorHouse   06/13/2011

ISBN: 978-1-4567-8315-0 (sc)
ISBN: 978-1-4567-8320-4 (dj)
ISBN: 978-1-4567-8321-1 (ebk)

Printed in the United States of America

Any people depicted in stock imagery provided by Thinkstock are models, and such images are being used for illustrative purposes only.
Certain stock imagery © Thinkstock.

This book is printed on acid-free paper.

Because of the dynamic nature of the Internet, any web addresses or links contained in this book may have changed since publication and may no longer be valid. The views expressed in this work are solely those of the author and do not necessarily reflect the views of the publisher, and the publisher hereby disclaims any responsibility for them.

Contents

Introduction and Acknowledgements 1
Foreword 7
List of Illustrations 11
Chapter 1: 1794-1805; Early Life 13
Chapter 2: 1805-1822; British Naval Career 18
Chapter 3: The Ottoman Empire and Greek Revolution 34
Chapter 4: 1822; Arrival on Hydra and actions on
    'Thermistocles' 53
Chapter 5: 1822-1823; Nauplio and actions on 'Leonidas' 72
Chapter 6: Byron and The London Greek Committee 86
Chapter 7: 1824-1826; London and construction of the
    'Perseverance' 111
Chapter 8: 1826; 'Karteria' 129
Chapter 9: 1827: January to June 143
Chapter 10: 1827: July to December 163
Chapter 11: 1828: January to April 183
Chapter 12: 1828: May to June and the Aftermath 200
Chapter 13: Legacy 214
Appendix 1 219
Preface 221
Memoir 223
Notes 237
Appendix 2: Graphology Report by the late Patricia Marne,
    Graphologist, Essex, England 245
Appendix 3: Details of Personalities Mentioned in the Book 247
Index 257

Introduction and Acknowledgements

When this was originally written in 1985 the world was so different. No e-mails, only archaic computers, beer was around £1 a pint, there was no such thing as a "blog", and how did we get around without Sat-Nav? My business life dictated that the manuscript lurked in a black hole under the stairs for nearly a quarter of a century until semi-retirement allowed me to dust off the curly-edged paper. Most of what I had done as a much younger man was perfectly reusable, as was the original Introduction. I hope they will forgive me, but I have lost contact with many of those I thanked, having moved at about that time from Hampshire up to Warwickshire.

Plouha. Cotes du Nord. France. April 1985

Captain Frank Abney Hastings is an unknown name to any in England other than a handful of scholars and historians. To the Greeks he still remains a hero of their nation.

To write a book on such a subject has been a fascinating exercise in research and has provided the author with several opportunities to work in the country for which Captain Frank lived and died. It has been a work where many have been involved, and my gratitude goes to all of them—I am sure that those whom space does not allow me to personalise my thanks will forgive me. Many authors and historians have been studied in presenting this biography, but four stand out above the others; Finlay and Gordon, both participants in the Greek Wars of Independence, and the modern "historian" Douglas Dakin and C.M. Woodhouse.

Maurice Abney-Hastings

The idea for the book came from the late Right Honourable the Countess of Loudoun, Lady Barbara Abney-Hastings, who was invited to Greece as the head of the family in 1971 for the 150th Celebrations of the Greek Wars of Independence (1821-1833). Lady Loudoun helped with research and contacts, and she and her late husband, Peter, provided constant encouragement and assistance. I was extremely grateful for their involvement I must record my gratitude to the Management Committee of the British School at Athens for electing me as a student, and allowing me to work in their extensive library and enabling me to access the fragile ship's log kept by Captain Frank. Dr Roger Just and his staff at the library were more than helpful, but a special mention must be given to Professor Joan Hussey of Cambridge University who worked at the School for many years annotating and publishing a record of the Finlay and Hastings papers.

Assistance was given by many other bodies including the Huntingdon Library in California, the National Historical Museum and the Benaki Museum in Athens for which I thank them. So many individuals have provided many small favours without which this work would not have been possible.

In Athens the mainstay of research was the Historical Families Association through their President John Delyannis and his charming wife. Thanks to my kinship with Captain Frank, I, like my sister before me, was elected as a member. Most of the names, including Delyannis itself, of those in this book have been encountered by me in Greece as members of the Association. One family in particular, that of the historian Dimacopoulos, has given both help and friendship. Without the assistance of his daughter, Lilica, herself an historian of repute (she now edits a national newspaper, Estia) the validity of this work would certainly be less.

To you all, those mentioned and many others, I am completing this work in Plouha, Cote du Nord in France, with you in my thoughts.

Maurice Abney-Hastings

Now I return to the 21st Century! Life is so different nearly 25 years on, but thankfully the events of history remain static. Of course, turning a dusty old manuscript into a book has required a great deal of help and encouragement, but where to start?

As always, family encouragement is required and I have certainly received this from my son and four daughters. But without my friends the completion would not have been possible! To Peter Pritchard, gratitude for the hours spent over dusty papers, maps and charts, old and new. Also thanks to Dianne Williams, who has acted as research assistant, read, amended, edited the manuscript and made suggestions and contributions throughout the last eighteen months.

In the little Warwickshire town in which I live, there have been several supportive friends including Mihael Mavrommatis, who helped with the interpretation of old place names and also undertaking the odd translation; Rita and Mike Lindegren, Andy Mitchell and David Henderson—many thanks for your suggestions and support, especially with the preparation of the presentation.

One great supporter of the whole project is local historian and Curator of the Ashby de la Zouch Museum, Kenneth Hillier. He has agreed to arrange an exhibition in June 2011 about Captain Frank, only two miles from the family home of the Greek hero.

I have returned to Greece twice in the last two years in order to update the original manuscript and obtain visual material for the book. The people we met in Greece were absolutely marvellous and without their help, life would not only have been less fruitful but much less enjoyable! I hope that I do not miss anybody, so here goes!

I wish to thank the Reverend Canon Malcolm Bradshaw of St Paul's Anglican Church Athens, where Captain Frank's heart is immured. His memorial is close to that of Richard Church with whom he argued so much during their campaigns but between whom there was enormous respect.

Special thanks go to Mr Nicolai Voulgaris, a previous Mayor and Nomarch, and his interpreter Constantine Alexandris, who were so helpful when I visited Messolongi Mr Voulgaris explained the importance of Captain Frank and his actions when he drove the Turks from the island of Vasiladhi. Mr Voulgaris showed me the impressive monument in the Garden of Heroes and a portrait in the Museum.

Thanks the academic staff of the National Historical Museum, Athens. They provided me with copies from their archives and were extremely helpful. Thanks go to the British School at Athens for assistance, encouragement and hospitality. The Director, Professor Cathy Morgan, proved to be a mine of information about everything Greek; the School Secretary, Helen Clarke MBE, arranged valuable meetings and contacts that without her it is quite possible a second trip would have been required; the Archivist, Amalia Kakissis, who was invaluable in accessing collections and records. Sincere thanks to you all at the BSA.

I need to thank Captain Dimostheris Fanourgiakis HN, commanding officer of the Hellenic Naval Training base on the island of Poros where Captain Frank is buried. He greeted me with great honour and allowed me to visit Captain Frank's monument on the site of the old battery.
.
Thanks also to Vice-Admiral John Paloubis HN (Rtd), Trustee, and to Mrs Anastasia Anagnostopoulou—Paloubis, Director of the Hellenic Maritime Museum, Piraeus. The Museum has a model of the *Karteria*.

Sincere thanks to Dimitri Capaitzis, maritime historian, senior marine engineer and ship broker. He mentored and guided me throughout both visits to Greece and introduced me to many other interesting people. Especial thanks to Telemaque Maratos, President, and Spyros Nicolaou, Secretary, of the Society for the Study of Hellenic History for their interest, hospitality and support. Especially I must express my gratitude for the invitation to present Captain Frank to members of the Society and invited guests at the Old Parliament on 27th March 2009.

To any I have forgotten, my apologies, but to all involved with me over a 25 year period, my gratitude.

To those who wish to have updates about Captain Frank, visit www.captainfrank.co.uk.

Maurice Abney-Hastings
Warwickshire—October 2010

Foreword

Frank Abney Hastings is one of a small group of people who occupy a rather peculiar niche in history: nowadays virtually unknown in his own country, Hastings remains a national hero in another. His story might have been very different.

Born in 1794, the descendant of two wealthy and ancient landed families from Leicestershire and Derbyshire, the Abneys and the Hastings, and son of a military man, General Sir Charles Hastings,Frank was sent at the tender age of eleven years to join the Royal Navy as a Volunteer First class on his Majesty's Sloop, the '*Neptune*' in Admiral Lord Nelson's fleet. On the 20th October 1805, still only eleven years old, Frank saw action in the Battle of Trafalgar.

Over the next fourteen years his rise within the navy was swift. He sailed for another year on the 'Neptune' under his hero, Captain Freemantle, patrolling the Mediterranean; in 1806 he joined the crew of the 'Seahorse' under Captain Stewart, again patrolling the Mediterranean, and was officially appointed Midshipman in 1808; in 1810 he joined the 'Victory', flagship of Admiral Saumarez' Baltic Fleet, on which he served until 1812 as Senior Midshipman; then, between 1812 and 1818 he served off the coast of the Americas on a series of vessels—the 'San Domingo' the 'Atalante', the 'Anaconda', the 'Elk' and the 'Pelican'—taking temporary command of the 'Elk' and being appointed Lieutenant on the 'Pelican'. Importantly, while serving on the 'Anaconda' he also commanded land forces as an artillery man in the disastrous Battle of New Orleans which convinced him of the futility of attacking land forces without heavy artillery—a lesson he would put to good use a decade later. Finally, in January of 1919, still aged only 24, he received command of his first ship, the 'Kangaroo'. Frank Hastings naval career seemed assured. Some people—no doubt fondly—were even talking of another Collingwood or Nelson. And then disaster struck.

On the 18th June 1819, while entering the harbour of Port Royal, Jamaica, Hastings overlaid his anchor cable on top of the cable of the fleet's flagship, the 'Iphizerea'. It was a mistake, and he could have expected to be reprimanded, but unfortunately the 'Iphizerea's' captain, Hyde Parker, hailed him within everyone's earshot, calling him a 'damned lubber' and yelling that he ought to be ashamed of himself. Frank promptly handed over command of the 'Kangaroo' and challenged his superior officer to a duel. He was duly charged with insubordination and his name removed from the List of Commissioned officers—and that was the end of Frank's career in the Royal Navy.

At twenty-five years of age Frank Abney Hastings was thus left (fairly literally) a loose cannon: trained (one might almost say bred) to be a warrior; equipped with the experience of fourteen years' active service in the Royal Navy; endowed with a substantial personal fortune; and possessed (as would soon become apparent) with a sense of adventure and a yearning for a cause—but with nothing to do, or at least nothing to do in his native England or for his native England. In 1820 he thus took himself into self-imposed exile in France, first to Normandy where he had friends, later to Paris and then Marseilles. There he found his cause and his employment, for in 1821 the Greek War of Independence broke out—a cause that was beguiling adventurers, idealists, romantics (and not a few scoundrels) from every part of Western Europe. And so in March 1821, for a fee of fifty pounds paid in gold, Frank Hastings set sail with his friend, George Jarvis, son of an American diplomat, aboard a Swedish brig bound for the island of Hydra to fight for the liberation of Greece.

This is the story that Maurice Abney Hastings follows in his book. I doubt that any wars are particularly glorious on the ground, and wars of liberation are no exception. Had the Greek War of Independence been fought in the twentieth century rather the nineteenth, we would be talking about 'ethnic cleansing' on both sides. But amongst the cruelty, barbarity, confusion, incompetence, treachery and naked pursuit of booty and power, there were also acts of bravery, self-sacrifice and even gallantry. As a professional soldier, an officer and very much a gentleman, it is with the latter that Frank's name can be associated. And certainly it was a war that involved him with a cast of larger than life characters: the Greek politicians and leaders, Kapodistrias and Mavrokordatos; the war lords Odysseus and Kolokotronis; the writer and historian, George Finlay; the wily and venal Admiral Lord Cochrane (a fellow soldier of fortune who went on to fight for the liberation of Chile, Bolivia and Peru); and of course Lord Byron with his preposterous helmet, robes (and money).

On their arrival in Hydra, Frank and his American friend, Jarvis, were not exactly welcomed. Marvrokordatos and the Greeks were suspicious. Conversely, it is hard to imagine a man more temperamentally at odds with his Greek fellows-at-arms than Hastings: austere, punctilious, methodical (though prickly when it came to matters of personal reputation)—indeed, more than a little priggish. He was appalled by the Greek sailors' lack of discipline; he was appalled by their treatment of prisoners; he was appalled by their naval tactics; and he was particularly appalled by the state of their equipment. He set about rectifying the latter two failings, and although he might not have seemed destined to be a popular man with the rank and file, his improvements to the Greeks' artillery, his tactical use of fire-ships, and above all his conspicuous acts of personal bravery won him not only success but a good measure of popular admiration. But his greatest contribution was perhaps as a technical innovator. Mindful of the British defeat at New Orleans, he saw heavy artillery as the answer to besieging fortifications, and that meant a new form of vessel—steam-ships that could fire hot cannon. He persuaded the Greek government to purchase two steam driven paddle-ships, contributing the amount of £5,000 from his own pocket towards the first, with six more to follow, and in 1824 he returned to Britain to oversee their construction. In the event only four were built (due to a misappropriation of funds), and three of those were seriously delayed and never performed properly. But in

1826 Hasting returned to Greece as commander (that was a condition of his participation) of the revolutionary vessel, the 'Perseverance', soon to be rechristened the 'Karteria', under which name it entered the mythology of Greece.

The 'Karteria's' success was phenomenal. It pulverized the Turkish land forces besieging Athens (although the Greek army was unable to lift the siege); it captured and destroyed a Turkish brig-of-war and four schooners at Trikeri near Volos; it sank the Turkish admiral's brig and captured three Austrian vessels at Salona; it captured the fortress of Vasiladhi near Messolongi. Hastings and his 'fire-ship', the Karteria, became national heroes. And then, on 25th May 1828, with the Greek War of Independence virtually concluded, Hastings was hit by musket fire in the left arm. At first the wound was considered minor. It was not. Hastings died ten days later at the age of thirty-four.

Ordinary Greek sailors who had served under him arranged the first of his many funerals held on Egina. His body was then preserved in brandy and a year later the Government of Greece held his official burial ceremony on Poros. One hundred years later the Government of Greece struck commemorative medals bearing his likeness and with the words 'Greece grateful 1828-1928', while streets in Athens and Piraeus still bear his name. Perhaps Frank Abney Hastings might have become another Collingwood or Nelson; perhaps he might have gone to a quiet grave in rural England (although that seems unlikely). But a fouled anchor set him on the path to become a hero of Greece, and perhaps this book will make both his adventures and misadventures and the history of which they form part a little better known in Britain.

Roger Just
Professor of Anthropology
Eliot College
University of Kent at Canterbury

List of Illustrations

1. a) Family Tree.
   b) Willesley Hall, 1901.
2. Passport as issued in Marseilles on 7th March, 1822; courtesy of The British School at Athens.
3. Portrait by Karl Krazeisen, 1828.
4. a) Daniel Brent's plan of The Perseverance; courtesy of the National Maritime Museum Archives, Greenwich, London.
   b) Layout of the Karteria from an original drawing by George Finlay.
5. Figurehead of The Karteria; courtesy of the National Historical Museum, Athens.
6. The Battle of Phaleron by Theophilos; courtesy of Evangelos Angelakos.
7. Hellas and Karteria by Krazeisen, 1828.
8. Pistols bequeathed by Hastings to Captain EH Scott RN; courtesy of Squadron Leader Darryl Plumridge.
9. Memorials to Hastings at Poros, Athens, and Mesolonghi.
10. a) Commemorative Medal, 1928; b).Commemorative Stamps, 1983; c) Model of the Karteria; courtesy of Hellenic Maritime Museum, Piraeus.

Chapter 1

1794-1805; Early Life

The lush pastures of the borders of Leicestershire and Derbyshire at the end of the eighteenth century were comfortable in the hands of two families, the Abneys and the Hastings, who had been there for five hundred years. The estates of the Hastings family stretched from Castle Donnington to Ashby de la Zouch and those of the Abneys from the borders of their illustrious neighbours south-west through Willesley to the village and manor of Measham.

A boy was born at Willesley on St. Valentine's Day in 1794 who was to be described by the Duke of Northumberland as having the potential of another Nelson or Collingwood; a boy who would go to sea at the age of eleven, serve at Trafalgar and eventually be the first person in maritime history to introduce a purpose-built steam warship into naval warfare. The child, Frank Abney Hastings, was to die in Greece at the age of thirty-four fighting for the cause of freedom against oppression. He is still remembered in that country as a naval officer who altered the course of their history allowing the foundation of a new nation.

An examination of the antecedents of the child is perhaps the only way in which to comprehend how a lad from such comfortable, rural surroundings should end his life serving for a foreign country and becoming a hero of that nation but almost unknown in his own. Although his early years at Willesley Hall were normal enough, his family certainly could not be described as anything other than extraordinary. If English mythology is to be believed even Robin Hood, reputed to be of the family which became the Earls of Huntingdon, was of the same ancestry as Frank Abney Hastings who was a direct descendent of the first Earl of Huntingdon.

Frank Abney Hastings was the son of General Sir Charles Hastings, the natural son of Francis, the tenth Earl of Huntingdon, after whom he was named. The Hastings family has a long ancestry dating back to the Norman conquest of England and has direct descent from the Plantagenet kings of England. The family fortunes were always closely linked to the royal court and changed with the political and religious climates of the time.

Frank's mother was Parnell Abney. She came from a family which, whilst not as high ranking as that of Hastings, was certainly one of the oldest in the land. Their records show a John d'Albeny as receiving lands from William the Conqueror, and have been kept since that time. The estates of Willesley, which bordered immediately on the Packington lands inherited by Charles Hastings, had passed into the hands of John Abeney in 1310. The parents of Parnell were a judge, Sir Thomas Abney, and Lady Parnell who, in her own right as an heiress to the Villiers' family, possessed great wealth. The gallant soldier, member of the Hastings family and owner of adjoining lands, must have seemed the ideal match for their daughter.

The marriage settlement brought with it the Willesley Estate, near Ashby de la Zouch, and to describe the young couple, who took up residence there after their marriage in 1790, as comfortably placed would be an extreme understatement. Charles Hastings spent considerable time refurbishing the house and estate.

Their eldest son, Charles, was born in 1792 and Frank in 1794. The two boys lived a very happy life surrounded by the magnificent countryside, and being quartered in the nursery wing of Willesley Hall overlooking the stable block, the woods, the tumble-down water-mill and the lake.

The older of the two, Charles, was a bookish child and never really became close to his more energetic and adventurous brother Frank. This must have displeased the father whose own life was as a professional soldier and man of action. He certainly looked more kindly upon the younger son's manner. Frank was never happier than when hunting for hare in the woods around the estate in the company of the woodsmen and their children.

Many of the traits seen in Frank Abney Hastings come from his illustrious ancestors; his sense of duty and loyalty, his hatred of oppression, his caring for those beneath him in social rank, his slightly puritanical trait and, perhaps most common throughout this remarkable family, an outward coolness and aloofness hiding great feelings of emotion. Like so many before him, Frank was to show on many occasions that his own personal feelings and prejudices were stronger than the will of authority. He was always aware that the Earl of Huntingdon was his grandfather and his own line was secured in heraldic terms by the awarding of an Abney-Hastings coat-of-arms in 1806. His financial life was equally secured by the wisdom of his mother, Parnell, who, while agreeing in the terms of her marriage settlement that the lands should go to the normal male line, made provision from her personal fortune for female and younger male children.

About the time that General Hastings received his Knighthood, he discussed the future of his sons with his close cousin, Sir Francis Rawdon. It was agreed that the nature and temperament of young Frank indicated a naval career was one to which he was likely to be most suited. By adopting a course which meant spending much of his life out of England, Frank would be unlikely to eclipse any sporting or political career activities of his elder brother, Charles. An approach was made to a mutual friend, Captain Thomas Freemantle, at that time commanding His Majesty's Sloop the *Neptune* in the fleet of Admiral Lord Nelson.

After a season of energetic fox-hunting, the decision was announced on Frank's eleventh birthday, 14th February 1805 that he was to be sent to Portsmouth to join the Royal Navy as a Volunteer First Class.

A few weeks later he was loaded into a carriage and waved sadly off by his mother, a little girl called Eliza Harriet Moore who had been adopted by the family, and by the many estate workers and their children who were so disappointed to see the departure of the lively and attractive child. General Hastings decided to visit Portsmouth not only to accompany his eleven year old son to join his first ship but also to gather intelligence reports on the French situation.

Frank's mother, with whom he was a definite favourite, must have been heartbroken to see her small son leave the comfort and safety of Willesley Hall with her husband, not knowing when—and if indeed—he would return. Even the journey to Portsmouth was an adventure for the boy. They sometimes stayed in the gracious homes of friends and, if that was not convenient, stayed at coaching inns. In all, the journey took six days. Portsmouth at the time was a hubbub of activity—marines, sailors and the ladies of the town milling around; press gangs returning from their forays into the country dragging their unfortunate victims with them, and officers and gentlemen surveying the scene from their carriages.

Young Frank was taken to the naval outfitters to acquire the uniforms required by a volunteer mid-shipman, and to numerous other shops to obtain the items needed for his new career; medicines, some preserved foods; books to continue his general education and to start that of navigation, and the instruments of that art.

In Portsmouth Dockyard ships were crammed in and swarmed over by hundreds of carpenters and shipwrights. The condition of many of the vessels was poor after months of blockading the channel, or crossing the Atlantic from bases in the West Indies. Older vessels were being carefully broken up to utilise the timbers, now in short supply since the American Revolution (1776-1783) and the wood taken to use on those ships being repaired. One of the most important members of the team was the caulker, whose job it was to replace the oakum between the seams in an effort to make the wooden hulls watertight.

The rush was almost one of panic. The '*Victory*' had sailed with most of the fleet six weeks earlier, and was chasing the French Admiral

Villeneuve to the West Indies and back. It was of paramount importance to strengthen the fleet and put pay to any plans by Napoleon to invade England.

Young Frank Hastings could never have seen such sights and must have experienced emotions of both fear and elation at his first sight of the 'Neptune'. She was a 2nd Class Battleship, built in Deptford in 1796 (launched on 28th January 1797), and had just been completely refitted. At 185 ft in length, with 51 ft in maximum beam, she was probably the largest vessel in harbour in April 1805. The 'Neptune' carried a total of ninety eight guns, comprising twenty eight 32-pounders, twenty eight 18-pounders and forty two 12-pounders—an impressive and mighty fighting machine in the eyes of an eleven year old boy. The 'Neptune" was not dissimilar in size to the 'Victory', being only one foot shorter in length but in fact having slightly greater weight. Even today, to a small boy, HMS 'Victory' at Portsmouth is awe-inspiring—without the knowledge of battle looming ahead.

Equally awe-inspiring must have been Frank's first Captain, under whom he was to serve for nineteen months, Thomas Francis Freemantle. Although the Captain was short in stature, with a rotund appearance and had somewhat rustic features, he had an aura of strength and power commented upon by those who met him. His demeanour was certainly enhanced by the knowledge that he was one of Nelson's closest friends and confidants. Perhaps Freemantle sympathised with Frank, having himself joined the Navy at the age of 12 in 1775 from his country home at Aston Abbotts in Buckinghamshire.

Chapter 2

1805-1822; British Naval Career

General Hastings had taught his son well, and the boy knew all the details of the brave and heroic deeds of his new master. Nelson had failed to locate Villeneuve's French fleet in the West Indies, and was obliged, after a fruitless voyage, to return to Europe with all haste only to learn that the French had taken refuge in the harbour of Cadiz on the south-west Atlantic coast of Spain.

'Neptune' had reached the Cadiz station slightly before Nelson, and on September 29th Captain Freemantle wrote to General Hastings. The letter contained much of interest, and as far as the author can ascertain, this is the first time of publication, other than as a report on manuscripts of Reginald Hastings of Ashby de la Zouch in 1934:

"1805, Sept. 29. <u>Neptune</u> *off Cadiz—*
". . . . This same sort of life is very wearing to the spirits, every day is almost alike; we stand in towards Cadiz, look at the French and Spanish fleets and then stand off again. Lord Nelson arrived here this day but as yet we have had no intercourse with him, as it was late before he joined. We shall now be quite strong enough for everything in Cadiz, and indeed can afford to detach some ships to the Mediterranean, which I suppose will be the case if we are to act with the Russians. The weather here is delightful, only a little too warm, but we shall not have that to complain of a month or six weeks hence. I don't think politics seems much altered since I left town, I mean domestic ones. My good friend Lord Nelson is looking better than ever I saw him in

my Life, and has gratified me by giving me my old station with him, namely his second, which is infinitely more pleasant than being more astern. We have a very fine fleet here, and you may rely the French and Spaniards will not attempt moving whilst we can keep off the ports. Sir Robert Calder is going home and writes himself for a court martial. He is really so good a man, and so fair to serve with, that I take a warm interest in this affair and hope he will come off with credit, although I certainly have my fears. Here we shall remain until the French fleet escape in some dark, windy night, and indeed we are much better off than serving in the Channel at this time of year. Of your boy I can say nothing but what ought to make you and Mrs. Hastings very happy. He is very mild and tractable, attentive to his books, and dashing when with the youngsters of his own age. I declare that I have never once had occasion to hint even anything to him, as he is so perfectly well behaved. I hope to get to Gibraltar some of these days. The sight of such a place will amuse the boys so much. If you have an opportunity, write to General Fox about him, as he can then be on shore two or three days. I think if you were to see the Neptune you would find her very much altered since you were on board. We are now scraping the ship's sides in order to paint it like the Victory. The fellows make such a noise I can scarcely hear myself."

The English fleet grew as more ships arrived from Portsmouth, and on the morning of 20th October, 1805 the two mighty fleets were in sight of each other with Nelson's being off the Cape of Trafalgar. To Frank Hastings, volunteer, age 11 years, it was the first taste of action where at last he would see his idol, Freemantle, in action.

The combined French and Spanish fleets were in a north-south crescent, and the English Fleet headed towards them in two columns from the west. Nelson was in command of the northernmost column, and Admiral Collingwood of the southernmost in his flagship the 'Royal Sovereign'. 'Neptune' was in the northern column lying immediately behind 'Victory' in line with 'Temeraire' and 'Euryalus'.

By noon Collingwood came within gunshot of the Spanish flagship, 'Santa Ana' in the south, and a half hour later 'Victory' was in range of the French. A holocaust of bombardment raged, but inch by inch the English Fleet broke through the enemy lines. Virtually every ship was damaged. At 13:00 the *'Neptune'* was hit in the powder store and almost lost. Frank Hastings was praised for his part in quelling the fires. At 13:15 Nelson was hit by a musket ball and calmly carried below to avoid any panic. By 14:30 Admiral Villeneuve had surrendered his flagship, the *'Bucentaure'*. By 16:30, victory was clear. Many enemy ships had been sunk, others had fled whilst more were still being taken as prizes by the English. During this time the Admiral Lord Nelson died.

The first naval battle of Frank Abney Hastings has been perhaps the most important of all times. His whole life was to be affected by the glorious action of Trafalgar and he had acquitted himself with great gallantry.

The next year was something of an anti-climax. The *'Neptune'*, under Freemantle, spent her time patrolling the Mediterranean station. In autumn, 1806, the *'Neptune'* returned home, and Freemantle entered Parliament as the Member for Sandwich and was appointed as a Lord of the Admiralty. This great man, who so influenced Hastings, subsequently became a Baronet, a Rear Admiral, K.C.B and Commander-in-Chief of the Channel Islands. In 1818 he was given the Mediterranean command based in Naples. A year later, after receiving his G.C.B, Freemantle died suddenly in Italy and was honoured with a State funeral.

Frank had left the *'Neptune* on her return to Portsmouth in 1806, and joined the vessel of another of his father's friends, the *'Seahorse'*. Rated as Class 5, the *'Seahorse'* was almost as long as *'Neptune'* (146 ft), but much lighter and less beamy. She carried thirty-eight guns, twenty-eight 18-pounders, two 12-pounders and eight 9-pounders but she was fast and seaworthy. Again Frank found himself stationed in the Mediterranean but this time under Captain John Stewart. It is interesting to note that while Stewart was not considered an excessive disciplinarian, he recorded any punishments which by today's standards would be considered barbaric. These actions would certainly have been witnessed by Frank as it was often the duty of the midshipmen to count the number of lashes given. An example is the following entry in the Captain's Log, 1807—*"Sailed Thursday 8th January*

15th January punished:
Dennis Malcolm	—	*24 lashes for insolence*
Hugh Roger	—	*12 lashes for drinking and neglect*
George Young	—	*12 lashes for drinking and neglect*
Peter Cunningham	—	*12 lashes for drinking and neglect*
David Isaacs	—	*12 lashes for drinking and neglect*
3 marines	—	*12 lashes for drinking and neglect*

Then sailed south"

Despite these incidents, the 'Seahorse' was a happy ship, and spent most of her duty between Toulon and the Ionian Islands. The enemy varied between the French Fleets sailing to and from Corfu, and the marauding Turks in the East. Apart from occasional skirmishes little of note occurred and young Frank had time to study navigation and gunnery in which he had a passionate interest. The only real action was when the 'Seahorse' attacked two Turkish men-of-war much larger than herself, drove one off and captured the other, the 'Badra Zaffer'

Many letters to General Hastings confirmed that his son Frank was a dedicated young Naval Officer, and it was the Duke of Northumberland writing from Alnwick Castle who said of Frank:

"I hope he likes the sea as well as ever, and flatter myself that he will in time prove another Collingwood. I should have said Nelson, but that I would prefer his being a great living naval Character to a dead one".

In the many reports and letters from Captain Stewart to General Hastings, he records his delight in having such an able young man aboard. In 1808 he was able to announce the official appointment of Frank Abney Hastings as a Midshipman. Although Freemantle had been Frank's hero, it was certainly his time on 'Seahorse' under John Stewart which taught him his profession during his three and a half years aboard.

It would have been with some relief, however, that he learned that the halcyon days in the Mediterranean were coming to an end, and that he was being transferred to the '*Victory*' on the Baltic station as Senior Midshipman.

Admiral Saumarez had accepted command of the Baltic Fleet in 1808 aboard the flagship '*Victory*', on which he had served thirty years previously as a Lieutenant. Although Saumarez had never received the acclaim of his fellow officers, such as Hood, Collingwood, or Nelson, he was praised for his Baltic work and negotiations with the Russians. Frank spent two years aboard the '*Victory*' under Saumarez. He does not appear to have created a great impression upon him, perhaps due to the rather shifty, pompous bearing of his commander. Frank left the '*Victory*' on 31st January, 1812, after almost seven years of continuous service, and took nine months of what must have been well-earned leave.

He naturally spent some time at his home in Willesley Hall, but with most of his formative years at sea he found little in common with his friends, and in particular with his elder brother Charles. Much of his leave was spent in London pouring over records of artillery research, visiting the Ordnance factories and even passing time at the Carron armaments factory in Scotland.

Between October 1812 and May 1813 he sailed aboard the 3rd Rated vessel '*San Domingo*' off the American coast under no less than three Captains—Gill, Thompson and Pichell—before transferring to the eighteen-gun sloop '*Atalante*'. Under the bluff Captain Fred Hickey, Frank Hastings was very happy. At last he was sailing with a small crew and able to use his own authority. The pleasure declined as the autumn gales, and winter cold of the North Atlantic depressed all aboard. By early November the crew were half-frozen each time they came on deck to change sail, and the morale of the ship fell.

On 8th November, 1813, Captain Hickey decided conditions were too poor to remain at sea and headed with great difficulty into the monstrous seas for Halifax in Nova Scotia. Much of the rigging was torn away by the green seas washing over the decks and one by one the seams of the ship sprang leaks. For nearly two days the slow progress to Halifax continued, until in sight of the harbour, the order came to lower the ship's boats. Fishermen and pilots alike from the harbour realised the trouble which the *'Atalante'* was experiencing and came out to assist but all efforts to take the sloop in tow failed. After hours of courageous strain, the task was abandoned, and the *'Atalante'* sank into the seas. Thankfully nobody was lost, although it is reported that several died later from cold and exposure.

A few days later the captured American Privateer, the *'Anaconda'*, entered port under the command of Captain George Westhall. Fortunately for Frank Hastings there was a vacancy on board for a Lieutenant, and he joined the 100 foot sloop on 24th November. She had been taken from the Americans only a few weeks earlier in Chesapeake Bay, and was under instructions to refit, and join the fleet gathering in the Gulf of Mexico.

During the next few months Lieutenant Hastings impressed Captain Westhall with both his command of men and his knowledge of artillery. It was natural that when the British decided upon an offensive against New Orleans in late 1814, Westhall should recommend Hastings to Sir Thomas Trowbridge, Commander-in-Chief of the Naval Brigade and Colonel Dixon, Commander of the Artillery. Frank found himself for the first time commanding forces on land—members of the Naval Brigade.

New Orleans, the chief port of the Gulf of Mexico, is at the entrance to the strategically important Mississippi Valley, and on December 13th the *'Anaconda'* was part of a fleet of fifty which anchored in Lake Borgne to the east of the city. Some 7,500 British troops under the overall command of Sir Edward Pakenham were landed, and many were veterans of the successful Peninsular campaign of the Napoleonic wars. The Naval Brigade, with one group under Frank Hastings, made a significant number of the fighting force.

The American area commander, General Andrew Jackson, had already established his troops in the fortified area of Baton Rouge expecting the British to move up the river. On learning of the landings, he moved some 5,000 men down to New Orleans. When the English forces were only seven miles from the city he checked their thrust with a night attack on December 23rd. Jackson then withdrew his troops two miles to Chalmette where he built defences of logs and cotton bales along the dried-out Rodriguez Canal.

On 8th January 1815, Pakenham advanced with 5,000 men on the American line and Hastings, with the Naval Brigade under Trowbridge, attacked the northern flank. The main body arrived first and experienced withering fire from the Tennessee and Kentucky Rifle Brigades. The Naval Brigade, hampered in the marshy ground around a cypress swamp, presented an easy target for the American artillery. The British fell back and regrouped, only to be spurred forward by their generals for a second assault which proved equally hopeless.

Within a short period of time the situation became obvious, and the invading troops scattered in disarray to regain possession of their anchored ships. In total the British had over 2,000 men killed and wounded including Pakenham and two other generals. The Americans lost only eight men and twelve wounded. To add to the British misery, when the troops retreated to their ships, they learned that the war had ended two weeks previously with the Peace of Ghent signed on 24th December 1814. Although the Peace Treaty did little more than finalise the war of 1812 as most of the issues had disappeared with the overthrow of Napoleon I, the battle did restore American pride in its own troops and made Andrew Jackson a national hero and later President of America.

To Frank Hastings the Battle of New Orleans demonstrated the futility of attacking established land forces with inadequate heavy armaments. He realised that for any chance of success in such an operation it was necessary to have a method of landing the heavier ships' guns using the long-boats.

The '*Anaconda*' remained in the West Indies for the next eighteen months until she was sold back to the Americans in June 1815. Frank returned to England, and after a short leave at both Willesley and at his father's town house in Harley Street, London, presented himself at Chatham as senior of four Lieutenants aboard H.M.S. *'Orlando'* under Captain Clavell. He was delighted to find that his boyhood friend, Edward Hinton Scott, had also joined the ship and they were bound for the East Indies and China Sea with the main duty of keeping the waters and harbours clear of pirates.

Shortly after their arrival on station further orders came for Hastings to take temporary command of H.M. Sloop *'Elk'*. This followed the sudden promotion of Captain John Reynolds to H.M.S. *'Cornwallis'* on the dismissal by court martial of Captain Robert O'Brian. Hastings commanded well, and on his return to England in May 1817 could well have looked forward to a permanent command. The system of favours and more settled, peaceful times acted against Frank. After a prolonged leave of over six months, spent again in Willesley and London, he was disappointed to learn that he had only been given a Lieutenant's post aboard the Cruizen Class Brig-Sloop *'Pelican'* under Captain the Earl of Curzon on the Jamaica station.

In December 1818, only one year later, he was back in London and turned to Lord Melville, the First Lord of the Admiralty and a friend of his father, for assistance:

"My Lord,

"I feel that in addressing your Lordship I am taking upon myself an unwarrantable liberty, perhaps no excuse can justify it. I throw myself on your Lordship's well known demeanour and trust that you will not attribute it to impertinence but an anxiety to attain that eminence in any profession which is the desire of every enterprising officer. Although fortune has not favoured the kind intentions your Lordship expressed towards me I am not less grateful, more particularly as I am sensible that neither the length nor merit of my services alone entitle me to expect preferment. Then the Marchioness of Hastings was so good as to offer me her intercession with Sir H. Blackwood, I made appreciation to your Lordship through Mr Hay for employment in the East Indies. Since then Sir H. Blackwood has informed me that 'twould

be impossible for him to render me any service having several relatives of his own to provide for this has emboldened me to solicit employment in the expedition your Lordship has planned to the Northward in a favourable season. If I am so happy as to enjoy your Lordship's good opinion sufficiently favourable to induce you to grant any request no exertion on my part shall be found wanting to qualify myself for this arduous undertaking. Till the period of sailing my labours shall be directed to the acquisition of such knowledge as is likely to prove serviceable. You may perhaps find those more capable, but none more devotedly willing to acquit themselves with credit".*

"Frank Hastings"

Whether Frank's next appointment had anything to do with the letter is not known, but a month later he received command of the *'Kangaroo'*, a survey brig purchased a few months previously, with instructions to deliver her to a survey officer in the West Indies. Frank Hastings had received his first command. The future looked good—served at Trafalgar, the Battle of New Orleans, well spoken of by all his Captains and experienced in all major areas of the world. Added to his specialist knowledge of artillery and the family connections, an observer could well have favoured a long and successful career for the twenty-four year old Commander. A fascinating series of letters between Warren Hastings and General Sir Charles Hastings lasting well over a decade showed the interest taken in Frank's career and many of the highest personages in the realm looked to him as a future senior naval commander.

Writing from his home at Daylesford House, Warren Hastings, one of the leading figures of the period, wrote:
"You will live to see your son standing on the summit of glory as a British Seaman. Sir Charles Imhoff tells me he never saw one so improved in knowledge, manners or manliness. I congratulate you and Lady Hastings on this proof of good, innate character, and of his attachment to his profession".

An incident on the evening of 18th June, 1819 brought all this to an end and paved the way to exile and service in a foreign cause. Running into the harbour of Port Royal, Jamaica, Hastings brought the *'Kangaroo'* to anchor between the brig *'Sheerwater'* and the flagship of Rear-Admiral Sir Home Popham, the *'Iphizerea'*. The captain of the flagship, Captain Parker, saw that the anchor cable of the *'Kangaroo'* had overlain his own, and was forced to veer out his own cable to prevent being dragged down upon Hastings' ship. This was certainly not an uncommon occurrence in the days of sail. Although Hastings would undoubtedly have anticipated a dressing-down for carrying too much sail whilst entering harbour, he did not anticipate Parker's response.

In Hastings' own words:
"He thought proper to hail me in a voice that rang through the whole of Port Royal, saying 'You have overlaid our anchor—you ought to be ashamed of yourself—you damned lubber, you—who are you?'"

Frank certainly over-reacted to this slight upon his character, and his seamanship and, after handing over command of the *'Kangaroo'* to the survey officer, sent a challenge to a duel to Captain Hyde Parker, whom he described as a rude and uncouth person. Parker wrote officially to the Admiral who called a court inquiry but to make matters worse Hastings refused to give evidence.

Sir Home Popham wrote to Hastings on 21st June—*"Captain Hyde Parker of H.M.S. 'Iphizerea' did by his letter to me of 20th Inst. represent that on this evening of 18th the 'Kangaroo' under your command was brought to anchor in a most unseamanlike manner forcing the 'Iphizereaon' on board of which was my flag flying, to sheer her cable as the only means of preventing the 'Kangaroo' getting athwart her hawse. In consequence of this representation I considered it was my duty to insist upon a Court Inquiry which was held this day on H.M.S. 'Sybille' for the purpose of inquiring into this and other parts of your conduct during the time you have been at Port Royal.*

The Court proceeded to execute my orders but they have represented to me that you have refused to answer any questions which the Court put to you re your conduct on the evening of 18th inst. I have therefore to request you will inform me on what ground you have refused to answer the questions alluded to"

Frank's reason was quite simple—he strongly felt that the question of his seamanship was entirely separate from that of issuing a challenge to Parker. After the incident and after he had handed over command of the *'Kangaroo'*, he specifically waited a couple of hours before calling for the duel. He was by then on half pay and decided this was the right time to issue the challenge. He felt, probably quite rightly, that if he had answered questions about the incident, the two matters would become interwoven, whereas he was prepared to answer criticisms of his seamanship first, and the affair of honour on a different occasion. Having been refused permission to return immediately to England on H.M.S. *'Tartar'* to present his case to Melville, despite requests from officers of that ship, he instead sent a letter with them to the Lords of the Admiralty:

"24th June 1819
"My Lords,

    "Being unable to passage on H.M.S. 'Tartar', and as no other vessel is about to proceed to England I beg leave to detail to your Lordships the circumstances which have led to an enquiry into my conduct. The officers' statements which go home in H.M.S. 'Tartar' will inform your Lordships of this unfortunate affair. As I have not seen them myself I feel that it will be necessary to intrude a little on your Lordships' time.

    When anchoring H.M. S.V. 'Kangaroo' at Port Royal late in the evening of the 18th. we drove near H.M.S. 'Iphizerea'.

    By her veering out a little Cable we were enabled to hold on clear of her. During the period that we were near the 'Iphizerea' Captain Hyde Parker hailed me in the most intemperate manner and said: 'You have overlaid our anchor—you ought to be ashamed of yourself—you damned lubber, you—who are you?'

    I have reason to suppose that Captain Parker was not on deck when we anchored and therefore could not be a judge whether we had overlaid her anchor or not, and as a proof that we had not done so we moored upon a good berth without even lifting our first anchor which I trust has been established by the Court of Inquiry.

When duty permitted me for a moment to reflect on the language used by Captain Parker my first impression was to apply for a Court Martial. I interrogated my officers, but the anxiety under which circumstances had placed them prevented their hearing the most material part of the language and consequently I felt that I ought to first establish the charge, and thus increase the enquiry I had already received, and it only remains now for me to appeal to the candour of your Lordship whether in the circumstances I was placed any other course remained than that which I pursued. There were officers of the Army on board who could not be ignorant from its publicity of the insult that had been offered one, and from my being on half-pay they would have construed forbearance into cowardice. Had I communicated to the Commander-in-Chief the language which had made use of, I feel persuaded it would have met his decided disapprobation, but whatever reprimand it called forth it would have been known to few whereas the insult was known to all. In fact the short time I had to deliberate left me no choice but that of disgracing in the eyes of the world the rank to which your Lordships had been pleased to appoint me, or of adopting the proceeding which has led to this explanation.

It now becomes necessary to explain to your Lordships that part of my conduct which relates to the Court of Inquiry, and endeavour to prevent its being suspected that I intended in the slightest degree to treat that court with disrespect. I beg therefore to relate on what grounds I declined answering any questions.

Early on the morning of 21st Inst,. I received a note from the Admiral's secretary making the Admiral's request that I should attend Sir George Collier on board the 'Tartar' who had been directed to enquire into my conduct, but it appearing to me that the inquiry combined so intimately the proceedings whilst I was employed and after I became on half-pay, as to prevent the possibility of their being separated. More particularly as no complaint had been made by Captain Parker until after I had resigned the command of the 'Kangaroo' I felt that I could not answer to any questions which related to the one without making myself responsible for the other, and on receiving a letter from the Admiral desiring me to report my reasons for such refusal. I distinctly stated that I was ready to submit to any inquiry which he might be pleased to direct into my conduct during my command of the 'Kangaroo'.

Having thus detailed to your Lordships the particulars of every circumstance which it has been the object of the Court of Inquiry to investigate I confidently rely upon the protection of your Lordships".

His confidence was misplaced and by the time he arrived back in England on September 6th a decision had already been made as to his future. Letters to General Sir Charles Hastings from his son, and back to Lord Melville were of little avail, and Melville wrote to Sir Charles:

"*I received the official report from the Admiral respecting the misconduct of your son in sending a challenge to the Captain of the Flag Ship because the latter reprimanded him (very deservedly as it appears from the report) for the manner in which he had brought his sloop to an anchor. There was some doubt as to his being on full pay and amenable to a Court Martial at the time of his conveyancing the challenge, and Sir Home Popham therefore submitted the whole matter to the board of the Admiralty. In a case of insubordination which under all circumstances was of so aggravated a nature there could be no question as to the duty imposed upon us, however much we might grieve, than being compelled of directing the name of Mr. Frank Hastings to be removed from the List of Commissioned Officers in the Navy*".

Unfortunately for Frank, his cousin and mentor, the Second Earl of Moira, along with his father had become involved with great political upheavals which had upset certain powerful people in Government. It was always Hastings' claim that the matter would have been less severely dealt with for any other officer. Pleas to re-open the case failed. Even Captain Parker and Sir Home Popham spoke for his reinstatement later.

Almost to the point of his final departure for France and Greece, Frank went on appealing, and although he had lost his records of service as Midshipman on the ill-fated '*Atalante*, all his other Captains wrote to Melville.

Edmund, Earl of Curzon wrote *"His public conduct did honour as an officer and private to be expected from a gentleman of birth"*. John Clavell under whom he had served on the *'Orlando'* stated *"He was seamanlike, gentlemanly and an exemplary officer"*.

Captain George Westhall of H.M.S. *'Anaconda'* wrote in great detail of his bravery during the Battle of New Orleans, and there is no record of any slight misdemeanour other than that at Port Royal. It was all to no avail and Frank Hastings was to go on to make a decision to take a major part in the birth of a nation, which would lead to his own death

Frank's father publicly supported him, as did his influential kinsmen, but certainly the involvement of Lord Moira with politics and the potential Government did little to help his cause. During the winter months of 1819 and early 1820 Frank lived in misery in his Leicester Square apartments. Frequently visiting the Admiralty to plead his case without success, he became more and more depressed—the dashing, popular young naval celebrity withdrew into his shell. The company of the racier, effete young men about town did not substitute for that of his sea-going friends with whom he had been so close. Even the frequent company of the ladies of London did little to alleviate his black moods. He used much of his time to write down his theories of gunnery and the work he did during this period was eventually to be used by Lord Byron and Lord Cochrane prior to publication in 1828 by Ridgeway. In the spring of 1820 Frank made the momentous decision to move to France.

In part this was caused by a genuine thirst for knowledge of the language and France's innovative development and techniques with artillery. He felt that even his own family had turned against him in the battle with the Lords of the Admiralty. This animosity was short-lived, as General Sir Charles Hastings wrote of Frank in his Will of 1823: *"As my youngest son, Frank Hastings, has been provided for by a clause in the Marriage Settlement I shall entrust him to the care of his mother and brother, and I grant him my blessing and entire forgivings"*.

An additional influence on his decision to move to France was a friendly acquaintance with a group of young writers, poets and disciples of Byron and in particular a French brother and sister, Maurice and Françoise Renée, who were in London to complete their education. The pair took Frank under their wing and invited him to spend summer 1820 at their father's home in Caen to perfect his knowledge of the French language. Having heard so many tales of his grandfather's time in that beautiful Norman capital, the decision came easily. Having settled his affairs in the City with his brother and paid his respects to his parents at Willesley, Hastings went into self-imposed exile, for undoubtedly this is how he regarded the gesture himself.

Life in the ancient city came easily. Charles Renée proved an admirable tutor of the language and the constant companionship of the two siblings brought forth a deep affection for them. The three young people were inseparable and it was clear to the father that he would shortly be able to welcome the exiled English aristocrat as a son-in-law. The summer ran into autumn and winter and, for the first time in the life of Frank Hastings his wanderings had ceased and been replaced by an inner peace never before, or later, to be observed.

During the hunting and balls of the winter, the tall fair-haired Englishman was popular. The elders of Caen saw in him the same linguistic and social skills of his grandfather, the 10th Earl of Huntingdon half a century earlier. Frank and Maurice assiduously studied literature and culture and were no less accomplished in the hunting field. A cloud came onto this blissful scene when Maurice developed a chest infection after one of their energetic outings at "la chasse". Shortly into the new year of 1821 this developed into tuberculosis. The young man declined in health, and on Frank's birthday, on February 14th 1821, Maurice Renée died. All the indications were that this date was to have seen the engagement between Frank and Françoise but the planned celebration was superseded by great misery for the family and for Frank.

His relationship with both Françoise and Charles, her father, deteriorated—perhaps they felt that Frank's love of hunting and the involvement of Maurice in his escapades were in part responsible for the illness and death. Having found peace and affection, Frank was once again plunged into despair and decided to move nearer to Paris to study French artillery methods. He never forgot the Renée family and five years later wrote in his Will:

"To Monsieur Charles Renée of Caen I bequeath £500 as a token of my affection for his deceased son".

Clearly a token of quite considerable proportions being the equivalent of five year's salary for a ship's officer and perhaps an indication of a feeling of guilt at his involvement with the death of Maurice.

Paris seemed to be the change Frank needed and he came into contact with many adventurers of no fixed abode. In particular he was to meet a brigandish young man who was to influence his future life, and death. Nicolas Kallergy, called Nicolo by his friends, was a swarthy Greek, born in Russia and, in return for many hours of lectures from Frank on gunnery, Nicolo regaled Frank with tales of bravery in the new Greek cause. It became clear to the exiled naval officer that here at last would be another opportunity to sail into battle and, if the writings of Byron were to be believed, a battle more glorious in its destiny than that he had first seen at Trafalgar.

Frank soon returned to London in a completely different spirit from that of deep depression in which he had left. For the final time he approached the Admiralty to offer his services back to England but even with the support of Sir Home Popham and Captain Parker, this was not to be. Still with great enthusiasm, he set about organising his financial affairs to enable him to return to sea. His optimism, or even arrogance, led to the conclusion that if the English Navy did not want him, that was their loss and he was quite capable both financially and academically to form his own navy every bit as good as the one which now rejected him.

Chapter 3

The Ottoman Empire and Greek Revolution

Like so many others, Frank Abney Hastings moved to the steamy, sordid and exciting French port of Marseilles but the cause for which these young adventurers gathered was one of which they knew relatively little. Perhaps the Byronic romance, perhaps boredom, or even a Christian mistrust of Islam had driven them there. It is certain that none really knew who the Greeks were which is hardly surprising as the country had been ruled by the Turks since 1453. Prior to that there had been six centuries of the great Byzantine Empire which was in effect the Greek antecedent of the Eastern Roman Empire. Greece at this time did not exist as the modern country it is today. It was made up of different regions separated by rugged countryside.

Byzantium rose to power in around the Sixth Century with Constantinople as its capital and came of the doctrinal differences between the Christian Churches of Rome and orthodoxy to the east. The situation in 692 at the Ecumenical Council of Constantinople was that the Greek Church tried to impose its dogma upon Rome, which was ignored by the Latin Bishops who boycotted the Council. Also three of the Sees of Christianity at Antioch, Jerusalem and Alexandria were in Muslim hands. So it was that total schism existed between the East Roman Empire and that based in Rome.

During the next three centuries the situation changed little overall apart from continuing challenges to the Byzantine territories. These pressures came from all sides. The Muslims, Venice, Rome and even Russia took part in the power struggle. The boundaries of the two Empires had been drawn up by the Treaty of Aix-la-Chapelle in 803, and Constantinople had little alternative but to acknowledge Charlemagne as Emperor of the West. This had not stopped the conflicts between the Popes and the Patriarchs of the Greek Orthodox Church.

By the turn of the millennium the Muslims were gaining in strength in the eastern countries of the Mediterranean and in 1070 the Seljuq Turks took most of Egypt, and many rich cities of the eastern coast. The most successful of the Seljuq tribes was that of Othman which settled in North West Anatolia, and despite such set-backs as taking four years to overthrow Armenia, the Turks continued to gain territory under their mighty ruler Sultan Alp Arslam. Ignoring the wishes of Byzantium the western European nations—from fear and greed rather than religious motivation—decided that the only way to counter the Turkish growth was by the use of Crusades, and the war-like Normans were amongst the early participants.

The Constantinople administration perceived that their main threat came from the Normans and their imperialistic aims. They therefore made agreements with the wealthy shipping state of Venice and also with the Seljuq Turks, who by then had settled at Nicaea, that area of Turkey and north Iran lying to the south and east of the Black Sea. The Crusaders made great advances in early years, and against the wishes of the Emperor in Constantinople they took back Antioch and Jerusalem with great barbarity. They then marched towards the Seljuqs who only saved themselves by surrendering to the Emperor alone. The western forces did return some of the lands to the Byzantine Empire but in many they formed their own little kingdoms. For example, the Norman warrior, Robert Bohemond, had himself crowned as Prince of Antioch. Inevitably the power struggles between them started. So it was that the Byzantine Emperors were weakened not only by their original losses to the Turks but also by their so-called saviours.

Seeing this weakness, there were many who again assailed the Empire. The Turks from the east, Magyars from the north and even the Venetians took islands and towns off the western coast of Greece. France and Germany saw the possibility of the Byzantine Empire crumbling and readily answered the call of the Pope in 1145 to the second crusade. Once more the status was maintained with another agreement between the Seljuqs and the Emperor and the crusade collapsed in disaster. A rift had now opened in the Christian Churches, not only between Rome and the East but within the Catholic Church itself and in 1159 two Popes were elected.

Using the confusion on all sides Emperor Manuel of Constantinople took the opportunity to reassert the power of Byzantium. With great diplomacy he even took the chance to try and re-unite Christianity and in 1169 he set up a Russian Orthodox Monastery on Mount Athos having attributed to religious unity the only hope of holding back the Islamic advances. It was unfortunate for Manuel that the great and barbaric leader of the Kurdish tribes, Saladin, had launched his campaigns at the same time and in 1170 Egypt fell to him. Shortly after his death the third crusade was launched by Pope Gregory VII and gained support from both Emperors, Barbarossa in Rome, and Isaac Angelus in Constantinople. The main successes of this crusade came from the English troops of Richard I who took Cyprus and parts of Palestine before making a truce with Saladin and returning to the England, supposedly and mythically guarded by Robin Hood.

The former allies of Constantinople, the Venetians, again turned upon them and re-took the western islands and from that power base joined forces with the Crusaders. In the Byzantine capital anarchy reigned with several claimants to the throne warring between themselves and this was the opportunity the greedy western Europeans had awaited.

They entered the historic city of Constantinople and found it to be suffering from abject demoralisation—its people could no longer fight. With disgraceful thoroughness the Normans, German and English proceeded to rape, loot and pillage on a scale unknown before and even the Cathedral of Sancta Sophia was torn apart by those Christian troops lusting after the ornate gold surrounds to the altars. The population was slaughtered on an unprecedented scale and neither Greek nor Muslim could ever forgive the 'Franks' for the horrors they perpetrated.

The Crusaders proceeded to carve up the spoils of an Empire and immediately appointed a Latin Patriarch and Emperor, although it never was the complete Byzantine territory. The Venetians retained most of the islands to the west and Epirus and Nicaea were ruled by the legitimate Greek descendants of Byzantium monarchs. Meanwhile the Ottomans, descendants of Othman, had become the rulers of most of the Asia Minor mainland and were only held back from the spoils of the Empire by the Mogul tribes beating on their back door to the east. During the next two centuries Empires rose and fell. The Latin Byzantine Empire had lasted less than a hundred years and the Greeks with help from a succession of mostly treacherous allies regained some of their old territories.

For a time it seemed that the Byzantine rule may have continued over the reduced lands and Manuel II had been given promises of support by a number of nations against further encroachment by the Turks. Additionally the Mogul problem in the East grew to the point where the Mogul leader, Tamerlaine, captured the Ottoman Sultan Bayazid. Civil war broke out between the sons of Bayazid in the Ottoman Empire and it did not become reunited until 1413 under Sultan Mehemet.

The once great Byzantium had only one course open to save itself from the ensuing years of Turkish assault and that was to capitulate again to the Latin Empire and for Greek Orthodoxy to succumb to the Roman Church. Against the wishes of the Russian and Greek Churches and the people who remembered in their folk-lore the brutalities of Latin rule, the Emperor gained a temporary respite by taking this step in 1439. The younger brother, Constantine XI, who inherited the throne in 1449, must have known that his reign could not last. Attempts were made by Constantine and the Patriarch Gennadius to obtain support from the West but apart from small brave groups of foreign mariners none was forthcoming.

The European nations were too apathetic to see how serious the situation was. This situation was to be exactly repeated nearly four hundred years later. The Byzantine Empire, once the greatest force in the world, collapsed in May 1453 after a two month siege by the Ottoman Emperor, Sultan Mehemet II.

The rivalries between the Latin and Greek Churches had played a major role in allowing the energies of Byzantium to become so depleted that overthrow by the Ottomans was inevitable. It is sad that on May 28th, the night before the final collapse, the two Churches came together in worship for a moving service at the ornate Church of the Holy Wisdom—they, like the rulers of other nations, did too little and too late. History does not record the fate of the last Byzantine Emperor, Constantine XI, but to this day some superstitious Greeks await the coming of their ancient sovereign.

Remarkably much of Constantinople survived. It was the Muslim custom to raise to the ground the towns they conquered and in many respects Sultan Mehemet II acted with considerable diplomacy. Gennadius was appointed as the new Patriarch under the Sultan and the actual instillation was performed with full Byzantine Rite by Mehemet himself. More importantly to the survival of the concept of Greek nationality, this did nothing to reduce the power of the Orthodox Church. The Cathedral of Sancta Sophia, so shamefully and blasphemously desecrated by the Crusaders, was converted with great consideration for feelings to a most glorious mosque and many Greeks were given high office. Whilst there were instances of destruction and barbarity, these were only in keeping with the harsh times.

Attempts to regain the areas for Christianity were made but none with any degree of success. It took two centuries for the Turks to obtain a tenuous control over all the lands of the old Empire. During this period the Ottomans systematically took away the pride from the vassal races of Greeks, Slavs and Armenians and non-Muslims became second-class citizens in every sense of the term. Even the Arab word for non-Muslims used by the Turks was 'rayah', meaning cattle.

The Sultan himself was an absolute monarch although Muslim law and the Koran dictated the general principles, and he had in effect two cabinets below him from whom advice could be sought. One 'cabinet' was involved with interpretation of the Koran in matters of theology, law and education, and the other was a civil service administering the provinces and the military.

One of the laws of Islam was the responsibility of continuing expansion of territories and it was this that eventually brought the Empire down. Originally the Ottomans only had two Provinces over which to rule through a military Governor but this grew with time and territorial acquisition to more than thirty. In Greece alone there were eventually eleven 'sanjaks' of which six were on the mainland. The duties of the Governor were simple; to raise taxes, keep peace and raise militia as required and life for Greek peasants under the 'sanjak boys' was every bit as equitable as for their western counterparts.

The Governors were directly answerable to the Sultan and they maintained an elite corps called the Janissary. Christian families were required to pay Tribute to the Sultan by having one male child in five between the ages of eleven and eighteen taken away for service and of course many girls and young boys were taken for service in the Muslim harems and households. These once-proud races made little objection to these indignities and, in many cases, service in the Janissaries was preferable to life in the meagre fields.

Other financial taxes were imposed; a tax on every person, tax on the proceeds of land and taxes on import and export which were double for the non-Muslims. This latter point made little difference as most trading was conducted by Greeks, Armenians and Jews who flourished despite taxation. The Churches which after the original warrants given to Gennadius by Mehemet enjoyed considerable autonomy were required to raise their own taxes for the Sultan.

Provided that the Orthodox Churches collected and paid their taxes they were allowed almost total religious freedom. In part this situation was condoned to maintain the power of Orthodoxy and the Patriarchs of Constantinople and to maintain the rift with

Rome. Additionally there was no great desire for conversion of the population to Islam as this would leave fewer serfs to till the fields and pay taxes. In many regions the Church continued in its role of local administrator and in many others they shared this duty with their Turkish masters. The Ottoman Empire flourished under a succession of mainly good Sultans and despite frequent attacks from Venice, Austria and even Russia, whose claim to rightful succession to Byzantium was based both on Orthodoxy and the marriage of the last Emperor's niece to Ivan III, Grand Prince of Moscow.

By the middle of the 17th Century the system of administration by which the Ottomans had ruled was in a state of collapse. In part this was due to the characters of the Sultans and the constant wars with their neighbours but in part it was also due to the changes in the Janissaries which had ceased to become the elite corps at the service of the Sultans and had taken on more the role of local tyrants.

Members of the corps had relaxation in their laws which had once barred marriage and after a time it became a hereditary organisation whose loyalties lay only with their families and the seizure of property and land. The Christian populations dwindled and once fertile acres became barren. The uncomfortable but at least fairly peaceful relationships between Christian and Muslim deteriorated and the main sources of income for Constantinople from people and agricultural production gradually declined. The Sultans could not cope with the situation and at least two of them gave serious consideration to the wholesale slaughter of the Greek race.

Although this did not come about on a national scale the level of depopulation was enormous and had the effect of creating the realisation of a need for some form of strength from unity. Many who previously spoke other languages, the Slavs, Albanians and Rumanians especially learned Greek from the Church as a second and in some cases, first language. Many took to the hills to avoid the excesses of the regime and formed themselves into armed bands or 'klefts'. In rural areas the Chief brigand (kleftis) achieved considerable power and some Provincial Governors were unable to deal with the situation on their own. The Janissaries were of little use

Commander of the Karteria

against the local brigand heroes and they were themselves in a state of turmoil and often open revolt. The rulers came up with the idea of creating a Christian Militia known as the Armatoli. These groups were provided with armaments and, unfortunately for the Turks, often the Armatoli decided to join the klefts in a life of piracy.

Towards the end of the 17th Century a Greek, Panagioutaki, was made the Dragoman of the Porte, a post roughly equivalent of a Minister for the Interior. Other posts followed shortly, the most important of which was that of Dragoman of the Fleet, second only in naval hierarchy to the Captain Pasha. The wealthy and powerful merchants and traders of the Greek Orthodox faith lived in Constantinople near to the residence of the Patriarch in an area called the Phanar, and they became known as the Phanariots. It was inevitable that with their own compatriots and relatives holding the top posts they should in turn receive positions of influence.

In allowing this to take place, the Turks created a situation which gave birth to the eventual revolution against, and collapse of, the Ottoman Empire. Their rather naïve and simplistic view of the world meant that they actually encouraged the Phanariot rise in administrative power which led to their own downfall. From the ranks of these merchant administrators arose the new Greek aristocracy which was to play the major internal role in the subsequent wars of Independence. Families whose names were to become, and still are, those of national heroes in Greece became famous; Ipsilantis, Mavrokordatos, and Delyannis. Even Kolokotronis, the great folk-hero of the wars, came from a family employed by Delyannis.

Like so many, Kolokotronis was a 'kleft' who had won fame as a brigand and was subsequently employed by the Phanariots to protect their property at home while the masters increased their riches in Constantinople and elsewhere. It was one of the greatest mistakes of the Turks that they allowed this ascension to high position of power by the Phanarriots abroad as well as within the Ottoman Empire. Personal and trading links were built up by these Greeks with foreign governments as well as trading houses. These links were to serve them well in the future in raising public interest and awareness of the Greek cause.

The Phanariots were quick to observe the rise of free intellectual thought sweeping the western world and many either moved to European capitals or sent their children there to be educated. With their newly acquired learning and wealth they started new schools both in Constantinople and in Greece. Throughout the 18th Century they developed a mixture of the peasant tongues and the semi-classical Greek of the Church into a national modern Greek language. Much of the driving force of this came from ex-patriot Phanariots and many literary works in the new Greek found their way back from London, Paris and Vienna. One author in particular, Korais, who lived in Paris used the syntax of French grammar freely when transcribing Church and Classical Greek into a modern form but more importantly to his writings, he proposed the revolutionary and anti-clerical ideals so rampant in his adopted country. Many consider him to be the intellectual father of Greek independence.

The Greek peasant had little in common with these wealthy, worldly-wise strangers from the Phanar district of Constantinople. Whilst in modern Greece children are taught of the emergence of these patriots, in truth there is little to suggest that the majority were more than profiteers and collaborators with the Turkish regime. This mistrust was to continue throughout the revolutionary period.

The earlier part of the 18th Century had been one of almost constant warfare for the Turks against the Venetians, Austrians and Russians. The middle of the Century was one of comparative peace. The Western world was too preoccupied with its own changes in balance of power and especially the increasing dominance of Russia in world politics. The Empress of Russia, Catherine the Great, embarked upon a programme to include the Ottoman Empire with her own. Although a German by birth she achieved her throne by arranging for the Orlov brothers to murder her husband Peter III and these same characters were sent by her to the Peloponnese to incite rebellion against their Turkish masters by the Greek peasants. Her first war with the Turks came in 1768 as a result of the Turks agreeing to help the French by attacking the southern areas of Russia—an event which had happened periodically for centuries—and Catherine's response of creating internal dissent.

After the Peace Treaty of 1774, Catherine's desire for the Ottoman possessions were exacerbated and she formed grandiose schemes with Joseph II of Austria to create a new state between Russia and Austria and a Greek nation ruled by her grandson Constantine from the capital of Constantinople. With these ideas to the fore she again went to war with Turkey in 1787 but the Austrians soon abandoned her and again it ended in failure in 1792. The main effect of this short attempt to take power was to create awareness in Britain and especially in France of the potential use of so-called Greek nationalism to achieve expansionist ambitions.

There were more genuine results of the new awareness with Greek cultural centres springing up in many cities, the most important of which was that created by the influential writer, Korais, in Paris.

During the war another influence arrived on the scene—Ali Pasha of Tepelini was appointed as Provincial Governor of Epirus in 1788. A three way tussle for power started in this Western outpost of the Ottoman Empire. Russia realised the vulnerability of these southern Balkan areas. France created a Consulate at Ioannina, the capital of Epirus and Ali Pasha himself saw an opportunity far greater than that inherent in the post of Governor. Ali Pasha had been born in Albania in 1744 and through his mother was a kinsman of the infamous Kurd Pasha of Burat; perhaps through this connection he learnt that once surrounded by loyal and murderous brigands he held the key to power.

This involved the systematic murder of anyone who stood in his way and his use of politics was skilful enough that he managed to convince Sultan Abdul Hamid I in Constantinople that this was done to maintain peace within the Ottoman Empire. His rewards came with responsibilities over ever enlarging territories and, by the turn of the century, he and his son Veli ruled most of the Balkans.

After his appointment in Ioannina he brought the Albanian chieftains into line by giving some authority within his administration and others he killed. To the north of his capital city were the mountainous areas of Souli where the Greek Christian warriors had a fierce reputation and presented Ali Pasha with something of a problem. Two attempts to crush them and the Suliot leader, Botsaris, proved disastrous and it was not until Ali received help from other areas of the Empire that he was able, by a mixture of blockades and attack, to crush the Suliots. The tribesmen agreed to leave their homelands and move en masse to Parga—from there many went to the Ionian Islands—and Ali was rewarded with even greater lands for his command. His son Veli was given the Greek heartland of the Peloponnese and ruled Morea in a manner similar to his father.

Much as Ali had done in the north, Veli set about a programme to move the dangerous klefts from Morea and the most powerful of these was Theodore Kolokotronis. Like so many who were to become national heroes, Kolokotronis had started his life as a typical brigand living off stealing sheep and belongings from wealthy merchants. He was brought much more into contact with a different culture when the wealthy Delyannis family employed him as Kapo of their estates in Karitena—a post which largely involved him in protecting them from other klefts. Whilst he had returned to Morea as a kleft, he was to become a more political animal known to the Tsars, Napoleon and the British alike.

Veli eventually drove out the Moreot klefts and they, like many of the Suliots before them, fled to the Ionian Islands which had become the focal point of the gathering momentum of nationalism. The occupancy of the Ionian Islands had been disputed for years, with the greatest success coming from the Venetians but in 1797 Napoleon took over with the statement:

"Corfu, Zante and Cephalonia are of more interest to us than all Italy"

An unnatural alliance between Turkey and Russia came about the following year largely to protect their own territories but also to regain the islands. Ali Pasha, of course, had his own designs on the islands and had made independent agreements with the French. His plans were, however, foiled when in 1799 a Russo-Turkish Fleet took the islands from the Napoleonic forces and a Treaty was signed between the Russians and Turks in March 1800 at Constantinople forming the Septisinsular Republic.

In effect the islanders were given a measure of autonomy following negotiations between Turkey, Russia and England with Count Capo d'Istrias, a local nobleman, representing the population. Russia provided the troops necessary to protect the islands from Ali Pasha and the Septisinsular Republic remained under the suzerainty of Turkey. It was allowed to have its own constitution and all the trappings of independence but never really had either the wealth or abilities to be such. The importance to Greece was much more than practical. It was the first time in four centuries that Greeks had ruled in their own lands.

Count Capo d'Istrias, who had undertaken the negotiations, sent for his twenty-four year old son who was studying medicine in Padua (and later he was installed as Secretary of State) and the young aristocrat met the warrior leaders of the Suliots and Moreots, Kolokotronis and Botsaris. It is said they took an oath pledging that they would work together for the rest of their lives to free Greece. He certainly never forgot his pledge to the two klefts, even though it was to happen later than any at the time may have supposed. Ali Pasha, with support from French troops, had landed on Lefkas in 1806 but this invasion was repulsed by John Kapodistrias (as Capo d'Istrias had become known) and the klefts, an act which certainly strengthened the bond between them.

It was a miserable disappointment to all when in 1807 the Russian Emperor Alexander signed a Treaty with the French returning the Ionian Islands to them. The Treaty of Tilsit brought to an end this first tentative attempt at Greek independence but it did not end the friendships, alliances and hopes of those involved. Kapodistrias himself was wooed by the French to join their diplomatic service but instead he moved to Russia and eventually became the Joint

Secretary of State to the Tsar at the Congress of Vienna. His decision was undoubtedly based on the fact that he could see the rising land power of Russia against Napoleon and that, coupled with the increasing dominance at sea by the Royal Navy, clearly indicated that his beloved Greek Islands would not be under French control for long.

His opinion proved to be correct although, at one point, it seemed that the next occupants of the Ionian Islands would be the Austrians. In the event it was the son of a Quaker merchant from Cork, Richard Church, who led a British attack on Zante in 1809. Church had run away from his strict home at the age of fourteen to join the Army and at the age of seventeen was serving under General Abercromby as an Ensign in Egypt. By the time he was twenty-two in 1806, he had achieved the position of Captain-Commandant of Capri and was severely wounded in the head whilst defending the island from attack by the Napoleonic forces. After a period of recovery he was promoted to Major. As Chief-of-Staff to General Oswald he commenced the British take-over of the Ionian Islands which led to them becoming a British Crown Colony for half a century.

Kapodistrias at the Tsar's Court played his part in the international negotiations over the islands and at the time saw British protection as being the best for his long term objectives. Although his own idea was that they should be an independent state being protected by Britain rather than a Crown Colony. As a gesture towards the nominal independence for the islands, Richard Church was given the task of raising the first Greek regiment which was financed and largely led by Britain. This became known as the Duke of York's Greek Light Infantry and many of the klefts who had settled on the islands were to join. The most famous, Theodore Kolokotronis, was given a Commission in the British Army.

One of the unfortunate effects for the Greek cause of the negotiations leading to the Treaty putting the Ionian Islands under British protection was that the prospect of Greek Regiments was dashed. Church, recovering from another wound received during an attempt to seize Levkas from the French, had toured the Eastern

Mediterranean recruiting for his regiments and had subsequently returned to England and persuaded the authorities to raise a second regiment. To his great chagrin both were ordered to be disbanded in 1814, leaving Church to carry on his military career elsewhere in the Mediterranean—and awaiting the call from Greece. His klefti warriors had been trained in the only art for which they were familiar—warfare, and they too awaited a call.

Elsewhere in Europe the diplomats, merchants and intellectuals whose origins lay in Greece carried on a battle on a different front; that of influencing public opinion and negotiating with foreign powers. They did their job well and for the first two decades of the 19th Century Greece was included on the Grand Tours of aristocrats of many nations and these men gave hope to all they met. The Earl of Aberdeen, nicknamed 'Athenian Aberdeen', was to become both Foreign Secretary and Prime Minister after his visits. Frederick North who became the Earl of Guildford not only became a practising member of the Greek Orthodox Church but endowed a University of Corfu and of course Lord Byron, who was to have such an influence on the subsequent wars, made his first visit to Greece in 1809, the year Church took Zante. Even Lord Elgin by his desecration of the Acropolis and removal of the marbles, played a part by focussing the attention of the British people onto Greece It must be said that his motives in removing these antiquities from the dangers of the Turks were possibly impeccable and prevented their damage at the hands of the Turks, but the reason for their remaining in London has long since disappeared.

The ex-patriot Greeks formed themselves into groups to influence both Governments and important individuals. During the second decade of the eighteen hundreds, many merchants and intellectuals were to join the most powerful of these, the Philiki Etaria (The Friendly Society). This organisation had been formed in 1814 by a group of Greek merchants resident in Southern Russia and it was organised on the approximate lines of Freemasonry with three grades of membership. The word was spread by one member being given an apostolic role in a given area and usually with the task of recruiting a key individual. Gradually extra grades of membership were included to include both the peasantry and the klefts. It was, however, only the senior grades who were told the full extent of the objectives of the Philiki Etaria which included driving the Turkish out of Greece.

The one person they wanted as leader, Kapodistrias, refused on several occasions to join and when he was first told in 1816, he was violently opposed and reported the matter to the Tsar. Kapodistrias was still quite content with the British protection of the Ionian Islands giving a limited form of self government and said to the emissary of Philiki Etaria, Nicholaos Galatis:

"Anyone, Sir, who thinks to embark upon such an undertaking must be mad"

He went on to advise him not to mention the society to anyone and to advise those at home to leave it well alone:

"They must renounce their revolutionary activities, and continue to live under whichever government they find themselves until God shall decide otherwise"

Against his advice the movement gained momentum. The Phanariots joined in great numbers and the klefts enrolled their private armies in the cause. A particular triumph to their credibility came in 1818 when the Petrobey of Mani, Mavromichalis, joined with them and made peace with families around him with whom he had feuded over a long period to better await the call. But still the problem with the Philiki Etaria was that it was without a figurehead. Events in Ioannina in 1819 changed this.

Whilst on a visit to his family in Corfu from Russia, Kapodistrias was visited by the great chieftains whom he knew of old, Kolokotronis, and Botsaris. At the same time the British High Commissioner in Corfu, Sir Thomas Maitland, had persuaded his government to carry out an old Treaty and return the mainland town of Parga to Ali Pasha as the Sultan's representative. Although Parga was on the mainland rather than one of the Ionian Islands, since Venetian times it had been part of them to all intents and purposes. The entire population of Parga fled to Corfu rather than remain under Ali Pasha's regime and Kapodistrias, rightly horrified by the whole matter, tried to alter the British decision but without success.

He never again entirely trusted the British; nor did his friend, Kolokotronis. His attitude to the Philiki Etaria changed noticeably from this point and, whilst he was careful not to make any commitment on behalf of the Tsar, he certainly gave a warmer reception to the ideals. On his return to St Petersburg the following year, he received yet another deputation offering him the leadership headed by Xanthos, one of the founder members. The first meeting failed and Kapodistrias' secretary, Kantiotis, who was a member of the Etaria, arranged a second.

The records of this meeting are so scant that one must assume that Kapodistrias, normally so precise in covering himself by minuting every detail, may well have destroyed the records or perhaps given instruction that none should be kept. Whatever the reason, Xanthos came away with the distinct impression that the Tsar would eventually come to the assistance of any revolution and that Kapodistrias wished the leadership of the Etaria to Alexandros Ipsilantis. This decision was not well accepted by some members of the society, probably due to the fact that the two younger brothers of Alexandros were amongst early Phanariots who had joined but the older brother had always refused to become involved. There was no doubting his military capabilities as he was trained by the Officer School of the Imperial Guard in Russia, fought a number of campaigns and lost an arm at the battle of Kulm, and eventually risen to the post of A.D.C to the Tsar with the rank of General.

He always claimed that he visited Kapodistrias to seek his advice, although there is only his word for this and he later wrote:

"I thought my hour had come, and on the advice of Kapodistrias I accepted. It was at the beginning of the year of 1820 at a time when Constantinople had declared war without mercy against Ali Pasha of Ioannina".

The Tsar of Russia certainly approved one of his senior officers resigning to take the leadership of the Philiki Etaria if only to have some measure of control over the events looming so close. By March of 1821, Ipsilantis had gathered a small force around him and marched to free his country.

There was no doubt that Alexandros Ipsilantis had every reason to look forward to success. Although denied by Kapodistrias, it was generally accepted that Russian support would come. Perhaps more importantly, Ali Pasha, the Lion of Ioannina, was assumed to be for him and indeed for some time there had been rumours that he had actually become a member of the Philiki Etaria. Many of Ali's highly placed servants—his secretaries, many of his bodyguards, and his doctor, Kolettis—were certainly members and it is possible that he was influenced by them.

Ali Pasha was summoned to the Sultan, but declined. Following Ali's refusal to appear in Constantinople, Ismail Paso Bey set out to bring him to heel. His forces took Prevaza, capturing Ali's son Veli and moved north to take his stronghold of Ioannina with the help of the Suliot warriors of the northern hills. This latter group had no stomach for assisting the imperialist forces and Ali soon tempted them to his cause by his usual tactic of promising the earth—or large sections of it—in return for their loyalty.

It was these events which had prompted Ipsilantis to act with rather more speed than judgement in gathering his forces together, although he did take the precaution of sending leading Etarists to all the important centres of Greece. His own brother, Dimitrios, was ordered to the Peloponnese to take over as military leader of the various groups. Prince Alexander Mavrokordatos and Petrobey Mavromichalis readied themselves and the leading Klefts, Kolokotronis, Botsaris and Odysseus, encouraged others to join the Suliots in support of Ali.

The leaders in Morea were angry that the revolution would not be started in their lands and this turned to fury when the Turkish Military

Commander of the Peloponnese, Khursid Pasha, was ordered to march to Epirus to join the Sultan's quarrel with Ali Pasha.

As far as Ipsilantis was concerned the time was right. The Sultan had despatched his most powerful forces in the area to deal with Ali Pasha. He assumed that the Etarist leaders, under his brother in the Peloponnese, were awaiting the call. The leading Klefts were together with the Suliot warriors ostensibly in support of Ali. The route down through Rumania was eased by the assumed support of the revolutionaries of that land. Additionally he had done his preplanning well and even in the areas where it was probable that power would be Ali's, he had implanted Etarist leaders who would rise for the Hellenic cause when he arrived. Although he had risen to the rank of General with the Tsar, Alexandros Ipsilantis was still only 29 years old when in early 1821 he raised his army to march from southern Russia to relieve Greece.

It can only be assumed that this young professional soldier was blinded by patriotism when he looked at his forces. They consisted of 500 Greek students called his 'Sacred Battalion' and a motley collection of Serbs, Albanians and Bulgarians totalling no more than 3,000. They had some mounted soldiers and a handful of field artillery. This band had set off from the Russian-Moldavian town of Kirshinev for the borders of Rumania with only one clear promise of support on the other side—that from Olympios, who was pledged to meet him north of Bucharest with his troops. Somehow the Russians allowed this 'army' to cross the borders. Some accounts suggest simple bribery was used and others that Ipsilantis' eloquent pleading for the cause in which he believed so passionately, enabled the crossing in March, 1821. However unlikely they looked, the Greeks had invaded the Ottoman Empire.

In the event, support neither came from his supposed allies under Vladimerescu in Rumania nor from the Russians and whilst it cost Ipsilantis his life he proved that the Greeks really had a cause. Alexandros Ipsilantis was the founder of the revolution—without his leadership the Etarists could not have achieved their aim. It was the knowledge of his march into Rumania which allowed the other happenings in Greece to take place and it was his strategic deployment of the Etarist leaders which led to the eventual victory. He ended his life in misery in a foreign jail but he paved the way for the Greek nation. He was the greatest patriot of these early days.

The leaders in Morea were still incensed that their uprising had been delayed and recruits flooded to them when news spread to them of Alexandros Ipsilantis' march. Several chiefs took matters into their own hands and many individual acts of rebellion against the Turks took place. Fearing that this was a concerted effort on behalf of Ali Pasha, the Turkish Governors ordered the Bishops and Primates of the Peloponnese to meet in Tripolitsa to quiz them about the violence. Despite their protestations, by the time they arrived, their rulers were certain that the isolated acts were in fact the start of a rebellion. Such was their fear that their visitors were immediately incarcerated.

Knowing that Mani was ready under Petrobey Machalis and already troops were besieging the Turks at Kalamata, the Metropolitan Bishop of Patras gave the signal for revolution. At the Monastery of Aghia Lavra, he raised the Greek revolutionary standard. This signal from the north of the Morea gave Petrobey Mavromichalis and his 5,000 troops in the south the impetus they needed. They were not going to wait for a victorious Ipsilantis, as they assumed, to arrive by sea nor await news of Ali's efforts against the Turks in the north. Morea was in a state of revolution. Petrobey Mavromichalis wasted no time in establishing his leadership of the revolution in the eyes of the world. During the latter part of 1821 and early 1822, when the hundreds of adventurers gathered in Marseilles, the revolutionary factions in Greece seemed to concentrate more on their internal struggles rather than on ridding themselves of the Turks. None of this worried the romantics waiting to throw themselves into the Greek cause which they perceived as a revolution which truly had its origins in the glorious era of Byzantium.

Chapter 4

1822; Arrival on Hydra and actions on 'Thermistocles'

Frank watched from the harbour's edge as an old, black-hulled brig carrying a Swedish ensign dropped anchor at the port entrance. Her patched tan sails were roughly bundled up on the decks as the two ship's longboats were lowered on the davits to the water. The crew looked scruffy but well disciplined as they pulled the rowing boats round to the bows of the '*Trontheim*' and attached the lines to their wooden stern cleats. The anchor was hauled back out of the water and they started the laborious process of towing her between the breakwaters that marked the entrance to the inner harbour where she finally came to rest.

With interest, the onlookers saw the blond, giant of a Captain being rowed ashore to present his papers at the harbour office. Frank did not have long to wait outside the office for the Swedish mariner to reappear, and within minutes he learned that the '*Trontheim*' was unloading her cargo from Holland and taking another aboard for shipment to Constantinople and Odessa. Sitting later in the Captain's cabin, drinking foul-tasting spirit, the bargain was struck. His tedious wait was nearly at an end. For a fee of fifty pounds, payable in gold coin, Frank Hastings was to have the use of the Mate's cabin and would be dropped off on the Island of Hydra with his very considerable personal effects.

These not only included his navigational equipment, guns, uniforms and papers but also the complete works of Shakespeare, twelve volumes of Gibbon and fifty-two volumes of Sir Walter Scott. One of the latter works, Ivanhoe, always brought a little nostalgia and thoughts of home as it was written in Frank's home town of Ashby de la Zouch

The two weeks it took to unload the '*Trontheim*'s cargo and replenish it dragged heavily with the young man eager to be back at sea. Many of his new-found acquaintances in the harbour area pleaded to go with him. Most were penniless and were looking to the wealthy English gentleman for assistance. The majority he thought of as drunken wastrels doing little more than whoring, drinking and talking of great adventures to come, although a twenty-two year old American named George Jarvis did stand out from the rest. The son of Benjamin Jarvis, an American diplomat, George was born and brought up in Germany which gave him a Teutonic manner and attitude which appealed to Hastings. His romanticism towards the Greek cause, wearing a Greek costume and frequent use of his recently acquired Greek language appealed somewhat less to the professional seaman. However, his physical strength and general bearing outweighed this and Hastings agreed to pay the little extra demanded for an extra passenger.

The final days in the bustling French port were made busy with settling his affairs, moving out of the house he had rented for a few months, writing to his father and brother and making the necessary arrangements with the representative of his bank, Messrs. Coutts, to be able to draw monies in Hydra, Zante or Cephalonia. One hitch came in Frank's normally meticulous planning when, only a week before the scheduled departure date, Jarvis pointed out that it would probably be necessary to carry a passport. Unfortunately the British Consul, Alexander Turnbull, was away from Marseilles on leave with a Mr Richardson, the Chargé d'Affaires, being left with the responsibility of the Consulate.

Long arguments ensued over the ability of Richardson to issue a passport and only after threats to bring down the wrath of the

Marquis of Hastings and his father, General Sir Charles Hastings, upon the unfortunate diplomat did he agree. The passport was duly issued on March 7th, six days before departure, and very clearly stated "Issued in the Absence of the Consul". Hastings and Jarvis checked into the Hotel du Port for the last few nights in Marseilles and busied themselves loading their baggage aboard the 'Trontheim' and bidding farewell to the many envious adventurers with whom they had become acquainted. By the afternoon of March 12th the two men were settled into their somewhat cramped quarters aboard the 'Trontheim'.

The Swedish Captain must have questioned the wisdom of offering passage to such an experienced seaman as Frank. Such was Frank's delight at being back on board a ship that he could not help but interfere with the crew as they prepared for their next voyage. Thankfully for the Master this enthusiasm soon wore off and he was delighted when the pilot came aboard later in the evening.

Once more the crew members attached lines from the rowing boats to the 'Trontheim' and at midnight they started the one hour of strenuous exertion towing the vessel out of harbour. At one-thirty in the morning, the pilot was dropped off and the boats hauled back on board. Jarvis and the Captain could not help but laugh at the sheer delight and scarcely hidden joy of Frank Hastings as the dirty old ship pulled away from the land under full sail, propelled by the light south-easterly breeze. After three years, Frank Abney Hastings was back at sea. He was never to forget that moment; the sound of the wavelets lapping against the hull; the creaking of the timbers and the smells . . . . Stockholm tar, hemp ropes, fish-oil used to keep the sails supple, all mixed with the scents from the soap and wines in the cargo. By noon the following day the ship's crew were settling down to the routine of the vessel. The wind had freshened and it became necessary to haul down the royals along with the main and mizzen gallants. The carpenter was repairing one of the boats; warps and ropes were being maintained and stowed. All was well aboard the 'Trontheim'.

The wind dropped on the second day and progress was slow with the '*Trontheim*' averaging only 35 miles a day for the first eighteen days of the voyage, taking her round the toe of Italy and past Sicily. All this changed on April 1st when, almost from nowhere, a gale sprang up splitting the mizzen and causing the old ship to take a great amount of water on board. The sails were reefed and some taken down and the cargo was checked for any slipping. The '*Trontheim*' was now forging through the waves at nearly six knots, covering the remaining 400 nautical miles to the Greek island of Hydra in less than three days.

At daybreak on April 3rd, 1822, Hydra was in sight and, by 10:00am, the ship had rounded the north-eastern part of the island, coming to anchor in a small bay well protected from the heavy swell forced up by the gales. The ship's crew hoisted out a boat and to the great amazement of the fishermen tending their small caiques on the pebble beach, the two 'Franks', as all westerners were known, were offloaded onto the shore with their vast array of baggage. Hastings and Jarvis waved as the '*Trontheim*' set her sails again and pulled away from them.

If they had expected a friendly welcome from the fishermen they were to be most disappointed. Hastings exclaimed loudly to Jarvis: "*They look more like pirates and brigands than honest fishermen!*"—indeed they probably were! Certainly they all carried daggers which looked more appropriate to cutting throats than nets or fish.

At length one who spoke an accented form of Italian used by many in the Ionian island approached them and with difficulty they explained the reason for their strange arrival at Hydra. Neither was convinced that the fishermen really understood and they agreed that the only safe course of action was for Frank to remain guarding the baggage whilst Jarvis went to the town of Hydra to recruit help. Foolishly opening the belt containing his gold coin, a guinea was offered for the use of a boat and a man to take George Jarvis the three miles or so around the headland. This was willingly, too willingly, agreed and Frank was left sitting on one of his trunks, guns in hand, waiting for trouble. The cliffs around the bay were about three hundred feet high and offered no easy escape route if the men should attack him. His own journal of the events contains the only admission of fear in his adventurous life—more frightening than Trafalgar as an eleven year old, more frightening than the Battle of New Orleans, and more so than a shipwreck.

After an hour or so, he became so firmly convinced that he was soon to be attacked that he took his guns, £300 in gold coin and his sabre and started the difficult climb up the cliff. His hands were wet with perspiration caused by fear. The weight he was carrying and his lack of condition after such a long period of shore—life caused him to slip many times during the climb. Eventually he reached the top and looked back to see the ruffians breaking open one of his trunks.

Hydra was at that time a heavily wooded island. It was in the next few years that the demand for timber to build ships would strip it naked. Frank set off across the hills towards the town. Progress was slow under the weight he was carrying and by mid-afternoon he came across a shepherd's cottage. With the little Greek he had learnt from Jarvis during their voyage he asked for water and to his great relief was greeted in a most friendly manner and given both water and food for which the shepherd would accept no payment. Bidding his host farewell he was pointed in the direction of a convent about two miles distant down a small valley where again his welcome was warm.

He managed to explain in French his predicament and was given the loan of a horse with which to complete his journey and a guide to ensure his safe passage. After about an hour they saw Hydra ahead in the fast approaching gloom and his guide left him to finish his perilous journey alone. As he rode into the tiny village, Jarvis and the brothers Tombazis were standing on the road to greet him. He was immediately shown to the home of the Tombazis, the largest house in Hydra and with considerable gratitude sat down to recount his tale.

Jakomaki and Manolis Tombazis were part of a wealthy, ship-owning family which had been totally involved with the Philiki Etaria and the cause of Greek Independence since the early days and their merchant vessels were heavily armed as fighting ships. They relied on a little piracy and the prizes of their encounters with the Turkish supply vessels to make up for the income lost from more conventional trading. They talked well into the night in a mixture of French, English and Greek and gradually they were acquainted with the state of naval affairs between Greece and Turkey. The following morning (April 4th) the two visitors went down to the harbour with their hosts to look over the Hydriot Flagship, the *'Thermistocles'* and Frank insisted on taking his guns to try them out after the rigours of the previous day. All was well with his two pistols but the blunderbuss burnt in his hand and the shots fired into the crowd which had gathered around rather than safely out to sea. A villager standing a considerable distance away was wounded in the leg. Whilst Hastings admitted the wound was trifling he felt that he should give him £5 to avoid any ill feeling with his new colleagues. Jakomaki Tombazis reprimanded him strongly for his generosity, and pointed out that the police would have sorted the matter out without any cost. This display of kindness, however, caused the population of Hydra to regard Frank with great interest and shortly after the incident Hastings obtained a house and a boy as a servant without any problem.

Aboard the *'Thermistocles'*, Frank was horrified at the antiquity of the guns and proceeded to instruct the Tombazis brothers how to fix sights to them. Whilst he was willing to do the job for them, their pride would not allow this and in fact the job was not done until an armourer arrived in Hydra some weeks later. It is probable that although they got on well together, there was still a certain reservation as to the motives of the young foreigners. A couple of days after their arrival, Hasting and Jarvis appeared before the visiting 'ephors'—a cross between a magistrate and secret police—and they were questioned at great length about the navigational instruments, the weapons, and the purpose of their being there in the first place.

Clearly still holding them in some suspicion the 'ephors' told the Tombazis they could not take the foreigners aboard the *'Thermistocles'* until this was approved by the Greek President, Prince Mavrokordatos, and his government which at that time was based in Corinth on the Peloponnese mainland some 50 miles to the north of Hydra. Leaving their belongings at Hastings' house, the two men along with the servant were provided with a small vessel in which they made the journey to Corinth, arriving on April 19th.

Both men were speechless at the sights of utter devastation which greeted them. Hydra was relatively unaffected by the war but clearly the provisional capital of Greece had been the scene of months of pitched battle. They were met at the port by the President's secretary, Orlando who, having found them lodgings, took their letters of introduction from the Tombazis brothers and said he would return the following day to conduct them to the Prince. They were both received with politeness but the Prince clearly preferred the American. The attitude of Sir Thomas Maitland, the British High Commissioner at Corfu, had caused him to lose all faith and trust in the British. Neither received any promises from Mavrokordatos who said that he would have to consult with the appropriate ministers. In an effort to speed things along, Hastings himself visited the Minister of Marine only to be told that there was no "Marine" and therefore his papers were worthless and later called upon the Secretary to the Minister of War who stated that nothing could be done expeditiously at Corinth.

April 21st was a Fete Day at Corinth and to aggravate a difficult situation the servant had disappeared. Hastings resolved to return to Hydra as he feared that his servant, knowing where everything was stored, may well have been off on a piracy mission of his own. His idea was that he would return, place his valuables in safe-keeping in Tombazis' store, and then return to continue his quest to be allowed to sail on the *Thermistocles*. Once more he was frustrated by the realisation that the police still held his documents, including his passport, and without these he was told that he would be an illegal traveller.

Jarvis had been granted another appointment with the President, Mavrokordatos. He was told that he was free to travel and letters would be sent to Hydra to this effect. The President stated that he was worried about the possibility of his English companion being a spy for Sir Thomas Maitland. Jarvis argued Hastings' case and that evening when he set off for Athens he told his friend that everything was settled and that letters would be going out the following morning.

Frank Hastings was furious to the extent of almost quitting Greece when the next day he saw that the letters and permits covered only the American and not himself. In disgust he immediately wrote and delivered a letter to the Prince. The original was in French and the translation used is that undertaken by George Finlay and Hastings some time later:

"*Monsieur le Prince*

I have determined to take the liberty of addressing your Highness in writing as I found you occupied when I had the honour of presenting myself at your residence yesterday. I shall speak with freedom, convinced that your Highness will reply in the same manner.

I will not amuse you in recounting the sacrifices I have made to serve Greece. I came without being invited, and have no right to complain if my services are not accepted. In that case I shall only regret that my name cannot be added to the liberators of Greece; I shall not cease to wish for the triumph of liberty and civilisation over tyranny and barbarism. But I believe that without disrespect I may say to your Highness that I have the right to have my services either accepted or refused, for (as you may easily suppose) I can spend my money quite as agreeable elsewhere.

It seems that I am a suspected person because I am an Englishman. Among people without education I expected to meet some prejudice against Englishmen, in consequence of the conduct of the British Government, but I confess I was not prepared to find such prejudices amongst men of rank and education. I was far from supposing that the Greek Government would believe that every individual from a country would hold the same political opinions.

I am the younger son of Sir Charles Hastings, Baronet, General in the Army, and in possession of a landed Estate of nearly £10,000 a year. The Governor-General of India, the Marquis of Hastings, was brought up with my father by my Grandfather as brothers. If I were in search of a Position I might surely find one more lucrative with the British

Government in India, and less dangerous and more respectable than that of a spy amongst the Greeks. I venture to say to your Highness that if the English Government wished to Employ a spy here it would not address a person of my status while there are so many strangers in the country who would sell the whole of Greece for a bottle of Brandy, and this could apply to a Greek as for money traitors are to be found in all countries.

I quitted England because I believed the Government treated me in an arbitrary and unjust fashion in dismissing me from the Navy after fifteen years' service for an affair of honour. But in virtue of the Royal Prerogative I was dismissed without form, the affair having been misrepresented by an Admiral who, having had a personal quarrel with the Marquis of Hastings whom he conveyed to India, revenged himself upon me.

What I demand of your Highness is only to serve, without having the power to injure, your country. What injury can I inflict upon Greece, being alone on a ship of war? I must share the fate of the ship, and if it sink I shall be drowned with the rest on board.

I hope therefore that your Highness will give me a definitive answer, whether you will accept my services or not. I have, etc."

"Frank Hastings"

Once again Frank Abney Hastings had reacted to a slur on his honour. The same sense of personal pride which had proved his downfall in Jamaica now caused him to write such a pompous and potentially dangerous letter. Both he and Jarvis had expressed their unease about the power of the police at Corinth and the volatile Prince Mavrokordatos could easily have reacted violently against the innuendo suggesting that he had the thinking of men without rank or education. That evening Hastings was greeted as a long lost friend and was given the necessary letters. The two men retained a considerable mutual respect for each other after this and during the internecine struggles between the various Greek factions in the years to come, Hastings always looked favourably upon the claims of Mavrokordatos.

That same afternoon a French frigate arrived in Corinth under the command of Captain Chenchries carrying the nobleman, Count Philippe Jourdain whose work on exploding cannon balls and shells Frank had become familiar with and admired greatly whilst he was in France. Colonel Jourdain, as he was styled, saw the Greek cause as an opportunity to put his experimental and theoretical work into practice, much as Hastings himself. He also had an ulterior motive, secretly supported by the French Government, of leading the French cause to have the Duke of Nemours, the second son of the Duke of Orleans, eventually crowned as King of Greece.

The two men had much in common and they sailed together the following day, 25th April, for Hydra carrying papers with permission to join the *'Thermistocles'*. When they entered the harbour at Hydra, Jourdain immediately expressed his shock at the position of the shore batteries and the anchored fleet which left them totally exposed to a night fire attack. His reputation as a skilful artillery officer was greatly enhanced when he speedily explained the dangers to the Greek captains and reorganised the harbour.

Jarvis arrived back from Athens that same day and reported that whilst the Turks held the city, they were very short of water but seemed to have no shortage of wine. The three men moved on board the *'Thermistocles'* and were joined by several other foreigners including John Hane from Alton in Hampshire, who had been in Greece for nearly a year. As an artillery officer himself he was able to give Hastings and Jourdain a great deal of information on the methods adopted by the Turks and Greeks. He amazed them when he recounted several incidents where, both on land and at sea, the opposing forces had approached each other for battle and then withdrawn without a shot being fired. Even when firing did take place, the skills of the gunners on both sides were so poor as to render the outcome of such encounters dependant more upon luck than the art of gunnery. Again the 'Franks' pleaded with the Tombazis brothers to be allowed to fit sights to the *'Thermistocles'* guns and wheels on the smaller cannons to allow them to be used on small boats. Their response was still negative:

"We are grateful for your advice, but our own armourers must do the work!"

Their hopes were dashed on May 1st when the armourer arrived. He did indeed fit cocks to six guns but only made a perfunctory attempt to fit sights and none whatsoever to fit wheels to the boat's guns. Neither of the brothers who owned the ship was on board and, despite their assurances that the Greek Captain would co-operate with the experiments, this was not the case. Since the incident in Corinth where Mavrokordatos had shown his preference for the American, Jarvis had changed his attitude towards the English Captain to whom he owed his very presence in Greece. Frank wrote, somewhat petulantly:

"You take on the air of my superior, but, young man. until you have fought in battle, and until you command and are commanded with a proper disciplined service you cannot be more than an assistant to a real officer".

Reasonably enough, Jarvis reacted very badly to this insult from the autocratic Hastings, and hurled back insults of his own. He made the mistake of attacking the well-known pride of Hastings and pointed out that whilst his statements may be true, Frank himself was thrown out of such a service! Once again Frank resorted to challenging Jarvis to a duel— *"to rid myself of a meddling kind of charlatan"*.

Only the intervention of John Hane stopped the ridiculous farce but the friendship between Hastings and Jarvis never really recovered after this incident although that between Hane and Hastings lasted until the latter's death. Hane was to play a brave and important part in the heroic events of Hastings over the following six years.

Jourdain too was somewhat unhappy during the days of waiting on board the *'Thermistocles'* as his experiments with his shot were not going well. Whether a fault in design or one of manufacture, his shot was bursting immediately on leaving the cannon and clearly they were not made to resist the sudden impulsion from the powder. The Greek Captains in the fleet became more and more sceptical of the Franks aboard the *'Thermistocles'*. With some relief they sailed from Hydra on May 3rd to join the fleet of Admiral Kanaris off the easternmost islands bordering the Turkish mainland.

Their relief turned to absolute horror at the manner in which the ship was prepared for sea. The seamen came aboard as and when they pleased; none of the sails were properly prepared; no sheets were rove and, indeed, the bow lines were bent to the buntline cringles. The moment they left harbour they were hit by a squall and it became necessary to send men out on the jib boom to reef the sails and others actually had to be cut down. For the Philhellenes their first experience aboard a Greek warship was one of utter confusion and anarchy. Despite this setback which seemed the norm, they headed towards the east and battle.

In company with some thirty-six vessels they reached the island of Scio which lay only ten miles off the Turkish mainland and the fleet joined those of Admirals Kanaris and Miaoulis. News of Turkish atrocities had been filtering from the island and it was hoped that by keeping the Turkish fleet occupied at sea, they could not only prevent further dangers to the islanders, but that they could rescue as many Sciotes as possible.

Three days out of Hydra the *'Thermistocles'* anchored in the tiny bay at the front of the town of Psara, capital of the island of the same name. They were to spend two days there working ashore with the local mason to make a forge in which to heat the shot and, finally, fixing sights to the guns and preparing the ship for battle stations. On the afternoon of Wednesday, May 8^{th,} the *'Thermistocles'* sailed out of Psara to cover the 20 or so miles to Scio due east of them. At midnight they boarded a Turkish sachilever, a small vessel without any fixed armaments, and learned that the activities on Scio were perhaps even worse than they understood. They also gained information on the whereabouts of the Samian troops on the island and were able to decide where they could most safely land.

The following morning as the longboats pulled up on the beach of Scala Vollissou on the north-western coast of Scio, the sight which greeted them was one of such horror that even the hardened seamen amongst them vomited. Bodies littered the tiny road of the village, most of which did not have heads attached, and most of the corpses had been mutilated in a most brutal form. In one gutter lay the bloody heads of the victims, many without eyes. Stray dogs ran around gnawing at various parts of the human anatomy including male genitalia which had obviously been removed by other humans. In those cases where the head and torso of the islanders remained together the blood had been drained from gaping gashes in the throats. A peasant woman still wearing the colourful Sciote skirt lay naked from the waist up without her breasts which had obviously been used as sustenance by the now well-fed dogs. If nausea was not caused by the bloody spectacle then it would surely have come from the stench of rotting human debris, the decomposition of which had been accelerated by the warm spring sunshine of the Eastern Mediterranean. The Turks had quelled the attempts of the Sciotes to join the revolution.

Estimates of the numbers massacred vary enormously but certainly the original population was in the region of one hundred thousand. By August of 1822 this had been reduced to thirty thousand or so—even allowing for perhaps ten thousand working away from the island at the time of the start of the butchery and another similar number of refugees who managed to escape. Something approaching fifty thousand inhabitants of Scio were murdered. The party from the *'Thermistocles'* led by Frank Hastings was only able to find five living souls. Two men, two women and a child were taken aboard for transport to the comparative safety of Hydra.

This barbaric massacre affected the whole cause of Greek Independence in two ways. Firstly, when the news arrived in the Western world the indignation was such that people and Governments, which had up to then been disinterested and apathetic, became actively involved with the situation. The various Greek Committees throughout the world either found that they were at last receiving funds or, as with the London Greek Committee, were formed to raise monies to relieve the suffering of the Sciotes. The other more sinister effect was that the Greeks vowed to avenge themselves for the massacre and as retribution they themselves indulged later in similar scenes of inhuman barbarity. Several of these acts of violation against the Turks were to have a detrimental effect upon their cause. As a result, several Philhellenes were to leave the country later in disgust. In their defence, if there can ever be such, the Turks felt that they were only acting in a similar manner to which the Greek troops had acted the previous autumn at Tripolitsa. The main difference was one of scale and also that the horrors of Tripolitsa were perpetrated in the main against armed troops rather than against a whole civilian population.

During the next few days, the Greek and Turkish fleets indulged in cat-and-mouse manoeuvres in the islands off the Turkish coast. The main intention was to corner the opposition, ideally without wind, in the many narrow straits in the area. The Greek tactic, which was to prove so successful, was to fix a fire-ship loaded with highly combustible materials to the windward side of the enemy, light it, and scamper back to base in a longboat. These fire-ships, or brulots, became feared by the Turkish commanders but their own attempts to use the technique invariably failed. During the days following the landing at Scio many attempts were made by the Greek brulots to fix themselves to the Turks but either they failed or the Turks had enough prior warning to prepare themselves to put out the flames.

The constant harassment of the Ottoman ships did cause them to be separated from each other, with the men-of-war to the north of the islands and their smaller vessels thirty or forty miles to the south, with Greeks in between. The very light winds allowed very little opportunity for ships to come into effective firing range of each other. Although on most days there were reports of the '*Thermistocles*' firing upon the enemy and being fired upon there are no reports of them either being hit or finding their own target. One of the main preoccupations during this period was to keep the Greek fleet, now sixty strong, within a reasonable distance of each other.

This opportunity came when, on June 2nd, the Turkish fleet of thirty ships chased the slower Greeks through the straits between Scio and the mainland, only to lose them when the smaller vessels met with strong winds at the northern end and made the safety of Psara harbour. There they joined the '*Thermistocles*' and other more heavily armed vessels at anchor. The winds blew up into a gale and whilst the Turks sped north towards the Dardanelles, the Greeks remained in harbour replenishing food and water. There they learned from an Austrian vessel which had also taken shelter, that the main body of the Turks had headed north and then decided to turn back to take shelter in the Eastern straits of Scio. Admiral Kanaris gave the order to set sail on the evening of June 6th, with brulots prepared.

The night of June 6th was to the Muslims a great religious feast, the Bairam, and on that night many of the senior captains and officers had been invited aboard the Turkish flagship for the celebration. All the Ottoman ships were lit with flares according to custom and the twin-deckers of the Admiral and Vice-Admiral were made even more conspicuous by their sheer size. Amazingly the Turkish lookout ship had been taken off station and Admiral Kanaris decided to enter the straits with only two fire-ships. One was under his own command and the other under Captain Pippinos, leaving the other ships at the entrance of the straits to cover the withdrawal. With a favourable wind, no moon, no lookouts and a brightly illuminated target the journey was comparatively simple. Pippinos attached his brulot to the Vice-Admiral's ship but the skeleton crew left aboard were observant enough to see this in time and were able to control the fire long enough to unfasten the burning hulk and cast it adrift. The element of surprise was perfect aboard the flagship where interest was only centred on the noisy celebrations, allowing a good blaze to establish itself before the alarm was sounded.

Almost all the crew perished including Admiral Al-Zades who was mortally wounded by a falling mast whilst trying to escape and the two long boats rowed through the panic stricken fleet to be greeted at the southern end of the straits by the other ships of the Greek Armada. In triumph they returned to Psara where the whole population, including the clergy in full vestments, welcomed the heroes ashore. The bells of St. Nicholas' Church rang out and a procession of several hundred sailors, soldiers and islanders walked in procession up the hills to the Church for a service of Thanksgiving.

The Turkish fleet, in panic and confusion at the loss of their Admiral and flagship, sailed north to the Dardanelles and protection of their homeland and the Greeks pursued them to establish their bases on the Islands of Limnos and Samathraki, guarding the entrance to the narrow straits leading into the Sea of Marmara which has the city of Constantinople on its north-west shore. The *'Thermistocles'* had many skirmishes on the journey north and on several occasions put ashore to pursue the fleeing Turkish crews who had deserted their vessels on the shore. From prisoners, they learnt that the main enemy fleet had taken shelter on the island of Tenedos between Limnos and the mainland. Over the next few days many attempts were made to attack with fire-ships, but none was successful. Frank Hastings perceived that the main problem was the Greek interest only in destroying the enemy rather than, as he had done so many times in the American wars, capturing the enemy ship.

Knowing of the Turkish fear of the brulots following the Scio sinking, he devised a plan which he took to the stocky, taciturn Admiral Miaoulis. It must be remembered that the Admiral at that time was little more than a courageous and patriotic captain of a merchant brig, elected to his post by his fellow captains. Later he was to become probably the most professional of the Greek sea warriors.

Hastings' plan was to capture the largest Turkish frigate by going in with a brulot and three other vessels but, by burning combustible materials on the decks of the other vessels, lead the enemy to conclude that all four were fire-ships. When alongside the frigate, they were able to fire double shot into the rigging and also combustible balls on to the decks of the frigate. These were to be made to give out the maximum smoke but with little actual flame. In the confusion that would undoubtedly ensue, the Greeks would land boarding parties on the frigate, clear it of remaining Turks and tow it away.

Hastings recorded the result of his interview in his journal:

"The Admiral listed but replied on 'Kalo' (Good), without asking me a single question, or wishing me to explain the details: and I observed a kind of insolent contempt in his manner which no doubt arose from

the late success of Kanaris. This interview with the Admiral disgusted me. They place you in a position in which it is impossible to render any service, and they boast of their own superiority, and of the uselessness of the 'Franks' in Turkish warfare".

Hastings' plan was not put into operation and the crews of the Greek fleet, including the *'Thermistocles'*, continued the policy of undertaking many shore raids on the coast of Asia Minor, largely to plunder for booty. In many cases those plundered were members of the Greek community rather than Ottoman military or civil personnel. Shortly after the disagreeable affair with Admiral Miaoulis, the *'Thermistocles'* was pursuing some Turkish sachilevers off Mitilini on the island of Lesbos. The small but quite fast little vessels headed north and ran ashore on the mainland under the cliffs of Cape Baba. Groups of men from the neighbouring village gathered to watch as the *'Thermistocles'* closed on the land.

The Captain and crew, eager for prizes, chased in a longboat towards the shore but soon returned when they realised that the *'Thermistocles'* had drifted in range of the shore batteries. Within minutes of their return the wind failed completely and their vessel was soon in range of musket fire from the soldiers on the cliffs. Confusion took over and the total lack of discipline manifested itself by every man hiding from the fusillade of shot behind the bulwarks. None paid any heed to the orders given by the ship's officers; indeed the orders were neither comprehensible nor of any sense.

Occasionally a man would spring from his hiding place to undertake some small task and quickly throw himself back to the deck. The only person to remain impassively on deck watching as the ship silently drifted closer to both the enemy and the rocks was Frank Hastings. Oblivious of the shot whistling through the rigging, he searched for a way of altering their position of helplessness. His training and discipline served him well and he perceived a slight rustling in the sails and a minute flurry on the top of the sea. A tiny breeze was coming from the north.

Quickly he sprang to the foredeck and out along the bowsprit, hauling on the heavy jib sail as he went. Ten or fifteen minutes later, all this time under heavy fire, he had the jib over on the port side. Rushing back aft to the steering position, he swung the wheel from starboard to port several times, finally leaving it to port. Inch by inch the ship's head moved away from the shore and the light airs turned to a slight breeze. The *'Thermistocles'* was under way again, moving out of range of the enemy.

At the time of their departure, engineered single-handed by Hastings, there were over two hundred men ashore firing upon them and more were arriving all the time, excited at the prospect of the destruction of the finest ship in the Greek fleet. Even if she had escaped the rocks, it would not have been long before a major hit from the shore batteries would have sunk the *'Thermistocles'*. The Captain had shown no qualities of disciplined leadership and had proved to be thoroughly obstinate for not having a small anchor at the ready for just such an occasion despite numerous warnings from Hastings. The change in the attitude of the Hydriote officers and crew to the foreign seaman was both instant and dramatic.

After the scenes of excitement and congratulation had subsided, it became obvious that by his example Hastings had proved that there was no real substitute for order. To the Captain's great credit he admitted with true generosity that he blamed himself for his carelessness, obstinacy and greed, for allowing a stranger to risk his life to save a Greek ship. In traditional manner, Frank remained aloof from all praise and whilst he never gave any sign of friendship towards the crew members there were many who were to follow him in years to come. He was undoubtedly the engineered single-handed by Hastings.

The *'Thermistocles'* sailed south again for Psara and on one rather embarrassing occasion, spent most of a Saturday chasing a ship. Just before she came into range their target raised English colours. The system of payment amongst Greek armed merchant ships such as the *'Thermistocles'* was that the crew were rewarded in advance of a voyage for the period of a trip. The pay came one third from the owners, one third from the Captain and one third from the island where the ship was based. In times of peace the profits from the cargo and, in times of war, the booty, were divided in similar proportions. Perhaps this was the earliest form of co-operative.

The crew of the '*Thermistocles*' having finished their period of payment insisted on returning to Hydra. When they arrived in the afternoon heat of July 20th, word had arrived before them that 'Artigas', as the Greeks knew him, had saved the pride of the Hydriote fleet. His welcome was tumultuous and his reputation assured for the limited duration of his life.

Chapter 5

1822-1823; Nauplio and actions on 'Leonidas'

Whilst there was some euphoria at the saving of the *'Thermistocles'*, it was with considerable distress that the Hydriotes and their Philhellenic supporters learnt of the course of the war in their absence. In the north of Greece the Eastern Brigades of the Ottomans, under Khursid, had made spectacular advances securing most of the important mountain routes.

To the south the main Turkish army under Dramali had achieved equal success in his advance and the Greek Commander, Odysseus, had made little or no attempt to stop this. The suggested reason for this was that the Government of Mavrokordatos had long been regarded as weak and ineffective and, by allowing the advance of the enemy, Odysseus would create a situation whereby the present ministers would capitulate and allow him to bid for power. Indeed, on the evidence of many in Hydra at that time, the news also carried well-founded rumours that Kolokotronis, Ipsilantis and Petrobey had actually succeeded in the overthrow of the Government. This was not in fact the case, but there was enough substance to suggest that an attempt may have been made.

Whatever the situation, the confusion did allow Dramali to advance with little opposition from the outskirts of Athens, which had been taken by the Greeks on June 21st, move across the narrow strip of land separating the Peloponnese from the mainland and through Corinth towards Argos where the Government was then situated. Perhaps the rumours of the fall of the Government were caused by the fact that on the same day the *'Thermistocles'* arrived back from service in the east, the Ministers fled south from Argos to the small but well defended encampment near to Nauplio called the Mills, leaving the troops of Kolokotronis to defend the pass between Corinth and Argos known as Dervinaki.

Hastings, Hane and Colonel Jourdain set out from Hydra on the *'Thermistocles'* and sailed north up the beautiful Gulf of Argolis, now known to thousands of foreign yachtsmen as the Saronic Gulf, towards the important town of Nauplio. By the evening of July 26th when they arrived at the Mills, they learnt that Argos, the seat of Government, had fallen to Dramali and members of Government came aboard the Hydriote schooner and another from Spetses. The 500 troops of Petrobey had been deserted, leaving them without provision or cannons in the Argos Citadel and surrounded by Turkish troops who consisted largely of a crack cavalry regiment and totalled around 6000. The soldiers of Kolokotronis still dominated the hills and had taken control of the Dervinaki to the north of Argos cutting off any retreat by the Turks.

The vacillation of the Government had left some 20 pieces of field artillery at Navarin and the Turks at Argos had brought in four field guns. The main town of Nauplio was still held by the Turks and it was seen that if Dramali could reach the town before it capitulated under the siege then the hard won military advantages would be totally lost. Indeed it would also have been a great psychological blow for the Greek cause as it had long been the known intention to make Nauplio the seat of Government to replace Argos.

The main point of attack on the town came from an island fortress, the Bourdzi, set in the entrance to the harbour and this was still held by Greek troops from Kranhidi who were to prove totally unreliable. Jarvis, still quarrelling with Hastings, decided to go straight to Argos and the Dervinaki to assist with the relief of the former and the holding of the latter. On July 27th Hastings, Jourdain and a Dane called

Animet were rowed across to the Bourdzi fort carrying Jourdain's shells. They found an almost ruined old Venetian fortress mounting thirteen guns of various calibres and in various conditions. Its guns were aimed roughly at the entrance of the harbour rather than on the town, and it was completely dominated by the Citadel of Nauplio from which it was only two-thirds of a gunshot in distance.

The walls of the fortress were in a state of collapse and even the gun carriages were rotted away and the guns themselves quite rusty. They returned to the schooner that evening and explained to the Minister of War that it would only take an hour or two of concentrated fire from the Turks to render the Bourdzi a pile of useless rubble. The Minister expressed a little concern but ordered them back the following day as he wished them to create a diversion to allow supplies and troops to be sent to the aid of Ipsilantis in the Citadel at Argos. The tactic worked and, taking with them three of the field guns which had by then arrived, the Greeks set off in good heart. Shortly after, they met with resistance. The flag bearer was shot and the Greek banner was picked up by a Priest. As soon as the Priest saw the bulk of Turkish foot and mounted soldiers he panicked and retreated with the Ensign. The Greeks heard his cries of *"Retreat—save yourselves!"* and followed suit. Fortunately the confusion created on both sides did allow Ipsilantis to make his escape.

Hastings met him the following day at the Mills and described him as having an interesting and intelligent countenance but being worn out with fatigue and anxiety. On his return to the fort with orders to continue gunnery experiments, the 'Captain' of the fort refused him, heaping abuse upon the foreigners. Shortly after, a Mr Valiano arrived with his cousin and fifty men to relieve the troops. Again they refused to co-operate. It suddenly became obvious to the Franks what was happening—the reason for the Fort's old armaments being aimed at the harbour rather than the town, the refusal to carry out experiments with Jourdain's shells and the refusal to hand over the post to other soldiers. They felt safe enough—wrongly—in the Fortress and they were the nearest troops to the wealthy Turkish merchant's homes and businesses. They were frightened of losing the chance of booty.

With this knowledge Hane and Hastings resolved to do much of the work themselves and when they looked at the first gun they knew that it could not first be used without proving its safety. They had asked for water to be brought to see if there were any holes caused by rust but such was the unpleasantness from the Greeks that they decided to take a chance and unwillingly fire the mortar regardless of the hazard. As they suspected, the shell exploded at the mouth of the mortar but miraculously nobody was hurt. The troops still refused to carry out trials and prove the safety of their weapons. Another major problem they encountered was that when they eventually arranged the guns in the right position for a bombardment, the recoil of the gun was stronger than the crumbling wall of the Bourdzi. Several accidents were reported and at one stage they did more damage with their own weapons than the Turks over the water.

By August 2nd Jourdain and Mr Valiano decided that the fortress was untenable. Jourdain had been to the Mills to obtain spirits to dry his shells because he blamed wetness for their lack of success but he now refused to stay and try them. Although a large party quit the fort that evening, Hastings, Hane and Animet refused to go while there was any chance of success. The three spent the evening preparing what they called the 'bombs' and as they gradually gained in range and trajectory it became obvious that with trained men and more equipment, Nauplio could be brought to early submission. Their fear of Greek duplicity was well founded.

Despite visits and repeated requests for aid to the Minister of War, nothing was forthcoming. With Greek successes in the north, the garrison at Nauplio was more concerned with helping the escaping Turkish troops. On August 6th the three 'gentlemen'—a term used to differentiate themselves from the Greeks—saw little more they could do and left the Bourdzi. They came alongside the schooner with most of the members of the Government aboard but were refused permission to come alongside and in fury Hastings grabbed the chain plates, swung aboard and pulled Hane and Animet behind him. His complaint of apathy and lack of support was recorded as being greeted with a shrug of the shoulders and: *"What can you expect from people without education?"*

The very words that Hastings had sent in his letter to Prince Mavrokordatos earlier in the year!

Nevertheless they demanded to see the Minister for War the following day and this having been agreed to, they were given quarters on board an accompanying brig. They met with the Minister next morning, and using a mixture of threats to leave and promises of things to come, the Minister agreed to give them official Greek Commissions in the immediate future. This was supported by a Greek, Nicholas Kallergy, who had met all three on a number of occasions and had formed a very strong friendship with them. He agreed to take them into his artillery and this was enough to satisfy the Franks who said they would go down to Mylos to await the notification of their official status.

Valiano had left the Bourdzi with Jourdain to take up residence on the lovely island of Mylos some sixty miles to the south-east of Hydra and they were amazed at the Turkish plunder on the island where many members of the Government and their staff had taken refuge. Even Hastings, who strongly disapproved of looting, added to his considerable library by purchasing sixty-five volumes of French works for thirty-five piastres.

Their visit to the comparative safety of Mylos was cut short on August 14th, when Hastings realised that a bout of dysentery to which both Hane and Animet had succumbed had lasted too long for it to merely have been one of the regular attacks. He was so worried about the state of their health that he hired a boat and set off for Hydra. Their condition must have made the journey seem longer, although northerly headwinds caused the small craft to tack all the way and they did not arrive until the following evening.

By then the two friends were very weak and a cause for great concern. Hastings, described by those who did not know him well as something of a 'cold fish' wrote in his journal:

"Hane and Animet were still more ill than before we left, but I could not procure them any medical or other assistance from the Government. I *then saw myself charged with their support as they had no money, nor effects that would produce money, and I could not see my comrades absolutely die in want and sickness without proffering them succour"*

A 'cold fish' maybe, but for whatever reasons, duty or friendship or a mixture of both, Hastings spent the next two weeks both nursing them back to health and browbeating the Greek Government Ministers who came in and out of Hydra, to do something for them. Eventually the Minister of War agreed to look after them and they left Hydra to recuperate on Mylos under the supervision of the Government Medical Officer. It was actions such as these that explain the loyalty Hastings engendered in those with him and his supposed aloofness was merely the product of his training with the British Navy from the age of eleven.

With domestic matters now settled to his satisfaction, Hastings could now turn his mind back to his favourite occupation—fighting. Kalergy, who had already agreed that Hastings could meet up with his land forces told him that this would not come about for a couple of months and so the two of them joined another ship owned by Manolis Tombazis, the '*Leonidas*'. Shortly after they sailed the owner went aboard the Flagship and saw letters from Count Capo d'Istrias, now using the Hellenic form of his name, Kapodistrias, who in his post of a Minister to the Tsar of Russia informed the Greeks that both he and the Tsar would be attending the Congress of Verona. A few days later another letter arrived stating that Kapodistrias, who had served the Russian Government for so many years, had resigned his post and would actually be attending the Congress as a Greek.

This caused great jubilation, and the combatants were quite sure that the Russians had supported this action with the intention of making Kapodistrias the Sovereign of Greece. Hastings, as always, had very strong feelings on the subject and is reported as saying:

"Personally I should greatly rejoice at such a result, for the foreigners would be much better received by him than by the present <u>Canaille</u> (French—literally meaning riff-raff) that form the Government".

During the month of September the '*Leonidas*' remained on station guarding the entrance to the Gulf of Argolis and the supply route to Nauplio. This gave rise to many skirmishes and a great waste of gunpowder on both sides, but it did stop the Turkish Fleet supplying its beleaguered garrison in the town of Nauplio. It was during this period that Frank Hastings came to realise that unprofessional crews, part-time merchant ships converted to men-of-war, varying degrees of enthusiasm of the owners and the system of paying the crews in advance for a set period could never defeat the Turkish navy.

He continued in his vain attempts to improve the situation and in particular with his experiments of fitting wheels to guns but despite the logic of his arguments, he never obtained general agreement from the Greek Captains. He also became increasingly worried about their treatment of prisoners and realised that whilst the tide of public opinion in the West was firmly with Greece, any reports of brutality on their behalf could soon change this. Hastings needed this support in the West if he was ever to have his own properly equipped and staffed ship. There were many times during September when he came near to abandoning the whole cause.

Hastings' Journal—12 September 1822:

"I sometimes despair of the situation. The Greeks hold nothing so much in honour as disorder. Whilst on board with the Admiral today I saw something the horror of which will never leave my memory. A Turkish prisoner was brought on board to be interrogated, and after he had answered the questions the crew came and surrounded him, pulled him by the hair and beat him. He was then dragged several times around the deck by his beard and at length thrown living into the sea.

During this horrid ceremony the crew appeared to take the greatest delight in this spectacle, laughing and rejoicing, and when he was in the water the men in the boat struck him with a boathook. This shocked me so much I could not help letting them see I disapproved of it, although it was impossible to fully express my disapproval as this would have certainly exposed me to their revenge".

That same day Hane and Animet, having fully recovered from their illness, returned to the fleet but Hane immediately carried on back to the Bourdzi fortress with the rather better Ionian troops. Animet, hearing Hastings' story of the prisoner, recounted one that had taken place that morning on board the Brig Minerva which had transported him back from Mylos.

"This morning we captured a Turkish ship, and after sinking the ship with grape shot we picked up some of the wounded who floated along with two Greek women prisoners who had been aboard. The wounded were senseless, but the Greeks did not consider that to kill them was cruel enough, so they revived them. Afterwards one of the women cut the throat of two of them with her own hand. The others after torturing greatly they hung to death from the spars, and even then they heaped revenge upon their bodies. The Turks handled themselves with great courage, and the ones I saw made no complaints nor supplication or acted meanly in any way. One I saw trembled greatly, but he had already been half drowned, pulled round the deck by the beard and beaten—it was not surprising that his nerve should have failed him"

The following days did nothing that suggested that these were isolated incidents, or that the Greek Government showed any signs of getting to grips with the growing anarchy amongst its fleet. Hastings' journal records the increasing number of reports in the main Greek fleet indicating that the weakness and irresolution of the Government had really spread through the forces.

Sept. 25th:

"Arrived in Hydra. Pay for the crew for the month had arrived—they had all stated they would not leave without it. What marvellous patriotism is to be the form in Greece".

Sept. 27th:

"We received a report of a Turkish attack on Psara. This greatly alarmed the men on board who resolved gallantly to run away and leave their

countrymen to have their throats cut. They did not wish to get too close—Quelles Animaux!".

Of almost equal concern was the behaviour of the many foreign adventurers arriving, often daily, from Marseilles and Genoa:
"*I learnt that the 'Franks' on board other ships were conducting themselves in a manner not at all likely to gain the esteem of the Greeks—eating, drinking and smoking seems to be their principal occupation*".

It was certainly with some relief that Frank had dinner with his friend Nicholas Kalergy, Kalergy's brother and Count Metaxas on board the '*Leonidas*'. He learnt that Hane had done his job well at Bourdzi, and that the Dervinaki was still held by the troops of Kolokotronis, although they were still under great pressure from Dramali. Kalergy agreed that if Hastings recruited a small troop of men both he and Hane could assist him in the support of the forces in Dervinaki. A few days later Hane and Hastings met up at the Mills in the Bay of Nauplio and from his remaining supply of gold coin Frank recruited and paid some fifty soldiers to join them. They also procured horses for themselves and two Ionian Officers with them.

Many of the Ionian troops had fought with the Venetians and some with the French in the past and were certainly of a far higher calibre than those with whom Frank had previously had dealings in Greece. The short march from the Mills to Argos gave him great pleasure and brought back memories of leading his company of the Naval Brigade at the Battle of New Orleans some ten years earlier. Indeed the hot autumn sunshine and lack of resistance in the early miles added to the carnival atmosphere of the small army as it marched north.

They rounded Argos and headed towards the hills overlooking the main passes and saw scenes of great destruction. There is no doubt that Kolokotronis, Ipsilantis and Petrobey had fought long and courageously. They were not sure of the whereabouts of Dramali, although there was every possibility that he had escaped north to Corinth and this could have been allowed by the main interest of the Greek troops being in plundering the retreating Ottoman soldiers.

The interest of their leaders, especially the Commander-in-Chief Kolokotronis, was of a more political nature in trying to establish their power base.

By the time the weather in the mountains became cold, Hastings and his small force had aided the Greeks in sealing off the retreat for the surviving 5,000 or so Turks left from the original army of Dramali of 23,000. Virtually all their animals had either been killed or captured and it is clear that the Turkish army was defeated. Kolokotronis knew this well but waited to make his attack on Nauplion until it suited his own purposes and informed the Government that the decision was his and his alone. It again suited the warrior 'klepht' only to obey orders at his own convenience and naturally the other chiefs followed his lead.

The Greek army had thus disintegrated into a rabble little better than the navy. It was noted by the foreign observers that the army were concentrating on the booty to come from Nauplio, whilst the navy only survived by the incompetence of Mehemet, the Capitan-Pasha. The Greeks put all their faith at sea into the use of fire ships but they were the only ones not to realise that these were only successful under the command of somebody as brave and skilful as Kanaris.

Greed, incompetence and political ambition stood in the way of bringing the Greek Wars of Independence to an early conclusion by the speedy taking of Nauplio and setting up an effective Government in the ancient city. During the last weeks of 1822 in the minds of foreign combatants, foreign Governments and a number of more sensible Greeks was that Kolokotronis would be the perpetrator of another bloody massacre at Nauplio, an event that would totally discredit the Greek cause. The Greek occupation of Nauplio by early December was quite inevitable; the last Turkish attempts to bring relief from the North had been foiled by Kolokotronis and his many helpers, including Hastings and his Company.

On December 12th the fortress of Palamidhi overlooking Nauplio surrendered to the Greeks and it was obvious that the town could only hold out for a few days longer, especially as the Turks had learnt of the death of their Commander, Dramali. Fortunately for the history of modern Greece it was an Englishman, Captain Hamilton who saved another murderous episode and thus maintained their creditability in the outside world. Hamilton commanded the British Navy in the Levant, and his ship the *'Cambrian'* dropped anchor off Nauplio on Christmas Eve of 1822.

Immediately after Christmas, Hamilton was joined by Hastings and Hane who were able to give him first-hand accounts of the many atrocities committed by both sides and also traded naval and military intelligence of the situation as it then was. Hamilton, during his long periods with the British Navy in the Levant, had met many of the primates and chieftains and had a certain respect for them but he was also much influenced by his discussions with Thomas Gordon who had returned to England in disgust after the massacre of Tripolitsa. They were all passionate believers in the Greek cause and were all convinced that it another massacre was allowed, the support of the London Greek Committee, and other similar bodies throughout the world, would be lost.

Using the full pomp of His Majesty's Navy, Hamilton summoned the Moreot chieftains and Kolokotronis on board the *'Cambrian'* for a conference. Despite the Russian sympathies of the 'delegates' who still looked to the Tsar and Kapodistrias for aid, the bearing and strength of the English Naval Officer won them over. He was also acutely aware from his intelligence that there was no point in having support from the Government, such as it was, without that of Kolokotronis and he realised that any sign of compromise would convince the latter of his weakness. In the strongest possible language and in an honest and forthright manner, Hamilton told them that if they failed to take effective measures to execute an honourable capitulation the name of Greece would be rendered despicable in civilised Europe, and the Greek cause would be ruined. Having swung their opinion in his favour this energetic officer took immediate advantage of the situation.

He insisted that the Greek Government, supported by the troops, chartered ships to embark some nine hundred captors and he promised to take a further five hundred aboard the '*Cambrian*' for transport to the Turkish mainland port of Smyrna. In the negotiations with the Turkish garrison, this offer was gratefully accepted by the two Pashas in command on behalf of their troops but to their great honour neither Ali of Argos nor Selim actually agreed to sign the capitulation document. Due to this they remained prisoners of the Greeks.

Of the five hundred men taken on to the '*Cambrian*' sixty-seven died of Typhus before they reached Smyrna and the fever spread amongst the English crew causing the death of several. In his gallant and humanitarian actions, Hamilton had put himself and his own crew at risk. Regardless of this sacrifice, many Greeks felt that his actions went against the honour of the Greek army and certainly did not satisfy the lust for revenge after Scio. Hastings, who went on board the '*Cambrian*' again on January 5th 1823, saw the Turks embarked and wrote that evening: *"Much difference of opinion exists among the Greeks on the conduct of Captain Hamilton, but I feel convinced that he saved the lives of the Turks by his prompt measures, and thus did a great service to Greece"*.

A few days later Hastings returned to Hydra, and he there wrote: *"I found here, as at Nauplio, various opinions concerning Captain Hamilton's conduct, but respectable people here were in his favour."*

The last word on Hamilton's termination of the bloody campaign in the areas around the north of the Gulf of Argolis must be that of George Finlay: *"Captain Hamilton was the first public advocate of the Greek cause among Englishmen in an influential position, and he deserves to be ranked among the greatest benefactors of Greece"*.

During the early months of 1823, Hastings based himself at his house in Hydra and apart from odd trips on one of the Tombazis' ships to continue the 'cat-and-mouse' games in the Gulf of Argolis, life was somewhat dull for he and John Hane, both keen for more adventure. It was with considerable delight that in March they were told that Manolis Tombazis had been appointed Governor of Candia, that rocky island to the south of the Aegean now known as Crete.

The Cretans remain to this day a fiercely independent and nationalistic race, which is not surprising when one considers the variety of nations by whom they have been ruled. In the Classical Greek period, Crete remained separate from the other states and was conquered by the Romans in 67 BC. It became part of the Eastern Roman Empire in 364 AD, was occupied by the Arabs in 823, the Byzantine Greeks in 961 and was sold to the Venetians in 1204. After twenty-four years of fighting, the Turks took over in 1688 and, despite many attempts at liberation during the Wars of Independence and the uprising of 1866-1869, Crete did not become part of Greece until the Balkan Wars in the early twentieth century.

At the time of Manolis Tombazis' appointment, the Greeks knew that a strong revolutionary movement had been going for nearly two years led by the mountain chiefs and warriors from the Sphakia region in the west. They had received some support from the other islands, but it was felt that with a concentrated effort it would be possible to join up with the Sphakiots and take the main town of Candia on the northern central coast. To this end, Tombazis recruited well over a thousand troops and within these numbers were the more experienced Kranidhiot artillery men to whom were allocated a forty-eight pound carronade and some fourteen field guns of twelve and four pounds. The artillery he placed under the command of Frank Hastings and Captain Hane was appointed as his second-in-command.

The fleet of eight vessels left Hydra on May 30th and anchored in the protected Gulf of Kissamou to the extreme north west of the island three days later. The town of Kissamou capitulated with relative ease but then the old familiar problems with the undisciplined troops began. As was their normal custom, they wanted to murder their Turkish prisoners and loot the premises of Turk and Greek alike. On that occasion Hastings and Hane turned their artillery upon the Greek soldiers and threatened to open fire if any form of massacre should commence. To achieve this they even had to threaten to shoot the leaders of their own artillery men and whilst they saved the populace of Kissamou, they left themselves in a very vulnerable position.

Some days later the invading troops took the town of Khadena but this time the artillery refused to co-operate and despite strong protestations and pleading, the two Englishmen could do little to stop a blood-bath. Both complained vehemently to Tombazis and threatened to leave Crete. However the deed had been done and even the Governor proved powerless against the chiefs and soldiers. Despite this, Hane was to remain in Crete until April of the following year but the visit of Frank was all too short. By June of that year, 1823, his physical condition had deteriorated quite badly and he was subject to frequent bouts of fever. Hane, having himself been nursed back to health by Hastings, grew increasingly worried at the growing frequency of the attacks of fever and in some desperation he visited Manolis Tombazis and begged him to order their mutual friend back to Hydra as soon as possible. Equally worried at the possibility of losing not only a friend but his most trusted and reliable officer, Tombazis issued the order and arranged transport immediately back to Hydra.

On his arrival, Hastings, considerably weakened from the journey, was immediately attended by the senior doctor to the Fleet who, without doubt, saved his life by careful nursing. After a century and a half it is difficult to identify the nature of the illness but some Greek reports have it that Hastings lost most of his teeth from his fever which would indicate scurvy although others suggest that it was a form of Typhus. Whatever the cause, he was very ill for more than a month, and was only just recovered fully by October.

The piece of news that delighted him best during the period of convalescence was that Lord Byron, at the request of the London Greek Committee, had arrived in Greece. This stimulated him to finally formulate and record his plans for the Greek Navy and the use of steam-ships in the campaign and undoubtedly this impetus aided his recovery. He resolved that when his plans were complete and his health recovered enough, he would present them to Byron and seek his support. By October the situation was right for him to make his move and he first decided to visit Athens and establish a base there—having done this he set out for Cephalonia and Byron.

Chapter 6

Byron and The London Greek Committee

Byron's place in the history of Greece is undoubtedly very important but it is centred in two periods of time. The first of these is his early period when he wrote his most magnificent poetry about the country; the popular acclaim that these works achieved made many thousands aware of this nation to the east of the Mediterranean which for so long had been totally disregarded. His second period, which included his life and death in Greece, was that in which the wide regard for his name as a poet allowed the various Greek supporters around the world and especially in London, to raise money, political support and volunteers to join the cause.

Greek Committees had already been formed in Spain, Germany, Italy, Switzerland and France when Mavrokordatos asked a friend of his, John Louriottes, to visit some of the Committees to obtain funds. Partly they were hoping to obtain donations to the cause, and somewhat vainly they hoped to raise national loans. Whilst in Madrid, Louriottes met with a strange Irish ex-sea Captain and adventurer by the equally strange name of Edward Blaquiere who managed to convince him that London was the best place to raise a loan and naturally that Blaquiere was the best man to assist. The decision to move on to London could also have been aided by the fact that the founder of the Madrid Greek Committee, Sir John Bowring, had recently returned to London and had remained a passionate Philhellene.

With Thomas Gordon in London still working for the Greek cause, it was certainly an obvious place for a major Committee. Blaquiere, good to his word, introduced Louriottes to many known Philhellenes who were most impressed by his accounts of the progress of the war and also his hugely optimistic assessments of the potential wealth of the country once released from the Ottomans.

Even before the actual formation of a London Greek Committee, many individuals had written to Lord Byron in Italy, asking for his involvement and from correspondence with two particular friends, John Cam Hobhouse and Edward Trelawny, it is clear that he intended to join the struggle. These same individuals also asked Louriottes and Blaquiere to return to Greece both to tell the Government that they intended to form a London group and also to prepare an up-to-date report on the situation to assure them that monies raised would be going into the right hands.

With public opinion firmly behind them after the shock of the news of the massacre on Scio, on March 3rd 1823, Sir John Bowring, J.C. Hobhouse, Thomas Gordon and twenty-two other Philhellenes met at the Crown and Anchor in The Strand to officially form the London Greek Committee. One of the first actions was an agreement that they should invite Byron to be their representative in Greece. To this end when Blaquiere set off the following day for Greece he carried with him the letters and the pleadings of the London Greek Committee which he was asked to deliver in person to Byron.

The call appealed to the famous noble poet on many counts; his old friend Hobhouse had promised to join him, as had Trelawny. His relationship with Teresa Guccioli had been somewhat overshadowed by the arrival in Genoa of Lady Blessington, despite the fact that Teresa's brother Pietro Gamba was still very close to him. Perhaps most importantly he was tiring of life in Italy and of the constant demands on his wealth by many expatriate Englishmen in the area. Whatever the reasons Byron greeted Blaquiere and Louriottes with very great enthusiasm when they called upon him at Albaro, a suburb of Genoa, on April 7th. He gave them his promise that he would give serious consideration to their flattering proposals but all the indications were that he had already made up his mind to go to Greece once he had broken his relationships with Teresa Guiccioli and Lady Blessington.

By June he had found the courage to tell his close friends, male and female, that he was leaving them and undoubtedly in his own mind he felt that he would never return from Greece. At the same time he wrote to Edward Trelawny, who was on a visit to Rome, and asked his friend whom he described as his 'personification of my Corsair' to join him to sail for Greece. Byron threw himself into the preparations for his heroic adventure with a romantic fervour, his enthusiasm spurring on those around him. He designed the most magnificent comic opera uniforms for himself and his retinue and even had Greek classical helmets made, his own with the Byron coat-of-arms on the front, similar for Trelawny who had by then joined him and one for Pietro Gamba with the goddess Athena.

On a more practical side, he hired a doctor and procured medical supplies, sold his own sailing boat, the *'Bolivar'*, and chartered a three-masted clipper—the *'Hercules'*. On July 13th, watched from the terraced hillside gardens above the harbour by Teresa and the widow of Shelley, Mary, the *'Hercules'* slipped out of the port. She went little further as the wind dropped completely and one can only imagine the frustration of Byron, Trelawny, Gamba, the medical student Bruno, Bryon's personal servant Fletcher, his gondolier Tita, and Trelawny's black African servant as they wallowed hopelessly off the coast of Italy. After two days the American Navy took pity on them and the *'Hercules'* was towed out further to sea to search for wind. Even then, fortune was not with them. Perhaps they should have heeded their superstitions and not sailed on the 13th, because soon a violent gale sprang up, causing great problems for the horses they carried and much sea-sickness with the adventurers, especially Gamba and the decision was made by the ship's master, Captain Scott, to head back for harbour. A few days later they tried again and this time successfully sailed to Leghorn where they took on two additional supporters, a Greek Captain named Vitalis, and a Scottish Philhellene, James Hamilton Browne.

This relative of Lord Hamilton knew Greece well and had for a time been Assistant Secretary to the Ionian Senate until his pro-Greek sympathies became too much of an embarrassment to "King Tom of Corfu", the British High Commissioner to the Ionian Protectorate, Sir Thomas Maitland. This exceedingly incompetent and foolish British administrator was forced to dismiss Hamilton Browne to uphold his own policy of total neutrality to such an extent that he often seemed to favour the Turks.

With his intimate knowledge of Greek affairs, Hamilton Browne advised Byron to land on the Ionian Island of Cephalonia, rather than Zante as advised earlier by Blaquiere, on the basis that the British Resident for the Island, Colonel Charles Napier, was also known to have pro-Greek sympathies and had only obtained his post through his relative, Fox, and other influential friends in England.

Hamilton Browne's advice was sound as Byron and his group were warmly met by Napier when they landed in Cephalonia on August 3rd 1823. Although Napier was careful to adhere to the laws of neutrality, his interpretation allowed him to agree to Byron remaining on the beautiful Ionian island; an interpretation which was not agreed by Sir Thomas Maitland. Byron and Napier soon became the centre of political information and many factions flocked to them to present their particular case. The Suliot warriors had recently suffered a defeat in the north and had taken refuge in Cephalonia, their leader Bonsais, although both sending and receiving a letter from Byron, died after battle in August and Byron appointed his personal Suliot Guard as new leader. The Greeks were in turmoil; Mavrokordatos had been ousted as President by the Marmots who had appointed Petrobey as President and, after a short period with Theodoritos Bishop of Vresthena as Vice President this role went to Kolokotronis causing an alliance between Ipsilantis who had been completely overlooked and Mavrokordatos. The emerging nation was on the verge of civil war.

Byron felt equally worried about the London Greek Committee and even Blaquiere, who had promised to meet him on his arrival, had returned to England. The romantic hopes of leading a magnificent army to victory were fast fading as Byron came to the realisation that his post was one created for his name and money alone and that his only function was to act as a quartermaster for stores and funds raised in London. To his great credit, whilst thoroughly disappointed, he took this latter task with great statesmanship and refused to part with supplies until he was certain that the faction with whom he was dealing was going to be the true representative of the Greek people rather than of a particular local interest.

Having arrived and spent the first month at the Cephalonian capital of Argostoli, Byron was allowed by Napier to move his growing retinue to Metaxata where to the embarrassment of the British Government, he virtually set up court to deal with the many demands upon him. Trelawny, by this time having assumed the costume of a Suliot chief, was tiring of the political intrigue at Cephalonia, and was delighted when Byron sent him and Hamilton Browne on tour of Greece to try to ascertain the true political and military situation.

Frank Hastings, during this period, was recovering from his illness in Hydra and saw the arrival of Byron as a great opportunity to put forward his plans to somebody with the ability to cause them to be put into action. For six weeks, with growing strength, Frank worked on his theories which he vowed to take to Byron in October after visiting Athens. The memorandum he prepared after many re-writes for Byron was later modified but still used as a basis for the London Greek Committee, Lord Cochrane and the Greek Government. Just before his death, Hastings wrote an article which analysed the results of his plans when put to test—this was published as a small booklet by Ridgeway in 1828 (and used for many years as the basis of steam naval warfare throughout the world.

The original memorandum for Byron is written here in the words of Frank without alteration to more modern style, words or punctuation:

"Firstly, I lay down as an axiom that Greece cannot obtain any decisive advantage over the Turks without a decided maritime superiority; for it is necessary to prevent them from relieving their fortresses and supplying their armies by sea. To prove this it is only necessary to view the state of the Greek armies, and that of their finances. They are destitute of a corps of artillery, of a park of artillery, of a corpse of engineers, and of a regular army.

With all these wants, I ask, how is it possible to take a fortress but by famine? This, however, is difficult, even if the sea was shut against the Turks; for, from the state of the Greek finances, and the formation of the army, troops can scarcely remain long enough for a place furnished with a formidable garrison, and tolerably supplied with provisions, to reduce it. However, famine is the only resource, and it is by that alone that the fortresses now in the hands of the Greeks have been reduced.
The localities of the country are also such, and the difficulty of moving troops so great, that, without the aid of a fleet, all the efforts of an invading army would prove fruitless. But on the contrary, were an invading army followed by a fleet, I fear that all the efforts of the Greeks to oppose it would be ineffectual. The question stands thus: Has the Greek fleet hitherto prevented the Turks from supplying their fortresses, and is it likely to succeed in preventing them? I reply, that Patras, Negrepont, Modon, and Coron have been regularly supplied, and Messolongi twice blockaded.

Is it likely that the Greek marine will improve, or that the Turkish will retrograde? The contrary is to be feared. We have seen the Greek fleet diminish in numbers every year since the commencement of the War, whilst that of the Turks has undeniably improved, from the experience they have gained in each campaign. Witness the unsuccessful attempts with fire-ships this year (1823). The Turks begin to find fire-ships only formidable to those unprepared to receive them. Is the Greek fleet likely to become more formidable? On the contrary, the sails, rigging, and hulls are all getting out of repair; and in two years' time thirty sail could hardly be sent to sea without an expense which the Greeks would not probably incur.

We now come to the question; How can the Greeks obtain a decisive superiority over the Turks at sea? I reply; By a steam vessel armed as I shall describe. But how is Greece to obtain such a vessel? The means of Greece are much more than amply sufficient to meet this expenditure.

However, there are various reasons which it is not Necessary to detail, but which would probably prevent the Greek Government from adopting the plan. It therefore becomes necessary to ascertain how such a vessel might be equipped without calling on the Greek Government to contribute directly. If proper statements were made to the Greek Committee in England, I think it might be induced to bear some part of the expense. I will contribute £10000 on the condition that I have the command, and that the vessel is armed in the manner I propose. If this does not form a sufficient fund, I think that the deficiency may be made up by a loan; a guarantee being given that a certain portion—say one half of all prizes—shall be applied to the payment of interest and the extinction of the debt. The same proportion would be set apart to meet the expenses of the vessel, so that the Greek Government might be called upon to bear no other expenses but the wages of the crew.

I shall now explain the details of the proposed armament, and the advantages I think would result from it. It would be necessary to build or purchase the vessel in England, and send her out complete. She should be from 150 to 200 tons burden, of a construction sufficiently strong to bear two long 32-pounders, one forward and one aft, and two 68-pounder guns of seven inches bore, one on each side. The weight of shot appears to me to be of the greatest importance, for I think I can prove that half a dozen shot or shells of these calibres, and employed as I propose, would more than suffice to destroy the largest ship. In this case it is not the number of projectiles, but their nature and proper application that is required.

In order that the vessel should present less surface to the wind, and less mark to the enemy, combined with a greater range of pointing and more facility for the use of red-hot shot, the bulwark should be sufficiently low to admit of the guns being fired over it. From the long 32-pounders I propose launching red-hot shot, because, though perhaps not more destructive than shells, they give a longer range; and the fuel required to impel the vessel could easily be made to heat the shot. The idea being rather novel, startles people at first, because, as it has never been put n practice, they imagine there must be some extraordinary danger to which it subjects your own vessel. But this is not the case. The real reason it has never been adopted hitherto is, that on board a ship you cannot lay your guns before you introduce your red-hot shot, as on shore. This arises, of course, from the motion of the vessel. In other words, the danger arises from the possibility of fire communicating to the cartridge during the operation of running out and pointing the gun. If, however, it be prove by experience that, with proper precautions, the shot may be allowed to remain any length of time in the gun without setting fire to the cartridge, this difficulty (and it is the only difficulty) vanishes. In fact, during the siege of Gibraltar the guns were pointed against the block-ships after being loaded, it being found that one wet wad alone was sufficient security, and that with it the shot might absolutely be left to get cold in the gun. It may, however, be thought necessary to cast iron bottoms for the hot shot, of the same form as those of wood which I propose to make use of in loading the guns with shells. These may be placed over the wad, and then the gun may be well sponged, to drown any particles of powder that might by accident escape from the cartridge. With this precaution the shot might be left to cool in the gun, and there could therefore be no want of time to run out and point it. But this would be unnecessary if the gun worked over the bulwark, for it could then be loaded with its muzzle just outside the vessel, having been previously laid to its elevation, the direction being obtained by a slight movement of the helm. Thus there would be no necessity for touching the gun after the shot was once introduced. Perhaps the precautions I propose are in part superfluous, as hot shot are fired on shore without observing them.

Of the destructive effect of hot shot on an enemy's ship it is scarcely necessary for me to speak. The destruction of the Spanish fleet before Gibraltar is well known. But if I may be permitted to relate an example which came under my proper observation it will perhaps tend to corroborate others. At New Orleans the Americans had a ship and a schooner in the Mississippi that flanked our lines. In the commencement we had no cannon. However, after a couple of days, pieces of 4 or 6lb. and a howitzer were erected in a battery. In ten minutes the schooner was on fire, and her comrade, seeing the effects of the hot shot, cut her cable, and escaped under favour of a light wind. If such was the result of light shot imperfectly heated—for we had no forge—what would have been the effect of a 32-pouner? A single shot would set a ship in flames.

Having treated the subject of hot shot, I shall now pass to the use of shells. It has long been well known that ships are more alarmed at shells than at other projectiles. However, they rarely do the mischief apprehended from them, in consequence of the difficulty of hitting so small an object as a ship with a projectile thrown vertically. This uncertainty prevents bomb-vessels being employed against ships. If, however, shells be thrown horizontally, their effect would be equally great, and the chance of hitting the object aimed at reduced to the same certainty as if shot were used within a certain range. If the shell passed inside the vessel and exploded, the result would be the same as if it had been thrown vertically. My object, however, would be, to arrange it so as to make the shell stick in the ship's side and explode there. The result in this case would be much more decisive, and it would tear away part of her side, and might send her instantly to the bottom. In both cases it would probably destroy a number of the crew and set fire to the ship.

It remains, therefore, to ascertain whether shells can be thrown to a sufficient distance with precision from guns and carronades, and without any danger to your own vessel. The danger of transporting shells is considerably less than the danger of passing powder. It is, therefore, only necessary to prove how they may be fired without danger. The danger of firing a shell from a gun longer than a howitzer or a carronade is, that it might, by rolling in the bore, destroy the fuse and explode in the gun; also, that the fuse might break from the successive blows it would receive before quitting the muzzle. Now, both these objections are obviated by attaching the shell to a wooden bottom, hollowed out to receive its convexity. Each shell would be kept in a separate box.

We now come to the plan of attack. In executing this, I should go directly for the vessel most detached from the enemy's fleet, and when at the distance of one mile, open with red-hot shot from the 32-pounder forward. The gun laid at point blank, with a reduced charge, would carry on board 'en ricochetant'. I would then wheel round and give the enemy one of the 68-pounders with shell laid at the line of metal, which would also ricochet on board him. Then the stern 32-pounder with a hot shot, and again the 68-pounder on the other side with a shell. By this time the bow gun would again be loaded, and a succession of fire might be kept up as brisk as from a vessel having four guns on a side. Here the importance of steam is evident.

With good locks, tubes, Congreve's sights, and other improvements in artillery, I really see almost as much difficulty in missing a ship of any size in tolerably smooth water as in hitting her. In firing from a ship, the great difficulty is in the elevation; but when my guns were laid at point blank, or two degrees of elevation, neither shot nor shells would ricochet over the enemy.

With regard to any risk of the steam machinery being destroyed by the enemy's fire, there is of course some risk, as there always must be in military operations of the simplest kind; but when we consider the small object a low steamer would present when coming head on, and the manner in which the Turks have hitherto used their guns at sea, this risk really appears very trifling. The surprise caused by seeing a vessel moving in a calm, offering only a breadth of about eighteen feet, and opening fire with heavy guns at a considerable distance, may also be taken into account. I am persuaded, from what I have seen, that in many cases the Turks would run from their ships ashore and abandon them, perhaps without having the presence of mind to set fire to them. It would be necessary to have a Greek brig always in company to carry coals and to tow the steamer, for the steam would only be used in action"

The remainder of the memorandum was mainly costs for both the operation and furbishing of such a vessel. At its very simplest the whole scene must have sounded quite preposterous to men steeped in the traditions of naval battle. The very idea of a paddle-driven steamer going round and round in circles and alternately firing hot-shot and shells from the bow, the side, the stern and then the other side must have seemed alien.

Frank Hastings was convinced and, having had the weeks of inactivity recuperating from his illness, he was well prepared to argue his case. In early October he was well enough to move his base to Athens which by then was attracting many observers and adventurers to see the damaged but still extant classical splendours of the city. Not only did he intend to spend his time there learning to speak more fluent Greek but he rightly assumed that he would have a better opportunity to meet men of influence who could help his crusade for a steam-ship. Towards the end of the month he was settled into his house near the central square of the Plaka district, one of the few areas of Athens remaining today, and he set off for Cephalonia to present his case to Lord Byron.

On the surface he may well have expected to get on well with the poet. They were both from English aristocratic families, their homes in the Midlands were only a few miles from each other and Byron was only six years older than Frank. So little is recorded of their meeting, one can only assume that the differences between the two men were so great that they merely tolerated each other out of mutual necessity. It is also probable that Napier, by that time very close to Byron, was worried about the scheme. He and Byron had both agreed that he should at some stage be appointed as 'generalissimo' of the Greek forces and it could well have been that the plans proposed by Hastings, if successful, would have been enough to swing the balance without Napier's help. In the event Napier clearly demonstrated his lack of knowledge of the Greek military needs in a report and anonymous publication of his 'War in Greece' and the post of 'generalissimo' went eventually to Richard Church, allowing Napier to go to India to successfully seek fame, fortune and a permanent place in history.

Hastings was neither elated nor depressed at Byron's reception of his ideas, which suggested that the great man was continuing the policy he had adopted with all parties in the Greek conflict of listening carefully and giving no firm commitment. It was only when Byron discussed the plans with a visitor from Venice in November that he gave them his wholehearted support. This visitor, George Finlay, was to become the closest friend of Frank Hastings for the remainder of his life and also the greatest historian of Greek history, including that part which he and his friends were to influence.

George Finlay came from a solid Scottish middle-class family and was born in 1799 in Kent where his father, an officer in the Royal Engineers, was head of the Government Powder Mills at Faversham.

After his father's death when he was only three, George was brought up with his cousins at Castle Toward near Glasgow by his uncle, Kirkham Finlay, who was Member of Parliament for Glasgow Burghs and subsequently became Rector of Glasgow University.

Despite George's protestations as a teenager that he wished to follow his father into the army, the dour uncle insisted that he should study law. It was natural that he should commence these studies at Glasgow University and his three years there were followed by pupilage with a Glasgow firm.

His uncle, perhaps knowing the young man better than he knew himself, when he left to complete his studies in Roman Law at Gottingen, said to him: *"Well, George, I hope you will study hard at Roman Law, but I suppose you will visit the Greeks before I see you again"*.

So it was that the young man, full of ideals of liberty and democracy, was greeted in Cephalonia by Byron and Napier. The poet in particular admired the romantic young lawyer and indeed was to employ him for two months after he left Cephalonia for Messolongi as his agent. Finlay was to play an important role on behalf of Byron and the London Greek Committee in ensuring that supplies and equipment reached the right parties and, on one occasion, he had to personally divert victuals from the army of Odysseus to Athens, where both the food and military items were to prove of great use in the subsequent siege by the Turks.

It was during one such visit to Athens that George Finlay met Frank Abney Hastings for the first time. Hastings recorded the meeting in his journal with the comment *"He pleases me much"*. In part, of course, Hastings was grateful to the stranger who had convinced Byron that his naval plans were worthwhile. The two did not spend long together on this first occasion as Finlay was anxious to carry on his work of reporting the events between Kolokotronis and the Government Forces in what was by then a Civil War.

By the time Finlay returned to Byron a large number of Philhellenes had joined him either at Metaxata, or at Messolongi to await his arrival. One in particular, Colonel Leicester Stanhope, who was later to become the 5th Earl of Harrington, had seen distinguished service in the Napoleonic wars and having met Thomas Gordon, put himself at the disposal of the London Greek Committee. Whilst he is recorded as having many strange ideas such as founding printing presses and a postal service in the middle of a Civil War, itself in the middle of the Wars of Independence, Leicester Stanhope did have some influence over Byron. Having himself met up with many of the opposing Greek factions he had a full realisation of the effect of their internal struggles. He pushed Byron to call a conference of the various leaders, and indeed to move his 'court' to Messolongi.

Knowing that a man called Parry—subsequently shown to be a drunken rogue—was heading from England to Messolongi with an arsenal from the London Greek Committee and Stanhope having gone ahead to make preparations for its arrival, Byron left Cephalonia on December 30th, 1823. Unfortunately yet another of Byron's maritime excursions ended in near disaster; the ship carrying Pietro Gamba was taken by the Turks, Gamba throwing many of Byron's effects into the sea and only by a pure chance being released three days later. The small 'mistico' in which Byron was travelling was narrowly missed by the Turks but between that incident and actually landing in Messolongi his craft was twice nearly shipwrecked.

The adventures on the short journey did not dampen the poet's notion of great romantic heroes and he went ashore in a beautiful, highly decorated crimson uniform. The welcome was one designed for heroes; the guns saluted him and the people cried and cheered when they saw him. Within days his dream was shattered by the realisation that much of the sycophantic expressions of friendship he was receiving from so many corners was once again in reality a demand upon his wealth. Matters did not improve with the arrival of Parry whose first request was for more money.

Stanhope did his best to assist with the military preparations in the absence of Napier for whom Byron was waiting and he also busied himself in establishing a number of newspapers. These often met with Byron's disapproval as they were far too radical by nature.

On 21st February Stanhope, accompanied by Captain Humphreys, who had arrived with the by now infamous Parry, departed for Athens and other areas of Greece to establish the true situations of the warring Greek factions. Although Mavrokordatos, by now a tenuous leader of Western Greece, had spent much time with Byron and the Philhellenes at Messolongi, he was still not trusted nor was he considered a likely person to lead a united country in the final struggle when the finances were available from the London loans.

Stanhope soon made contact with, and came under the spell of, the Eastern Commander, Odysseus, who had also befriended both Trelawny and Hastings. George Finlay returned to Messolongi with many letters from Greek leaders asking him to attend a conference at Salona (modern day Amfissa), and also that he should use his influence with Mavrokordatos to ensure his presence.

Stanhope, who had been impressed by Odysseus' willingness to allow him to establish a museum at the Temple of Minerva in Athens, agreeing to allow the people to choose their own magistrates, agreeing to allow Sunday Schools and promising to build two hospitals, added his support to the proposed congress. The concept of the congress was that Mavrokordatos should represent Western Greece and the Islands, Odysseus Eastern Greece and Kolokotronis the Morea, and under the threat of Byron's withdrawal of the loan facilities they should be made to stop their quarrels.

It is a measure of the importance of Byron, that despite the constant pleadings of Mavrokordatos and Petrobey, he still refused to take the part of one side or another and the various factions agreed to attend the Congress of Salona called for April 21st, 1824. By April 16th most of the Greek leaders had arrived, each with their Philhellenic supporters, Finlay, Jarvis, Trelawny, Humphreys, Blaquiere, Stanhope, Frank Hastings and many others. Suspecting that Byron was not yet present could have been some form of plotting by Mavrokordatos, Stanhope instantly pleaded with Trelawny to return to Messolongi to see what was happening.

Byron had, in fact, been ill since he had been subjected to an epileptic type of fit on February 15th. He was reported to have gnashed his teeth, foamed at the mouth, rolled his eyes and lost control of his tongue. For many weeks he was not recovered from both the fit and the treatment with leeches administered by Dr Milligan and his old companion Bruno. The stresses of his position, his seeming inability to bring the Greeks together, the little effect upon the local Turkish garrisons by his rebellious and expensive Suliot warriors, the greed of all around him and the knowledge that his latest love, a beautiful fifteen year old boy he had brought from Cephalonia named Loukas, only gave him affection in return for monetary and other privileges, all took their toll upon the great poet.

His recovery was very slow but heartened by the news of the impending arrival of the first loan and the agreements for a Congress. By early April he was just able to take his evening rides again with Pietro Gamba. It was on one of these rides on April 9th that they were caught in a torrential downpour which brought on a fever but despite this he went out again the following day. The fever worsened and he was clearly not fit enough to travel. By Easter Sunday, April 18th, the doctors again decided to apply leeches. During that night he had occasional periods of lucidity, and on one occasion called Parry to his bedside, for although the artilleryman was undoubtedly a rogue, his abilities as a mimic and comic did amuse Byron.

In his periods of delirium he called to his troops whom he was leading into glorious battle, his greatest dream, but at 6.15 on the evening of April 19th 1824 Lord Byron died. He died, his body racked with fever and pain, splattered with the blood from the leeches and surrounded by many of his closest friends; companions in so many adventures past, and so many more to have come.

In Veritate Victoria

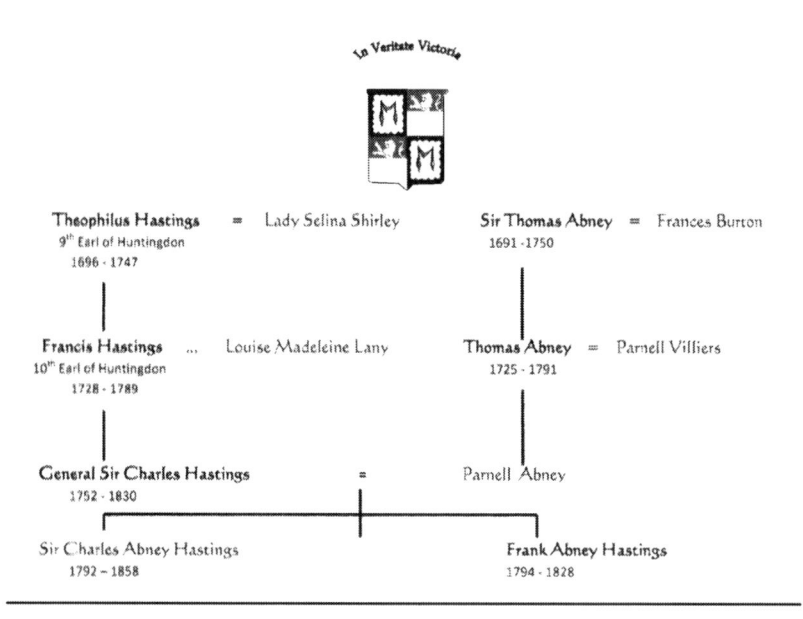

Theophilus Hastings = Lady Selina Shirley
9th Earl of Huntingdon
1696 - 1747

Sir Thomas Abney = Frances Burton
1691 -1750

Francis Hastings ... Louise Madeleine Lany
10th Earl of Huntingdon
1728 - 1789

Thomas Abney = Parnell Villiers
1725 - 1791

General Sir Charles Hastings   =   Parnell Abney
1752 - 1830

Sir Charles Abney Hastings
1792 – 1858

Frank Abney Hastings
1794 - 1828

1. a) Family Tree.

1. b) Willesley Hall, 1901.

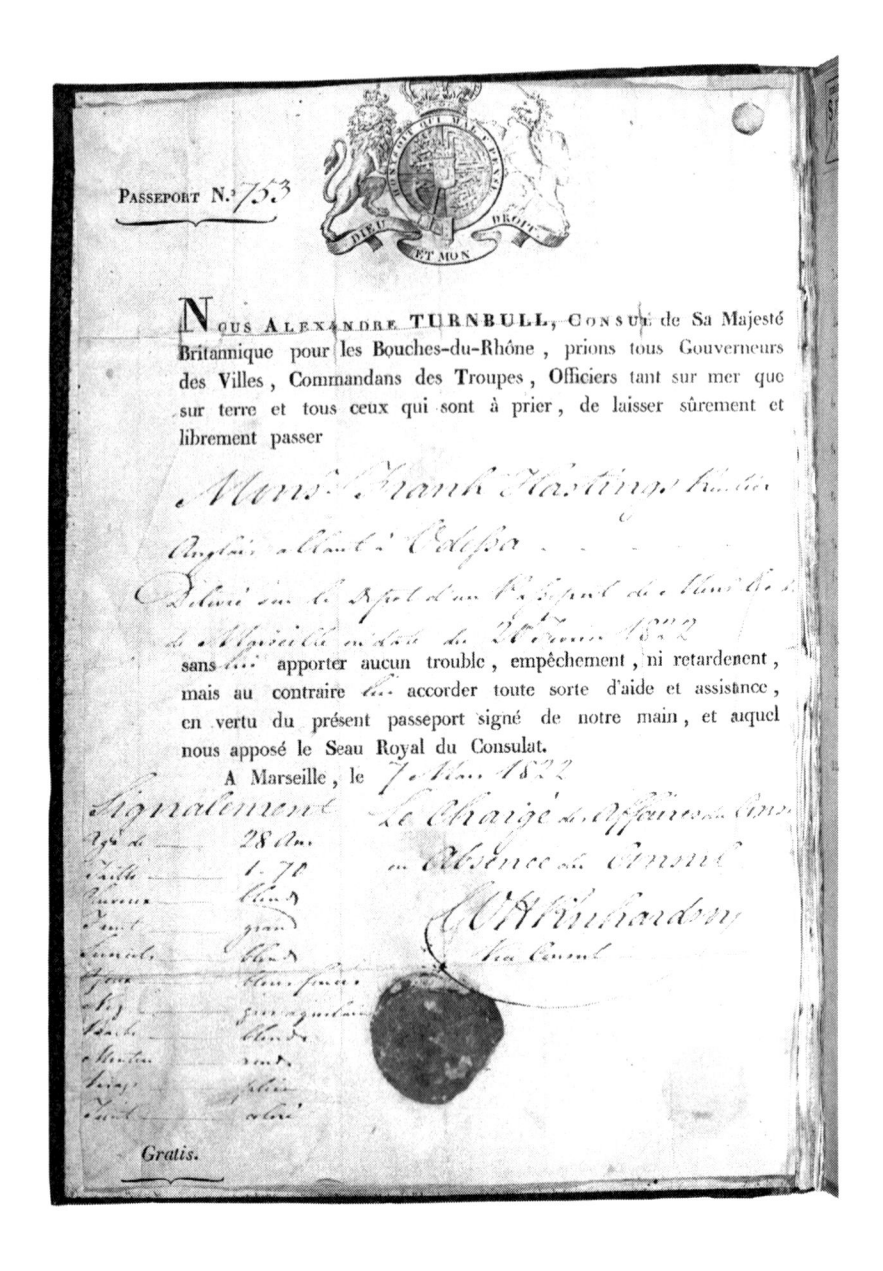

2. Passport as issued in Marsailles on 7th March, 1822; courtesy of The British School at Athens.

HASTINGS.

3. Portrait by Karl Krazheisen, 1828.

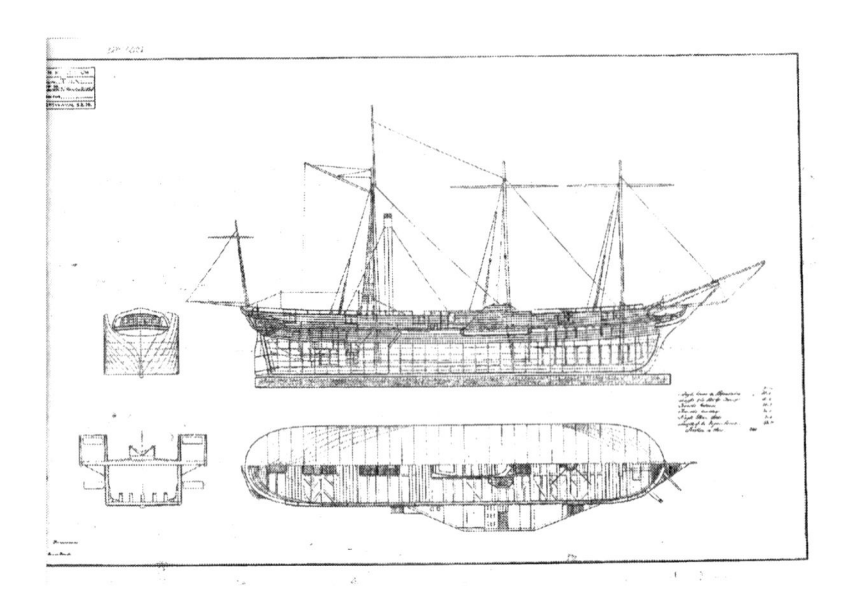

4. a) David Brent's plan of the Perseverance, courtesy of the National Maritime Museum Archives, Greenwich, London.

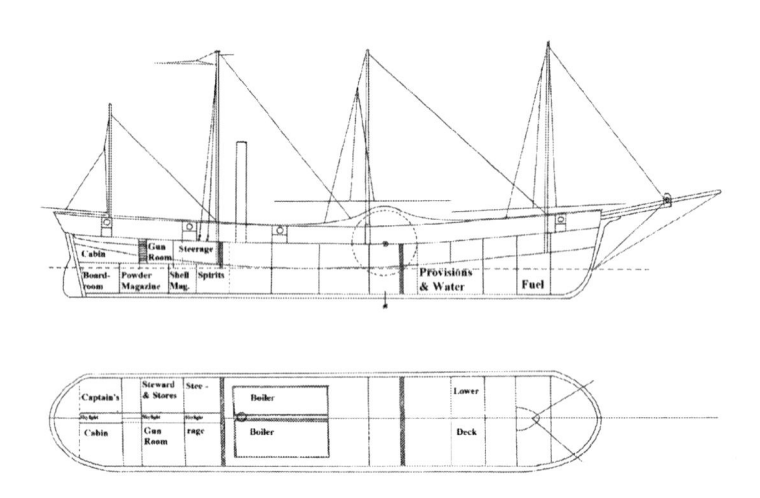

4. b) Layout of the Karteria from an original drawing by George Finlay.

5. Figurehead of the Karteria; courtesy of the National Historical Museum, Athens.

6. The Battle of Phaleron by Theophilos; courtesy of Evangelos Angelakos.

7. Hellas and Karteria by Krazheisen, 1828.

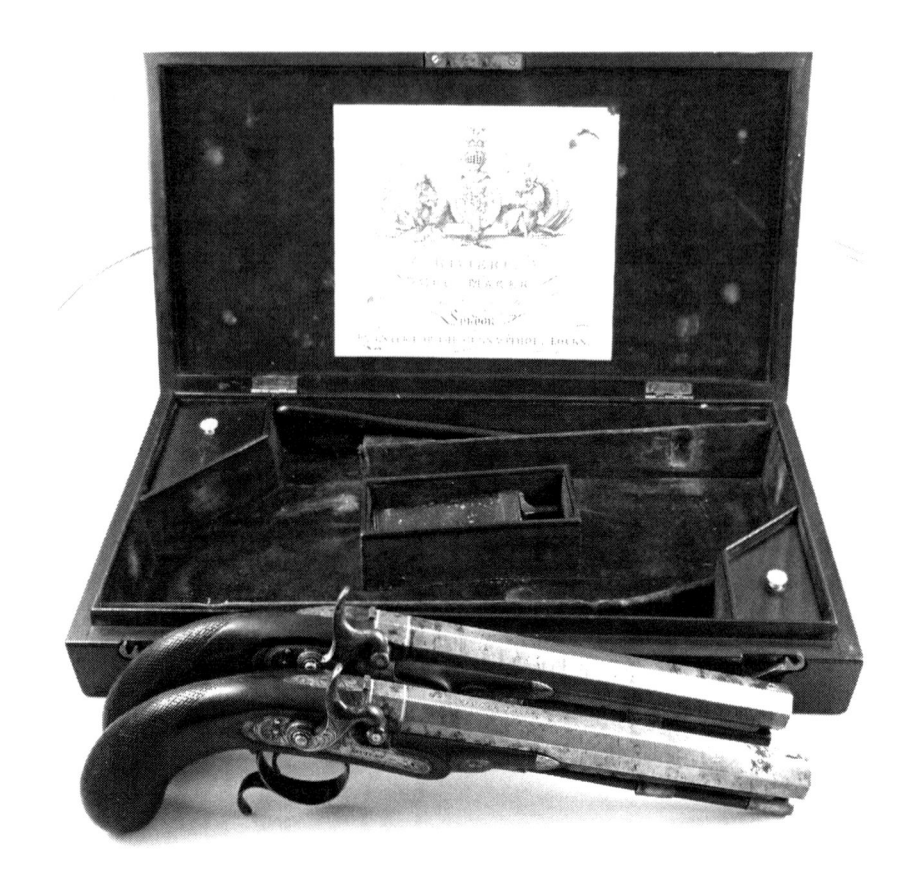

8. Hastings' pistols bequeathed to Captain Scott and now in the possession of Squadron Leader Darryl Plumridge.

9. a) Poros Memorial.

HERE LIES DEPOSITED THE HEART OF CAPTAIN FRANK ABNEY HASTINGS, YOUNGER SON OF LIEUTENANT-GENERAL SIR CHARLES HASTINGS BART: WHO, HAVING BEEN MORTALLY WOUNDED IN AN ATTACK ON ANATOLIKON, DIED IN ZANTE, ON THE 28TH DAY OF MAY 1828, AGED 34 YEARS. HE WAS BURIED IN POROS, WHERE AN OBELISK IS ERECTED IN THE OLD ARSENAL TO HIS MEMORY.

9. b) Athens Memorial.

9. c) Mesalonghi Memorial.

10. a) Commemorative Medal, 1928.

10. b) Commemorative Stamps, 1983.

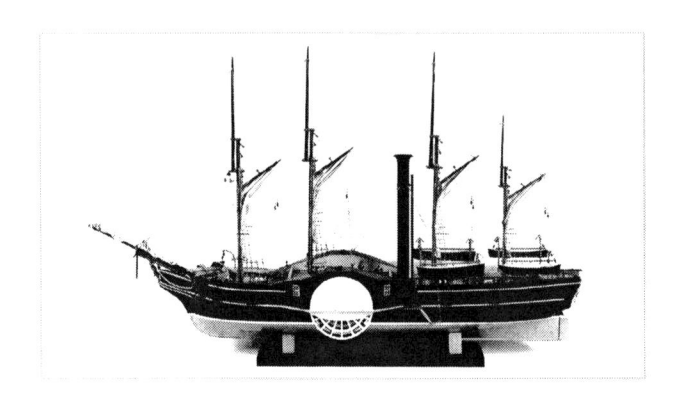

10. c) Model of the Karteria; coutesy of Hellenic Maritime Museum, Piraeus

Chapter 7

1824-1826; London and construction of the 'Perseverance'

The rocky inlet then known as the Gulf of Salona is a bite taken from the northern shore of the Gulf of Corinth. The town of Salona was connected to the coast by a ten mile track bordered by sparse mountains. The heights to the east of the track are dominated by Mount Parnassos and just to the south of that Trelawny and his party who left Salona on April 18th would have seen the Temple of Delphi above them and to their left. Once they had reached the coast, their route to Messolongi was to the west, along the northern coastline of the Gulf of Corinth and their destination was at a distance of about seventy miles.

Leicester Stanhope had become very concerned when Bryon and Mavrokordatos had not arrived for the congress due to start on the twenty-first but his worry was not for the health of Byron but his growing conviction that Mavrokordatos had found some means of dissuading the poet from making the journey. Trelawny being the closest personal friend of Byron at Salona was the best choice to deliver a letter and hopefully to return with him to take his natural lead at the congress. The letter from Stanhope that Trelawny carried was prophetic in that it begged Byron to leave Messolongi and not to sacrifice his health or even his life in that "bog".

Only a few hours from Messolongi, Trelawny was passed by a group of soldiers and was frightened that their sombre countenances may have indicated the loss of the town in battle. Catching a straggler he asked what the situation was and was told only the words *"Bryon is dead"*.

The effect upon the Congress of Salona, which lasted from April 21st to May 7th, was devastating and although the gathering was held with factions on the verge of civil war, some early signs of diplomacy did emerge. Whilst Georgios Koundriotis had for a little over three months been the nominal Head of State, it was left to Mavrokordatos to announce a three week period of national mourning for Lord Byron. The Government of Koundriotis was blocked at every move by the troops of Kolokotronis, who even maintained control over the seat of power at Nauplio, but Koundriotis did have the advantage of having been the only Greek appointed as a Commissioner by the London Greek Committee along with Byron and Stanhope.

Stanhope pleaded with the Congress for national unity. He was convinced in his own mind that his eloquence had succeeded and that his own plans for the formation of a true national Government would be accepted but in fact the only reason that warriors such as Odysseus went along with his suggestions was to obtain a share of the first Greek loan. Indeed Odysseus and his ruthless political agent, Sofianopoulos, had every reason to believe that Stanhope favoured them over the other claims and they realised that, without Byron, the struggle between Kolokotronis and the Government could only worsen. Hastings described Sofianopoulos as *"one of the most execrable villains that ever existed"*, and when one considers the actions of so-called patriots in both allowing and encouraging civil war at such a time to further their own aims, then perhaps Hastings was right.

The greatest sadness was that the ship, the *'Florida'*, arrived at Zante carrying the first loan only two days after the death of Byron. Had he lived long enough to influence the warring chieftains and had the finances from the loan been available, there is little doubt that the nation would have been united and that together they could have defeated the Turks, especially given the naval power so strongly favoured at the end of Byron's life by himself, Stanhope and Hastings. Thousands of lives would have been saved, towns and villages would not have been destroyed and the self esteem of the emerging nation would have been maintained. The final irony of the tragedy was that the very ship that carried the loan to Zante was the one that transported the body and effects of Byron back to England.

After much argument it was generally accepted that Bryon would have preferred to be buried in England—there were many who quoted him as asking to be buried without ceremony in Greece and his body and effects, guarded by Captain Hesketh, went from Messolongi to Zante. At the same time, having learnt of his appointment as Commissioner to the London Greek Committee and therefore trustees of the first loan, Stanhope set out to see the merchants in Zante acting as bankers for the loan.

It has been accepted practice that monies and supplies for the Greek cause were shipped through the Ionian Islands but, fearful of the rumours of civil war, Stanhope's support for Odysseus and his strange liberal and republican ideas, and under pressure from Sir Thomas Maitland, the merchant bankers, Banff and Logotheti, decided that the death of Byron nullified the appointment of Commissioners. They refused to release the loan until further instructions were received from London. Also awaiting Stanhope in Zante was a letter from his regiment which was the final blow to his political ambitions in Greece.

When he had arrived in Greece only six months previously he was on an extended leave of absence from the Horse Guards and on half-pay of £400 per annum as Lieutenant-Colonel. His letter recalled him to London and he too was to travel with the body of Lord Byron on the *'Florida'*. He is recorded by many as an eccentric and a crank but despite the strangeness of his ideals, Leicester Stanhope was an honest man who in a very short period made his mark on the birth of a new nation. Byron did remark that like so many, Stanhope had arrived in Greece *"like a sixth-former from Eton or Harrow"*, and went on to suggest that he and Napier would soon change that.

Humphreys carried on the work of Stanhope by visiting the Greek factions to persuade them to unite but he remained firm in his conviction that Odysseus was the man to unite the country supported by Trelawny and at that time Finlay. Other prominent Philhellenes, Hastings, Blaquiere, Parry and Jarvis stayed with their support of Mavrokordatos, whilst Kolokotronis looked to Russia for any support he may receive. Whilst all this political dealing was taking place, the official Government had less actual power than any of the factions and though many of the Ministers were willing to negotiate there were those, who for reasons of personal dislikes, would not deal with one faction or another. One particular case was Kolettis, a Primate from northern Greece, who had served with Odysseus under the Lion of Ioannina, Ali Pasha, and the two thoroughly disliked each other. Kolettis, although probably the most powerful Minister in Government, tried to have Odysseus assassinated, but this having failed, Odysseus removed himself and his troops to safety taking considerable amounts of Government funds with him.

In effect the constant battles between the Greeks in May and June of 1825 constituted what was to become known as the first civil war, and the defeat of Kolokotronis at the Mills near Nauplio did not only signify the temporary creation of internal hostilities but the loss of opportunity for Odysseus to seize control if the Government forces had been defeated. Part of the first London loan had eventually been released to Blaquiere, and the second loan arrived aboard the brig 'Little Sally' on June 13th, allowing payment in part to the fleets of Spetsai and Hydra.

In fact, with the armies and various leaders fighting amongst themselves for power, it was very much left to the ship-owners to continue the war against the Turks, albeit on a very low key at that time. Hastings in particular had warned Stanhope, Napier and Byron on many occasions that the real danger to the Greek uprising lay not with the unruly and lazy Turkish land forces, nor with its inexperienced navy, but more with the forces of Egypt.

The Greeks could never accept that Sultan Mahmud would ever be able to work with his vassal, Mehemet Ali of Egypt. It therefore came as a complete surprise when they learned that on June 19th, 1824, an Egyptian squadron of some fourteen vessels landed 2,000 Albanian and Egyptian troops on the island of Kasos. Over five hundred men were slain and well over one thousand women and children were taken into bondage and transported in the many small ships which the invading forces captured with little or no resistance. A few days later the Turkish fleet from the north attacked the island of Psara, which had served the Greeks so well the previous year.

On this occasion the invading fleet was over eighty strong, carrying six thousand Turkish and Asiatic troops and the island seemed powerless to stop the invasion. The island was well defended with both artillery and troops and over a hundred ships lay at anchor in the harbour when the Captain Pasha attacked. On this island, still crowded with the refugees from Scio, the troops of Khosref Pasha killed or enslaved over five thousand Greeks. By the time that Admiral Miaoulis had put to sea with the fleets from Hydra and Spetses, the Turks had returned to their homeland, and the town of Bodrum.

Still the Greek leaders ignored the threat. Throughout the early months of 1824 reports were filtering through that Mehemet Ali was gathering a mighty Armada at Alexandria. They still assumed that the greedy Viceroy had neither the will nor the available money to be drawn into the rebellion in the Ottoman Empire to the north. The man they had not allowed for was the adopted son of Mehemet Ali, Ibrahim Pasha, who had already proved himself to be a most able soldier. He was to go on to prove himself a great naval tactician in the Greek Wars of Independence.

Born in 1789 at Cavalla in Rumeli, Ibrahim was probably an illegitimate son of Mehemet and throughout his life was certainly regarded as his natural son. At a very young age he stood out from those around him. He was much taller, with a lighter skin and hazel rather than deep brown Arab eyes. At the age of twenty-six his father had given him command of his own battalion of troops and in 1816 they subdued the Wahabi tribes, his prize for which was to be given command of the whole Egyptian army. Having spent some time studying in France and possibly Germany, his first action on becoming Commander-in-Chief of the Egyptian forces was to remodel them along European lines. In doing so he proved to be an able, if severe administrator, and was admired by his soldiers and enemies alike, especially Frank Abney Hastings. Although born a world apart and fighting on opposite sides, the two men were very similar in their love of order, organisation and discipline and both, whilst being warriors of their day, had moments of great compassion to their foes. It was certainly Hastings who first realised the extent of the threat offered by Ibrahim and it was the Egyptian who first became most aware of the dangers should the naval theories of Hastings ever be put into practice. Whilst they never met other than at guns' distance, there evolved a powerful relationship of fear, admiration and jealousy between the two which in the end was to cost Hastings his life and cost the Greek nation to the Ottoman Empire.

On July 19th, 1824, Ibrahim sailed from Alexandria with a fleet of twenty-five men-of-war and over one hundred transport vessels carrying 10,000 men, 1,000 horses, over 100 field guns and huge amounts of supplies to last them through a long campaign. After some skirmishing in the eastern islands and a meeting with the Turkish fleet at Bodrum, Ibrahim and his army landed at Suda Bay in Crete to establish a base to commence war of a totally different dimension upon Greece.

Learning that the second instalment of the London loan was being sent and that the two new commissioners, Bulmer and Hamilton Brown, were travelling overland to be in Nauplio before the ship arrived, Hastings and Blaquiere realised that they had very little time left in which to bring the enfeebled Greek Government to its senses. They could both see that the threat from Ibrahim Pasha must be dealt with by an improvement of naval power, organisation of the land forces and uniting the chieftains, but that all these measures required money and commitment. The former would only come with the release of the second part of the loan and this would certainly not come about unless the new Commissioners were convinced that proper plans had been made to utilise the loan in a proper manner leading to what could reasonably be expected to be a victory over the Turks.

Jarvis, who seems to have forgotten his feud with Hastings, joined them, along with Hane and gave the two seamen the support of two men with military expertise. The plans they laid before the Greek executive were both extensive and comprehensive, and it is of great credit to the wonderful Irish oratory of Blaquiere that the Philhellenes finally obtained the support so desperately needed for their ideas. One of the most important modern historians of the period, Douglas Dakin, described Blaquiere as an 'international busybody' and whilst this may well be a true opinion, it is unlikely that without his success at Nauplio during July and August of 1824 the might of Ibrahim Pasha could have been overcome.

He convinced the Greeks of the honourable intentions of the London Greek Committee and even proposed that groups of twenty young men would be taken to England for education and he made great play of the University founded in Corfu by Lord Guildford. Jarvis left after a short time to carry on his military adventures in the East but the others remained to push forward their plans. The Greeks eventually agreed to purchase two steam ships, with Hastings now offering to contribute £5,000 towards the first, and was asked to return to England to supervise its building. In addition they agreed that if they could obtain the services of Lord Cochrane, recently returned to England from Brazil as a Naval Hero, they would build a fleet of eight frigates and perhaps a further six steam ships. On the military front, they agreed that they would approach Napier with the offer of Chief-of-Staff of the army and if he was not available then another soldier of similar stature should be contacted. It was inherent in these discussions that both the navy and the army would be formed on national lines and that these would gradually take over from the private forces which acted both independently and in an often opposing manner.

The most difficult task performed by Blaquiere was to make the members of the executive aware that if they were to expect further support, then it was necessary for them to put a face on their dealings with the West which indicated that Greece was indeed a true nation. In particular, he explained that many merchant houses in Europe regarded Greece as a nation of pirates and brigands, which to some extent it was, and that if they were to obtain truly international moral and financial assistance this feeling must be overcome. Using not too lightly veiled threats that the leading Philhellenes would also withdraw their assistance, Blaquiere at length persuaded them that the piratical behaviour of many of the ship owners must be stopped and that vessels sailing under the Greek ensign should open trade routes with the rest of the world. There is no doubt that an Irishman, Edward Blaquiere, supported by Hastings, Hane and two other Englishmen, Murray and Winter, had laid the basis for the international acceptance of Greece as a fully independent state. Unfortunately his far-sighted plans took many years, much bloodshed and a great deal of money to come to fruition.

Blaquiere had considered that he had done everything in his power at the Greek end of the struggle. He even carried with him schedules for the repayment of interest on the loans when, on August 29th, 1824 he boarded the Greek vessel the *'Amphitriti'* bound for London. His task was to give the London Greek Committee and the two agents of the Greek Government, Orlando and Louriottes, the assurances he carried and to seek theirs to carry out the London end of the bargain. Travelling with him were Hastings and Hane, whose responsibility was to build the first of the steam ships and arrange for her armaments to be ordered. They also had on board nine boys who had been the first selected to be taken to England for education. The *'Amphitriti'* sailed into the Thames estuary and into the River Medway on October 13th and so made a little piece of history by being the first ship sailing under the Greek flag to enter British waters. It was appropriate that the three men who had pushed for internationalism should have been aboard.

Their winter in England was one of great frustration and a growing disgust with members of the London Greek Committee, with the exception of Byron's friend, John Cam Hobhouse and Edward Ellice. The negotiations with potential leaders of the army were all collapsing. The Deputies, as Orlandoand Louriottes were known, could not agree to the terms of either Napier or Church and other approaches came to little. The main reason for the apathy was that the Greeks had made some advance as at that time they held Athens, Nauplio, Corinth and all the main strongholds in the Morea. They still virtually ignored the fact that Ibrahim Pasha and his vast army were waiting on Crete for their right moment.

The internal political situation appeared to be more stable with Kolokotronis securely in jail on Hydra, his soldier son killed and Odysseus, who had signed a three month truce with the Turks, had been incarcerated in the Frankish Tower of the Acropolis in Athens by one of his old followers, Ghouras. His trusted Lieutenant, Trelawny, who had recently married the beautiful thirteen year old sister of Odysseus, was firmly holed up in a cave in which he took refuge for many weeks. This being the situation in Greece, the Greek Government and their Deputies in London were not too interested in spending more money. They were convinced that the battle for Greece was nearly won.

Also they were enjoying considerably the wealth that they were receiving from the Greek loan. The less spent on battle, the more they could spend upon themselves, their friends and even those who had been enemies and from whom they now wished to obtain political support. George Finlay, having left Odysseus in favour of Mavrokordatos, was disgusted with the way in which the members of the legislative assembly handled the monies with which they had been entrusted:

"No inconsiderable amount was divided among members of the legislative assembly, and among a large number of useless partisans who were characterised as public officials. Every man wanted to head his own army, and hundreds of civilians paraded the streets of Nauplio followed by trained of kilted supporters like Scottish chieftains. Those who in the month of April 1824 were clad in ragged coats, and who lived off scanty rations, threw off that patriotic chrysalis before summer was past, and emerged in all the splendour of brigand life, fluttering about in rich Albanian habiliments, refulgent with brilliant and unused arms, and followed by diminutive pipe-bearers and tall henchmen.

Nauplio certainly offered a spectacle to anyone who could forget it was the capital of an impoverished nation struggling through starvation for its liberty. The streets were for many months crowded with thousands of gallant young men in picturesque and richly ornamental arms, who ought to have been on the frontiers of Greece".

Shortly after the scene at Nauplio with their new found, and misused, wealth which caused George Finlay to describe them so vividly, the young Scot contracted a fever from which he almost died. Several months of recuperation in Greece were followed by a similar period in Italy before he was well enough to return home to Scotland where he was able to complete his studies in law before returning to the Greek cause.

The apathy experienced by Hastings in London was such that it required all the boundless energy of the Philhellene before any member of the London Greek Committee would take any notice of the orders he carried from the Greek Government allowing him to start work on issuing instructions for the first steam ship. By November 1st he had created so much trouble for the Committee that, at the insistence of Ellice and Hobhouse, Bowring wrote to Hastings from the Committee room at the Crown and Anchor announcing his election as a member of the Committee. They wanted to enlist his services in returning to Greece to negotiate with the Government. On the same day another member, Lord Nugent, wrote to him expressing his hopes that Hastings would accept the invitation to join the Committee and that he would become "Our Commissioner of Remonstrance with the Greek Government on the subject of their miserable fainéants the Deputies".

Whilst he agreed to serve on the Committee, Hastings refused to return to Greece unless at the command of a steam vessel. He suspected the action by the Committee was designed to save them making any decisions about the steam ship. He returned to his family at Willesley Hall for Christmas and discussed with his father and elder brother the possibilities of returning to the British Navy. It was the events in Greece that avoided this situation and brought his plans back to the table of the Committee. Also there was growing unrest in

England about the amount of money which was being raised without seemingly being spent on the cause for Greek Independence.

Mavrokordatos who had again become President was still more concerned with strengthening his political base than with liberating his country. He had inveigled two young Englishmen, Fenton and Whitcombe, to visit Trelawny in the cave where he was holed up and under the guise of friendship Whitcombe shot Trelawney in the back and Fenton shot him again in the neck. Trelawny's guards immediately killed Fenton, but Trelawny, barely alive, agreed that he should give Whitcombe a hearing. The story which he was given was that Whitcombe's shot was an accident, and only that of Fenton was intended to kill him. Rather remarkably Trelawny believed this tale and after some weeks he freed him. The life of Trelawny was only saved by the eventual intervention of Captain Hamilton of the 'Cambrian' who insisted on sending his own surgeon to attend the wounded man and subsequently arranging to bring him and his child-bride back on board the English vessel. Trelawny's comrade, and brother-in-law, Odysseus, fared less well to the agents of Mavrokordatos and was found hanging at the end of a rope from the Frankish Tower in the Acropolis where he had been held.

But it was Ibrahim Pasha who really created the situation in Greece in early 1825 which the Government had ignored for so long and of which Hastings had so strongly warned. On 24th February the first wave of Egyptian forces landed on Morea at the town of Modon at the southern end of the Bay of Navarin. They met with very little resistance either at sea or on land, and three weeks later the second part of Ibrahim's invasion forces were disembarked at Modon and almost immediately the troops moved a few miles north to besiege the important town of New Navarin. Kalergy and his troops in the town were to fight bravely for two months before New Navarin fell. The news of the mighty invasion at last awakened the Greeks from their apathy.

News was immediately sent overland to London. Miaoulis started on preparation of fire-ships and Mavrokordatos moved his troops to Kromidi to the east of the bay in an attempt to prevent Ibrahim from spreading out over Morea. The Greek army at Kromidi was accompanied by a twenty-four year old American doctor, Samuel Gridley Howe, who was to become the Chief Surgeon to the Greek fleet, and to serve for a considerable period under Frank Hastings. Like so many other Philhellenes, Howe was inspired to offer his medical services to the country by the writings of Byron and was also prompted in his departure by an unhappy love affair at home in Boston, Massachusetts. He had been trained and qualified in medicine at Brown and Harvard Universities and it is difficult to imagine that the tall, slim, 'clean-cut' New Englander with *"hair as black as new hewn coal; eyes as blue as the Mediterranean on a sunny spring morning"* should within weeks of his arrival be speaking Greek, wearing the national costume and military regalia, and living 'rough' in the hills along with the klefts—the brigand chieftains.

In later life he was to become a medical specialist of world prominence but for the time Dr Samuel Gridley Howe was to throw himself wholeheartedly into his Greek adventure with fine and honourable results. Certainly of the many Americans who had come to the assistance of the infant nation, Howe must stand alone as one who made the most positive contribution.

When news of the invasion reached the London Greek Committee the effect was cataclysmic. At last they were obliged by public opinion and pushed into activity by the few men of true honour on the Committee. Hobhouse and Ellice again raised the question of the authority to build the first of the steam-ships and on this occasion the decision was quickly reached. On House of Commons notepaper, Edward Ellice MP, wrote to Hastings as Chairman of the London Greek Committee, giving the necessary authority to place the order for his ship and its engines. March 1825 was a delay of nearly six months from the intended time of ordering: a delay which could have caused the failure of the War of Independence.

At the same time the Deputies authorised their agents and accountants, Messrs. Ricardo, to pay £10,000 to Ellice for the provision of the steam-ship. Despite the protestations of Hastings, Blaquiere and Gordon, only £3,000 was ever paid and the balance was met out of Hastings' personal funds. The order for the guns, which Hastings had designed, had to be placed in Texas as it would have been illegal to fit out a warship in England and it was agreed that these should go direct to Greece aboard the first of the frigates which was under construction at Houston.

The old-established family shipyard of Messrs. Brent at Deptford was contracted to construct the ship, known at that time by her English name of *'Perseverance.'* When Cochrane returned to England from Brazil, Hastings immediately teamed up with him to use his influence to speed matters along. As it transpired, it was Cochrane's insistence that the engineering firms of Alexander Galloway of West Smithfield should be used to build the engines for the *'Perseverance'* and subsequent steam-ships which caused the greatest delays.

Galloway promised that the first engine would be ready in late August 1825 but it was not actually ready until April of the following year. The delays, at first put down to technical problems, soon were so numerous that Hastings and Cochrane became convinced that they were deliberate sabotage. It transpired that the son of Galloway was working in Alexandria for Mehemet Ali and was hoping to secure the valuable post of Resident Engineer there. Another factor which almost certainly influenced the disreputable behaviour of Galloway was that the British Government was about to bring in a bill specifically designed to forbid Lord Cochrane from again entering foreign service.

Thomas Cochrane, who later became the Earl of Dundonald, was vital to the Greek cause for the fear that his name inspired amongst enemy seamen. He had entered the British Navy at the age of seventeen in 1792, and served with great distinction against the French and Spanish In 1809 he was made a Knight of the Bath for his action in the Basque Roads when he attacked the French fleet with only five ships. Like Frank Hastings, his career was terminated by an affair of honour when he insisted on court-martialling a superior officer, Lord Gambier, and the Admiralty removed him from the lists. He had been a Member of Parliament for Westminster, sitting as a Radical and for a while he devoted his energies to the House.

He undoubtedly had many enemies and in 1814 he was accused of spreading a false rumour that Napoleon had abdicated for the purpose of making huge sums of money on the Stock Exchange. For this he was expelled from Parliament, had all his honours withdrawn, was fined £1,000 and sentenced to be pilloried. His constituents believed in his innocence, which he later established, and the order to stand in the pillory was never carried out. The public whom he represented raised the £1,000 to pay his fine and promptly re-elected him to Parliament.

In 1818, even at the age of forty-three, his hankering for the sea and adventure became too strong to resist and he hired out his services, quite illegally, to Chile. He led their fight in the struggle for independence from Spain and a few years later commanded the Brazilian Navy in a similar battle against the Portuguese. Realising his great worth as a naval leader in the fight for liberation, Cochrane struck a hard bargain with Greece. He negotiated for an advance of £37,000 to be paid and a further £20,000 on liberation and a further £93,000 to equip his expedition. It is an indication of the 'sincerity' of the man to the cause that his first action having extracted the vast sum, was to order a luxury yacht for himself.

Realising that public opinion in England was against his mercenary activities and that Parliament would soon stop him, Cochrane moved to Belgium to await the construction of his fleet. Prior to his departure he had visited Glasgow and Liverpool with Hastings to search for suitable second hand steam vessels which could have quickly been converted to warships but this sensible action was never taken. He did support Hastings well in pushing for the completion of the *'Perseverance'*, and on one occasion actually visited the Brent shipyard in disguise to ascertain progress on the vessel for himself.

It is perhaps sad that a man such as Cochrane should have sunk to such depths of mercenary greed, as he truly did have the gift of naval genius coupled with a bearing that inspired others. He was tall and commanding in person and had a lively and expressive manner which impressed him upon all those whom he was to meet. His worth to the Greeks was nothing approaching the price they paid for him and his actions never came near to either the expectations or the abilities of this remarkable man. Probably if he had been given the fleet he required on time his part in Greek history would have been glorious rather than ignominious.

The *'Perseverance'* was registered at Lloyds, London, in 1825, as a steam driven packet, i.e. to carry mail, private goods and passengers. According to the Register she was to voyage between London to Malta. Frank Hastings is registered as her Master and Captain and the owners are listed as Hastings and Company. It was illegal at that time to build foreign warships in England. The *'Perseverance'* remained on the Register until 1834.

During the winter the slow progress on the *'Perseverance'* continued and by February of 1826 Frank Hastings was confident enough to issue orders to John Hane to return to Greece in a collier from Newcastle, the *'Tiber'*, carrying fuel to Nauplio to be available on the arrival of the *'Perseverance'*. His orders were to show the documents to the Greek Government in Nauplio, and to solicit from them a suitable vessel on which to load the coal from the *'Tiber'*. Under no circumstances was he to unload the coal onto land, and was further instructed to stay on board the boat with the coal until Hastings or Cochrane arrived or further orders were received from Messrs. Ricardo, Cochrane or himself. Hane was also instructed to obtain permission from the Government to visit the Artillery and select guns of the largest calibres which were in good condition, obtain shells for them, and manufacture ship carriages for the guns.

Along with the main instructions, which were to be shown to the Government, Hastings also included secret orders for Hane—*"In the event of the Greeks being subdued by the Turks on your arrival at Nauplio"*. The secret document went on to advise Hane that if he encountered this situation, to proceed to Corfu and offload the cargo into store, discharge the *'Tiber'* and, having informed Messrs. Ricardo, await orders. Clearly he was not convinced that the Greeks could hold out during the two months it would take for Hane to arrive. He also told Hane to impress upon the Greek Government the need to collect fuel for the steam vessels. He was still certain that the fleet of six steam vessels really would be delivered at speed. In the event the second arrived a year after Hastings' ship, the third a year later—neither of these performed properly—the fourth, a smaller ship named '*Mercury*', arrived in October 1828 and the last two were never built due to the large scale misappropriation of the funds.

During early May of 1826 the final touches were being made to the '*Perseverance*'. For Hastings the name was appropriate as the vessel was now later in completion than originally thought. The '*Perseverance*' was of 233 tonnage and had a single deck with beams; she was 126 ft on the waterline, 159 ft overall when including a long bowsprit, and her maximum beam was 25 ft. Her rounded bow and stern gave her a somewhat barge-like appearance out of the water but once afloat with a draft of around 6 ft and with the 30 ft bowsprit angled upwards from the stem she took on an altogether sleeker and, to twentieth century eyes, more modern appearance. Her hull was constructed of wood and sheathed in copper in 1825. Slightly forward of the midships position her two paddles of 12 ft diameter were fitted and the housing for these was sloped to merge with the bulwarks fore and aft.

The 42 hp engines which had shown so many defects in their early trials, had, by May, been modified to the extent that they appeared to be acceptable, although they never did perform to their maximum capacity. The main problem was that they were simply not powerful enough to propel the ship which eventually weighed 400 tons. Part of the difficulty was caused by the way in which Galloway had manufactured the boilers. It had been hoped that wood alone would have been adequate to build up the pressure in the boilers but this proved not to be the case. Oil was satisfactory but consumption proved to be so great as to render this form of fuel impracticable. Therefore coal had to be relied upon to a great extent with all its inherent difficulties of supply and transport. The maximum speed of the '*Perseverance*' was only around seven knots in reasonable conditions and this was largely explained by the paddles being too high in the water and being almost certainly too heavy for their size.

Under sail the story was rather better and with as many as three jibs out of the bowsprit and the two after masts being fore-and-aft rig, she performed particularly well to windward. Whilst running before the wind with the large square-rigged sails and topsails on the forward two masts she was able to show a reasonable turn of speed. The crew under the strict training regime of the Master became very adept at shipping the paddles when the engines were no longer required and consequently the transition from steam to sail power did not present the problems incurred on earlier vessels of a similar type.

Below deck the ship was split into three sections, the midships area being almost entirely taken up with the engines and boilers. The forward section had an upper and a lower deck. The former accommodated the crew and the latter was a fuel store and the water and provision storage areas. Likewise the after section of the ship had two decks the lower of which housed the powder magazine, the shell magazine and the spirit room, whilst the upper deck was split into three sections. By far the largest of these was the Captain's cabin in the stern which occupied the total breadth of the ship and was around twenty feet in length. It was lit by skylights from above, as were all the areas in the stern section and also by galleon-style 'windows' port and starboards. Forward of the Captain's cabin on the starboard side was the gun room and opposite this a steerage cabin and store. Between that and the dividing bulkhead which separated the after accommodation from the engine area, were the cabins for the ship's officers.

The deck layout was of necessity cluttered, as it catered for the paraphernalia of a warship, a steam ship and a sailing vessel. She was also to become home to a regular complement of fifty-six men, and often many more with soldiers, refugees or prisoners on board.

One of the tasks Hastings had in his last few weeks was to select his crew. Many of those available to him were a very poor quality and destined to give a great deal of trouble in the succeeding weeks. However there were those such as William Scanlan, the Chief Officer, Edward Jermyn, the First Lieutenant, Gibbon Fitz-Gibbon, the Gunnery Officer and John Rosbreck, the Quartermaster Signaller, who remained with him for a considerable period, some to his death. For the seamen, stokers and engineers he had little choice available to him, and he was to leave England with an almost skeleton crew.

Finlay, who had been in correspondence with Hastings, had recovered from his illness the previous summer and while living at Castle Toward with his uncle he resumed his studies in law. He passed his final examinations in civil law in early 1826, and readily accepted Hastings' offer to allow him to share his cabin, the largest available area aboard the '*Perseverance*' and return to Greece.

By May 18th, 1826, everything was as ready as it would likely be, and to the great delight of Captain Frank Abney Hastings, the '*Perseverance*' under his command slipped out of the Thames Estuary on her trials.

Chapter 8

1826; 'Karteria'

For Frank Abney Hastings the ceremony that accompanied the departure of the *'Perseverance'* was a very private one. Cochrane, still worried about political repercussions, had made his clandestine visit to Brent's shipyard on May 13th 1826 and having been convinced that the next two steam ships would soon be completed retired quietly to Ireland to join the *'Unicorn'*, which, in company with the *'Union'*, was one of two vessels purchased by Messrs. Ricardo from the loan.

Although Hastings and some of the officers had been on board the *'Perseverance'* for several days, the majority of the crew were told not to report until the evening of May 17th 1826. It was almost exactly seven years since Captain Hastings had lost the command of HMS *'Kangaroo'* and ended his royal naval career. It was only his own perseverance, determination and loyalty to a foreign cause that put him back in his seemingly natural post of Master of a vessel. The almost surreptitious slipping of the ship down the muddy waters of the Thames, coupled with the aloofness and professionalism of her Captain, seemed a quite normal departure and even Finlay made no record of any display of joy amongst the Master or crew. One can only imagine the emotions of Frank Hastings as he felt for the first time the movement of the deck under his feet, and the response of the wheel to his touch. After his years of trials and hardships his private thoughts must have been sprinkled with a fair smattering of elation and exaltation.

The pleasure can only have been enhanced by the glorious spring weather, with a fair, south-westerly breeze that sped them on the morning of May 18th down the river past Sheerness and the Isle of Sheppey into the wide estuary bordered by Maplin Sands to the north and the Kent coast to the south. For the next four days the *'Perseverance'* sailed and on occasions even steamed around the southern part of the North Sea. This time allowed both master and crew to familiarise themselves with the handling capabilities of the ship and to familiarise themselves with the various procedures on deck which became so important at sea. There was some concern at the amount of fuel required to build up the pressure from the boilers, and this served only to re-emphasise the need for adequate access to fuel supplies.

Minor adjustments were made to the engine and boilers by Galloway's engineers who were on board and by then closely supervised by two of Cochrane's own engineer officers. The sail-makers and carpenters made the last minute alterations to the rigging and spars thought to be necessary and on May 23rd she returned to a berth in Rotherhithe to take on final supplies. The one member of crew who joined on the eve of final departure was Lord Byron's friend and travelling companion, Dr Bruno, who had left Greece in despair after the death of his mentor. He had made the decision to return and offer his medical skills to the cause so close to his old master's heart.

On May 26th 1826 the *'Perseverance'*, under the command of Captain Frank Abney Hastings, left England for Greece. Neither the ship nor her Master were ever to see the country of their origin again. Whilst several members of the London Greek Committee had made private visits to wish Hastings and his ship well, as had Frank's elder brother Charles, the actual sailing was still shrouded in secrecy to avoid any Governmental difficulties reflecting from the ever-growing body of opinion against the activities of Cochrane. To continue the deception the crew had been told, and rumour put about, that the *'Perseverance'* was in fact sailing for Ireland to join up with Cochrane and to perpetrate the canard she actually sailed along the south coast of England for several days. A few miles off Falmouth she rendezvoused with Cochrane's two frigates, the *'Unicorn'* and the

'*Union*', for final reports to be exchanged by signal. Once out of sight of land and other shipping Cochrane returned to Ireland, and the '*Perseverance*' turned south to the Bay of Biscay and Gibraltar.

The voyage to the Mediterranean was uneventful and even pleasurable with fair wind all the way. The only worry in Hastings' mind was the lack of experience amongst the sailors and the attitude of the five engineers on board. This latter problem became more acute once the ship had passed under the Rock of Gibraltar and into the Mediterranean. The wind which had carried them so comfortably from England virtually disappeared and they had to rely, for the first time, on the engines and the engineers. Both Hastings and Finlay were convinced that the poor maintenance and workmanship from the engineers was a deliberate act of sabotage but whatever the cause, after only two days of intermittent use one of the boilers burst.

As there was a great fear for the other boiler, especially if sabotage was the cause, both engines were closed down, paddles shipped and the '*Perseverance*' limped slowly for four hundred miles or so to Cagliari on the southern bay of Sardinia. There the troubles increased to the extent that Hastings asked Finlay to return with all speed to London to explain the situation to the Committee and if possible to return with engineers who could be better trusted.

The engineers on board did, after negotiating special payments, start the repairs using local labour and materials but the motley crew gathered together for the expedition used the time to sample the summer delights and cheap wines of Sardinia. Within days Hastings found himself summoned before Mr G Bomeester, the Consul General at Cagliari and was told that he must order his crew on board by nightfall each day. He was furthermore told to produce a full crew list so that any member remaining on Sardinia after the '*Perseverance*' left would be sent back to England at Hastings' personal expense.

The work on the repairs was slow. Of the five engineers, two had been identified as the ones who had committed sabotage and dismissed, the best engineer died on August 12th from a fever, leaving only two men who demanded more and more money. In total eleven men were sick and for some days Hastings himself was afflicted by what he described as Cholera Morbus. By August 26th, however, the engines were almost repaired and the remaining work could be undertaken at sea. It was with considerable relief to both the ship's officers and the residents of Cagliari that the *'Perseverance'* set off on the last leg of her journey.

With better winds and an engine which was gradually being improved, the journey to Greece only took two weeks. Hastings decided to stay for a few days on Cerigo, now known as Kythera, south of the Peloponnese, to finally prepare his ship before facing the Greek Government at Nauplio. He took the opportunity whilst there to write to J.C. Hobhouse, and to Messrs J. & S. Ricardo to announce the imminent arrival of the vessel at her destination.

He expressed his hope that Finlay, as his confidential friend, had described the horrendous conditions caused by the engineers and was pleased to report that the engines were now fully fit for work. He reported that without more men there was a risk that the fruits of all their labours would come to naught.

"The two men (engineers) I now have lately have worked hard and behaved tolerably well, even respectfully since I told Dunn that I always carry about me a brace of loaded pistols and should shoot him if he repeated to me the language he made use of in harbour." He went on to repeat his request for more engineers— *"Send me only Englishmen"—and also more crew. Send me more out than I need, the vagabonds will be sure to excel in nothing but drinking and will go home when they can no longer get drunk. I have had infinite trouble with my scoundrels, and I expect two thirds will quit me, but I do not know that I should want to keep more than one-third for the rest according to me seem quite determined cowards that they will do us no good if they remain".*

The disciplinarian in Frank Hastings comes out quite clearly in the letter but later he refers to the death of one of the seamen in a manner which shows the concern he always held for his men: *"Mr Thomas,* alias Critchley, died of a bilious fever on September 8*th* at 9.00pm. This was partly owning to his constitution, and partly to his having committed great disorders at Cagliari; he drank very hard. I shall send home to your direction all effects of his, that you may have the goodness to convey them to his wife. Of course we are no longer bound concerning him. I wished him to write if he had anything important to communicate ten hours before he died, but he refused until he was unable even to dictate. He then said he had some property he wished to make over to his wife. Dr Bruno sends for the satisfaction of his wife a statement of his case. I buried him with funeral honours".

The letters, which were virtually identical, went on to state the need for more money, and he complained that at that time he only had 2,300 dollars left which would scarcely pay the two months to those crew remaining along with six weeks for those who leave. Hastings added that if the money was not forthcoming he would again have to pay out of his own pocket.

"I am neck deep in the undertaking, and go through with it I must and I will whatever the consequence. Still I hope to meet every assistance possible from the parties concerned in England. With peoples co-operation both there and here we must succeed".

During the voyage which should have been so glorious for Frank Hastings, he had experienced troubles with the crew and the engines, illness and death on board and a sense that he was not to be given the support he so desperately needed from either the Greeks or their representatives in London. It was a measure of his almost outrageous optimism that the only clue to any depression was the fact that during the voyage he altered his Will. His stated reason for the change was that Finlay had advised him that he would be unable to make any legal transfer or legacy of his property from on board the '*Perseverance*' and could therefore only make certain requests.

His original Will had left sums to various friends; £2,000 to his cousin the Earl of Rawdon, £1,000 to Nicholas Kalergy, £500 to Charles Renée in Caen as a token of affection for his deceased son, £500 to John Hane, Alexander Ross his servant and to Lieut.

William Webb R.N. once a midshipman on *'Victory'*, later Lieutenant on *'Magnificent'*. To Captain Edward Scott RN he had bequeathed £1,000 along with his firearms, nautical instruments, watch and swords. The guns and swords he requested should be inscribed. *"This gun etc. was bequeathed by Frank Abney Hastings to his former messmate Captain Edward Scott"*. The balance was to go to the Vicar of Ashby de la Zouch, Rev. John Macdowell who was his Executor, along with his London Solicitor, Edmund Antrobus.

The codicil he made on board the *'Perseverance'* reduced Captain Scott's money to £100, but left him with the swords and other items. Alexander Ross was cut down to his wearing apparel, stores, wines and plate, Finlay was included with £500, and the balance was to be shared by Hane and Kalergy.

The news of Greek affairs they received on landing in Kythera could have done little to raise the spirits of Hastings or his men. A half-hearted treaty had been made between the British Foreign Secretary, Canning and the Turks which in part was supported for their own interests by the Russians and French, and in this Protocol it was suggested that Greece should become some form of independent state but within the protection of the Turkish Government. It was suggested that Mavrokordatos had in some way agreed with the proposal but lack of trust between the major powers encouraged them to carry on private and even more impractical negotiations. Both England and France had made proposals to Mehemet Ali, offering him Governorships of Syria and other inducements if he withdrew his support in the cause. Any real help from foreign powers was obviously not to be forthcoming and what little assistance might have been allowed would only have been for their own interests.

Throughout 1826, Ibrahim had been making his presence unpleasantly felt and in particular, despite the brave actions of Miaoulis in provisioning the besieged Messolongi, that town had been reduced to rubble by Ibrahim with thousands dying from starvation or wounds. Rather than agree to any settlement terms the garrison and civilians of Messolongi decided on the hopeless venture of breaking out through Ibrahim's lines to freedom. The ten thousand or so people having selected the night for their escape were betrayed to the besieging army who were awaiting them.

Men, women, children and a handful of soldiers, weakened by weeks of a diet largely consisting of sea-weed and racked with the pain of the many diseases, left the remains of their town. The slaughter was frightful. Only a thousand or so actually escaped, and some took refuge in the powder rooms where the following day they blew themselves up minutes before being over-run.

Following the fall of Messolongi, the Turkish troops had moved rapidly across country to the vicinity of Athens and by August occupied most of the town leaving the Greek and Philhellene troops trapped in the beautiful classical ruins of the Acropolis. Thus the important centre of Messolongi which had become world famous with the death of Byron and the cultural centre of Athens were both lost by the time the *'Perseverance'* reached Kythera. It was only the timely arrival of the new warship and the recent return to Greece of General Gordon which could have given hope to any but a blind optimist—fortunately both were to succeed!

Despite the worrying news, Hastings and his crew worked hard for two days in Kythera to prepare the ship for an official hand-over to the Greek Government at Nauplio. The ship was cleaned from stem to stern, carpenters repaired various *"pieces about the decks"* and even the engineers, perhaps fearful for their wages, ensured that the bulky machines were in full working order.

On a near calm day the *'Perseverance'*, for the last time under her English name, steamed north up the Gulf of Argos. Watchers from the shore—as word spread there were reported to be hundreds—on the afternoon of September 14th, 1826, must have reacted much as a man a century later when first seeing an aeroplane flying above him. For once the boilers behaved well under full pressure and the sleek vessel moved at considerable speed. Her two mighty paddles created a wide foaming double wake and her forty foot blackened chimney poured out clouds of darkened smoke. The waterfront at Nauplio was packed with incredulous onlookers as the *'Perseverance'* dropped her anchor between the fortress of Bourdzi—which four years previously to the day had been occupied by Hastings, Hane and Jarvis—and the town quay. At Bourdzi, Hastings had been seen as an outsider meddling with somebody else's affairs. His return to Greece in 1826 was as a hero arrived to save the nation.

The first boat to come alongside the *'Perseverance'* contained several representatives of the Greek Government and John Hane who had been patiently awaiting the return of his Captain. His voyage on the Newcastle collier to Greece had been slow and uncomfortable but nevertheless uneventful. The Greeks had accepted Hastings' orders and allowed Hane a barge to trans-ship and store the coal. Of great interest to Hastings was the not inconsiderable success Hane had achieved with the collection of additional fuels, armaments and shells.

Two days after her arrival the name *'Perseverance'* was removed from the stern of the vessel and in place went the Greek translation of the word, *'Karteria'*, by which she was to be known and through which her Captain was to become immortalised in the pages of modern Greek history. The *'Karteria'* was officially handed over to the Greek Government and as the first ship of the national Navy she was handed back to her Commander, Captain Frank Abney Hastings.

Many who saw her viewed the *'Karteria'* as some form of magic dragon, and rumours about her capabilities abounded. The most popular of these was that her paddle wheels would allow her to walk over land and that her fires and funnel would breathe death upon the enemy. In any event she was expected, even without her main armaments which were at that time crossing the Atlantic, to enter immediately into the conflict. It was with great difficulty and no doubt some considerable disappointment to the listeners, that the ship's officers and more informed members of the Greek community explained that it would be several weeks before the *'Karteria'* could breathe fire upon the Turks.

The first few weeks became a great adventure for the Government members and officials. They all wanted a trip on the *'Karteria'*.

Eventually Frank became exasperated at playing the part of a pleasure boatman and he sailed south to train the crew and try out the guns that Hane had so ably organised. Once more the crew, some of whom had remained and some who had been taken on at Nauplio, proved to be less than capable of the level of work and discipline required by the officers. Having heard from Finlay that the new engineers and several key crew members would be arriving in Nauplio in December, Hastings decided to drop most of his newly acquired crew members back at their home port and sail to Toulon to replace them with more reliable seamen. Before his departure he also wrote in exasperation to the Primates of Hydra and Spetses who had been complaining most vociferously about the lack of action from the 'Karteria' and pointed out to them that their understanding of the art of modern naval warfare was negligible, and that the 'Karteria' could not be ready until the 'Hellas' arrived from America.

His exasperation was growing too with Lord Cochrane, who had taken his huge sums of money, and had seemingly disappeared from the scene aboard the 'Unicorn'. The last news that Hastings had received was that the next two steam ships were nearing completion and that Cochrane was almost ready to join him. He could see the whole venture collapsing, with growing concern in London about both Cochrane and dealings in the Greek Bonds which had been issued to support the loan. Members of the Committee were using their knowledge and position to amass considerable fortunes on bond deals and added to this was the continued misappropriation of such money as did arrive in Greece.

In November Frank wrote to the 'Times' to warn the public of the misuse of funds by Cochrane. It is not known if he actually sent the letter—it was certainly not published—but his draft is extant at the British School of Athens. In this he places the main blame for the lack of steam ships upon the dealings between Cochrane and Galloway and their insistence on the use exclusively of the new experimental high-pressure horizontal cylinder engines rather than the proven conventional condensing engines. If the delays caused by fitting one engine of each type to the 'Karteria' had not occurred then Hastings was sure that he could have been in action in time to save Messolongi. He did not explain how the armaments would have arrived in Greece any earlier.

The only person exonerated in the affair was again Edward Ellice and the letter pointed out that Ellice and he had both been misled by Cochrane into believing that he would use part of the fortune available to him from the loan on obtaining at least some ready-made steam ships which could have been converted. The main cause of his complaint was absolutely factual:

"Lord Cochrane contracted to sail from England with a steam expedition two months after the signing of the contract. Fifteen months have now expired. To execute this he was to have £130,000 for the expedition and £37,000 for himself, yet not a vessel has sailed. Has he not forfeited the £37,000, this I demand of the public? Lord Cochrane has continually changed plans, and I suppose has eaten up the monies destined for the expedition, and I find myself here in Greece without a loan and I, after having expended much of my not overlarge fortune, am obliged to maintain this vessel at my own cost.

I demand that Lord Cochrane resigns, and returns the £37,000 to which in law or reason he can have no further claims. If he does not do this he will hear further of it. Lord Cochrane is my superior in age, in rank, in talent and in reputation; but not so in probity, a quality of some value in Public Character; here he has, and here he always will fail. Had he been an honest man Greece would now have been free. Should Lord Cochrane arrive here I shall resign the command of the 'Karteria' as I will never serve under the man who has done such irreparable injury to Greece . . . Let the public pronounce public character and must submit his reputation to the Public Tribunal—'twill ultimately render Justice".

Hastings was clearly in a position of great unhappiness where one of his boyhood heroes, Cochrane, had been shown in his eyes to be a person of little honour, and like any other in that and circumstance he had reacted against him. The relationship between the two never became anything other than mutual toleration at the best after that.

The problems with seamen dissolved to a great extent when the *'Karteria'* took on a largely new and foreign crew at Toulon. There is no complete record of their composition but certainly there were Swedes, Irish, English and French amongst those who joined the Greeks from the Nauplio enlistment. The difficulties, however, with the boilers continued and by the time the *'Karteria'* learnt at Syra, one of the Cycladean Islands, that the *'Hellas'* had arrived from America, his ship had developed several rather worrying leaks.

The *'Hellas'* had arrived in Nauplio on December 8th, 1826, and although a conventional frigate, by her very size and splendour she must have created as much disturbance to the onlookers at the *'Karteria'* a few weeks previously. The beautiful vessel had been the cause of many financial problems in America where she was built. The *'Hellas'*, under her original name of *'Hope'*, was ordered from the shipyard of Leroy, Bayard & Co., at the same time as a sister ship, the *'Liberator'*, was ordered from G.G. & S. Howland. Delays were the order of the day and the price went up in leaps and bounds until Messrs. Ricardo refused to pour any more money into the building programme. The Greek Deputies to the New York Committee eventually decided that the only way in which one ship could be made ready was to sell the other, so to raise the funds to complete the *'Hope'*, the *'Liberator'* was sold to the American Government.

The eventual cost of the *'Hope'* was £150,000, as compared with the price in England for a similar vessel of £60,000 and that of smaller ready-made ships advocated by Hastings of around £25,000 each. It seemed that in so many countries money was given to the Greek cause from the best of motives but so often this was squandered, wasted and misappropriated before reaching Greece where the same happened again, decimating the efforts of the true Philhellenes of all nations. Nevertheless, the *'Hellas'*, flagship of Admiral Miaoulis, and later for a short period of Cochrane, was a marvellous sight with well over fifty guns and more than a thousand tons in weight.

Hastings and his two gunnery officers, John Hane and Gibbon Fitz-Gibbon, rushed back to Nauplio to take on board their eagerly awaited armaments. Even the stoic Captain Hamilton of the

'*Cambrian*' was envious of the task ahead. He had transported Dr Samuel Gridley Howe to Nauplio to take up his post of Senior Surgeon to the fleet on board the '*Karteria*' and sent with him messages of goodwill to Hastings, expressing his admiration by saying that if he did not have a wife and family to support he would willingly have donated £1,000 to the success of the brave venture.

Of the eight 68-pounders which arrived aboard the '*Hellas*', four were carronades of the standard British Government pattern designed by Mr Gascoine, manager of Carron Ironworks in Scotland and the other four were designed by Hastings himself. The carronades were short iron guns attached to the carriage by a loop and bolt rather than by trunnion; they had less thickness of metal than other guns of a similar calibre, and at the muzzle a chamber for powder like mortar of the time. The advantage of these guns was the weight for the calibre but their great disadvantage was that with such a small charge of powder they were only really effective at short range. Hastings' plan was to use these at close quarters by using grape shot heated to fire into the rigging of his opponents.

His own designed four 68-pounders were altogether much bulkier, being three tons in weight and having a bore of seven feet four inches. As with most long guns they did have a trunnion fixing, but this was much further forward so that the centre intersected the centre of the bore of the gun. The mounting for his guns was a standard ten inch Howitzer carriage which fitted the purpose with a minimum of alteration and never caused any problems. The principal he proposed with the shells, as seen in his memorandum to Byron, was that they should be stored and moved around in a wooden cradle, although on several occasions at the height of battle this precaution was forgotten and they were put into the guns with the fuses towards the muzzle. This seemingly dangerous procedure, which was the main reason that guns of the type had not been used at sea, did not actually cause a single accident but realising that his theories would never be generally accepted if such an accident occurred Hastings always insisted that his safety method should be used where possible.

The engine fires of the *'Karteria'* heated the hot shot required, and these were brought on deck by two men in a machine resembling a double coal-box with long handles at either side. This allowed them to be tilted with ease at the muzzle of the gun to be loaded. Later a small furnace was mounted on the deck for speed and convenience.

Her trials completed with relative success, Hastings moved his ship to Spetses and once again John Hane left on another search for coal and supplies. Hastings bombarded the Primates of Hydra and Spetses with requests for coal and at one stage wrote to a G. Malakinis asking that he may be given 100 tons of coal from his ship to enable the *'Karteria'* to join the Government which had moved to Egina. Hane had carried with him a letter to Finlay who had gone directly to Egina, written by Frank at Spetses just before Christmas, which describes the difficulties he was still encountering:

"Engineers Dunn and McMahon quitted yesterday after nearly ruining the boilers. We are in a deplorable condition wanting coals, provisions, money; and the ship leaking to a degree inconceivable. However I shall endeavour to get to Egina to await your arrival".

During the latter months of 1826, another National Assembly had been sitting at Epidavros but again Kolokotronis spoilt any ideas of national unity by forming his own 'Government' at Ermioni on the mainland opposite Spetses and Hydra. It was assumed that the Egina Government was in favour of the involvement of England and Russia and that Kolokotronis, who had accepted funds from the French, was with them. Once more Edward Blaquiere was back in Greece on his diplomatic mission and yet again the name of Kapodistrias entered the arena. It was seen by Blaquiere that Kapodistrias was the only person who could enjoy the support of all parties and that the friendship between he and Kolokotronis over so many years would bring the warring factions together.

As an interim measure he assured Kolokotronis that both Church, who by then was on his way back to Greece, and Cochrane looked upon him favourably and thus guaranteed that when the overlords of the land and sea forces did arrive all the groups would lend their support. To some extent it was a bluff—Blaquiere was well aware that Hamilton was against the Kapodistrians on the assumption that the British Government would never approve a man who had worked so closely to the Russian Court for so many years. What in fact was not known to either Blaquiere or Hamilton was that the nephew of the British Foreign Secretary, Stratford Canning, had in November of 1826 had private meetings in Switzerland with Kapodistrias, and that by Christmas the British considered him to be the best leader from the point of view of British interests since Mavrokordatos.

Whilst the political intrigue was occupying the attentions of the Greek faction, the Turks continued their siege of the Acropolis although their troops under Mustapha Bey to the north had been cut off by Karaiskakis on the one side and Kalergy's forces on the other. During the hard winter's weather—the snow had arrived in the mountains unseasonably early—many hundreds of Greeks and Turks perished from lack of cover and food. In the Morea, Ibrahim Pasha had pursued a 'scorched earth' policy, and having removed all food and supply sources from his opponents he received further men and supplies from Egypt in December.

Hastings was furious. He realised that Ibrahim's information on the lack of readiness of the *'Karteria'* was sound, and also that neither Cochrane nor the other vessels were anywhere near the scene. More than anything this encouraged him to double his already considerable energies to put the *'Karteria'* into action. Having browbeaten, threatened, cajoled and bribed the Greeks for his fuel, and with guns still being fitted and tested, Hastings sailed for Egina and the Greek Government. By mid-January he put himself, his ship and his crew on battle orders and stood by for further instructions at anchor, off Egina.

Chapter 9

1827: January to June

Shortly before Christmas, some forty Philhellenes and three hundred Greeks led by the French Philhellene Fabvier had broken through the Turkish lines and entered the besieged Acropolis with supplies of food and powder. The arrangement had been that they would leave as soon as possible but Fabvier always maintained that he was tricked into a position whereby he and his troops had no alternative but to remain under siege.

The Greek Government, anxious to prove to the world that the men and equipment provided by the various Greek Committees were being used, decided in January to make a concentrated effort to relieve Athens. Rather than take the obvious course of cutting off the lines of supply on land and at sea for the Turks it was deemed more dramatic to make an all out attack. The main push was to be on Piraeus by General Gordon and his largely Ionian troops, supported from the sea. The French-trained and experienced cavalry officer, Colonel Burbaki, offered to mount a diversionary tactic by marching on the town of Elefsina to the west of Athens, and securing the hills around the lowlands surrounding Athens.

At the end of January 1827 Hastings was ordered from Egina to cross to Salamina to the north which lay a short distance from the mainland and Piraeus and there to pick up Gordon and his troops who had arrived from Megara. The day chosen for this activity was 2nd February; Hastings arrived at Salamina at around the same time as Gordon's troops and Burbaki advanced to the edge of the plain with eight hundred and supported on his flanks by two groups of a thousand under Vassos and Notaras. The concept was right—that whilst the three groups under Burbaki, Vassos and Notaras occupied the troops of Reshid Pasha, the naval force moved to Piraeus—but the plan failed.

Burbaki moved forward with great speed onto the plain to establish his defences amongst the olive trees and was met with a vastly superior force headed by Reshid himself. The two thousand men supposedly giving him support, rather than come to his rescue on either flank, dropped everything they carried and fled in a most disgraceful and cowardly manner. Burbaki's men fought gallantly against the appallingly overwhelming odds but more than half perished in a very short time including their leader. The head of Burbaki was severed by Reshid, complete with his cavalry helmet, and this was subsequently sent back to the Sultan in Constantinople as proof of the success.

An element of surprise still remained in that both Reshid Pasha and the Turkish Commander of Athens, Suraskier Kutayhi Pasha, assumed that the force of General Gordon would be taken around the south of Salamina and therefore attempt the landing at Piraeus at the most heavily defended point. No warship had ever attempted the northern passage around the island but using her engines, the 'Karteria' led eight other vessels, carrying a total of two thousand or more troops, through the narrow straits and at midnight on February 5th after a journey of only three hours, they anchored off Phaleron.

Short skirmishing took place and gradually the Turkish troops realised the extent of the landings and the fact that other ships and troops from Hydra and Spetsai were joining the invasion. They took refuge in the well fortified buildings of the Custom House and Monastery at St. Spyridon. Realising that there was no time to besiege these strongholds and a frontal attack would have been disastrous, the 'Karteria' was ordered into range of the fortifications the following day. For many hours she stood off shore and with guns and sights far more sophisticated than previously seen in Greece, Hastings commenced his bombardment of the two occupied buildings. Gradually the defences crumbled and the land-based troops were ordered to assault the Custom House and Monastery from the rear. The opportunity was clearly there with the main Turkish forces of Reshid at that time still operating on the plains against the remains of Burbaki's gallant army.

The Greeks, however, did not take advantage of the situation. This was left to Suraskier Kutayhi Pasha, who with great speed and military instinct, moved from Athens with a crack cavalry troop carrying with them two long five-inch howitzers which he set up in such a position that the guns of the 'Karteria' could not reach them. The Greek attackers had at the sight of the cavalry taken it upon themselves to yet again break into a disorderly retreat to the absolute disgust of Gordon and Hastings. Once it became clear that the advance upon the two strongholds had deteriorated into a disorderly retreat and also that the 'Karteria' was in some danger from the newly arrived guns, Hastings took his ship out of the bay to safety.

At this point Gordon moved his growing force into the hills of Munchya, and made camp on the peak and rocky sides of the outcrop overlooking Piraeus. It was not until February 11th that they came under strong attack when Reshid returned from his victory over Burbaki. With three thousand men he made many attempts to scale the hill using boulders and overhanging rock as protection and he also positioned five-inch guns in the defiles to ensure that any attempt to break out by Gordon would end in a massacre. Realising the difficulties the army was in, the 'Karteria' steamed back into Piraeus to divert the attentions of Reshid.

Using grape shot from all the 68-pounders on the Turkish artillery and reserves with great accuracy, Hastings created mayhem on land. Without any fear of injury the 'Karteria' was moved into a position so close as to allow the skilled gun crews to achieve an incredible success rate. Guns were destroyed, hundreds killed or injured under the firing, and many of the enemy were obliged to take cover back at the Monastery.

Reshid Pasha realised that the land forces of Gordon were now of secondary importance and that before he could take any further positive action it was necessary to either destroy the *'Karteria'* or force her away from Piraeus. To this end he brought five Howitzers within range of the *'Karteria'* and managed to position two of them between a tower and the Monastery to avoid the shot from the sea. The first three guns were quickly silenced, one of Hane's shots actually destroying the carriage of one before it was fired, but the two protected guns slowly improved their range with their shells.

One shell which did not explode on landing lodged in the carriage of a 68-pounder which was being sighted by Hane, and then exploded. Fortunately there were no injuries to the crew or Hane. Several other shells tore the ship's boats away and a further shell connected just above the water line on the transom ripping away two strakes of six feet each and badly damaging two others. It was only due to the insistence of Hastings that not only should his vessel have close caulked timbers in her hull but that the bulkheads fore and aft of the engine compartment should be water tight. The damage sustained by the *'Karteria'* in the bay of Piraeus would almost certainly have sunk any other vessel. Having succeeded in taking the attack away from Gordon, the *'Karteria'* withdrew.

At the entrance of the port of Piraeus on either side there were two pillars and as the damaged ship retreated she came within range of soldiers with muskets stationed on both pillars. The *'Karteria'* was raked with shot from over a hundred guns for half an hour. The remains of the ship's boats left by the shelling were virtually destroyed by the soldiers. No doubt the relief of Reshid on seeing the departure of the fearsome steamship after wreaking so much havoc was only matched by Frank Hastings and his crew at escaping the concentrated fire from the Turks.

Several hours later during the early morning of February 12th, the *'Karteria'* rounded the north-western point of Egina and pulled into the shingle cove a few hundred yards north of the town. The ship's carpenters and sail makers, aided by teams of locals set to work immediately to repair the extensive damage to the vessel. Dr Samuel

Gridley Howe worked alongside them to repair the equally bloody damage to the crew, virtually none of whom had escaped injury of some sort. Within the remarkably short time of three weeks the *'Karteria'* was again ready for sea and battle. On every subsequent encounter she was held in awe by the enemy who now knew the devastation the ship and the methods of her master could cause.

The failure of the army, even with the support of the *'Karteria'*, to relieve Athens from the front called for new actions. The Turkish supply route was from the north east down through the northern channel of the island of Evia to the fortress then known as Negrepont, now Halkida, where the munitions and victuals were loaded into barges for the short journey across to the mainland peninsular of Attica and the port of Oropos. It was decided in early March that to vanquish the forces of Reshid Pasha, Oropos should be taken and the vital supplies cut off from him. A German Philhellene, General Heideck was appointed to lead the Greek troops, some five hundred strong drawn largely from the men holding the hills of Munchya, and he was given the support of a small, but powerful naval fleet consisting of the *'Hellas'*, the *'Karteria'* and the brig *'Nelson'* under Admiral Miaoulis.

In the late afternoon the vessels arrived off Oropos, and whilst the *'Hellas'* and the *'Nelson'* anchored about a mile distant from the Turkish defences, the *'Karteria'* moved in to within close range of even the muskets. These were quickly silenced by judicious use of grape shot which scattered the defenders and the ship's 68-pounders turned their attention to the main walls of the batteries. These were of a type known as fascines, which were made of bundles of wood held together by rope and mud and having taken two flour carrying vessels as prizes, the *'Karteria'* opened fire with carcass shells setting fire to the fascines. Soon the powder magazine exploded and further shells silenced the remaining guns.

Miaoulis urged Heideck to land the troops under cover of both the increasing gloom of the evening and also the confusion caused by the *'Karteria'*. This Heideck declined to do until morning. The steam ship held her position until the action commenced in the morning but when it did, not only did General Heideck refuse to go ashore with the troops, he also refused to move closer to the '*Karteria*' to supervise the action. Without any form of leadership and discipline from within their own ranks, the Greek troops had no stomach for an all out attack on the Turkish garrison which had been reinforced during the night. In the afternoon, the cavalry of Reshid Pasha arrived throwing the Greek troops into further disorder and disarray and Heideck ordered them back aboard the ships for their return to Munchya. The affair which could have signalled the relief of Athens was a disaster and the presence of Hastings and Miaoulis ensured that Heideck's actions were reported back to the Greek Government. His military reputation never recovered from the extraordinary events at Oropos but again the skills of Hastings and the abilities of the '*Karteria*' were noted and reported back, ensuring that in future he should be given command of his own flotilla for all future actions.

The events at Oropos were, however, somewhat overshadowed by the arrival in Greece of the two men who had for so long been awaited, Church and Cochrane. These men, one by acknowledgement and friendship, the other by reputation, were believed to provide the only chance of bringing about a united Greece. After six years of waiting for the right time to return to Greece, Richard Church landed at Portoheli on 9th March 1827. This little port, set in an attractive bay on the Argostoli peninsular opposite Spetses, was nine miles from the Ermioni headquarters of Kolokotronis who had served so closely with Church many years before. The news of his old friend's arrival was soon received by the Chieftain, and during the night he marched the ten miles to greet him.

The reunion between the two was very emotional, and the atmosphere charged the more by the embraces between them taking place under the colours which Church had awarded to Kolokotronis twelve years previously. Blaquiere, as always for important moments, was present as he realised that through the reunion could come unity. Captain Hamilton had already anchored off Ermioni to assist in the major attempt to bring the parties together. The jubilant comrades at Portoheli were escorted back to Ermioni, and that evening dined with Hamilton aboard the '*Cambrian*'. Perhaps helped along by tiredness

Commander of the Karteria

from having marched much of the night and that day, and also by the lavish hospitality of Hamilton, Kolokotronis accepted that Church would not take any official office unless the two main ruling factions in Greece made peace and fought with a concerted effort. To this end it was agreed that Church should go immediately to the Government at Egina and arrange for neutral territory to meet.

He was very courteously received by both the officials and the military leaders and his offer to act as mediator was generally accepted. They chose the island of Poros as an acceptable neutral site for their subsequent meetings. On March 18th Captain Hamilton transported Church and his aides across to Poros where they were joined at anchor by Miaoulis in the '*Hellas*'. The following day Cochrane landed at Poros from the schooner '*Unicorn*', accompanied by the '*Union*' and the brig '*Sauveur*', where he was greeted with considerable pomp and ceremony. Miaoulis gave the official oration in Spanish, their common language, and indicated his willingness to put himself and his fleet at Cochrane's command.

Cochrane, from his months of preparation—he had studied many memoranda and reports from Hastings and Stanhope—had an immediate and correct understanding of the Greek political situation and like Church refused to take an active part in the proceedings until an agreement had been reached between the Greeks themselves. Under this considerable pressure from the Philhellenes—Cochrane's high flown oratory, Church's constant persuasion, Hamilton's superbly exercised neutrality between the parties and the fifth year of Edward Blaquiere's nagging, the Greek leaders had little chance of not accepting that they must come together. The site chosen was that of the classical temple and town of Damala, now Trizina, a few miles from Poros on the Peloponnese mainland, which was about half way between Egina and Ermioni, the seats of the two rival factions.

During late March and the first days of April it took all the diplomatic skills of Church, supported by Hamilton and Blaquiere, to actually make the parties sit down with each other. In turn they left Damala refusing to take part over some trivial matter and in turn each was persuaded back until on April 7th 1827 a United Assembly of Greece actually commenced.

Two days later the Assembly appointed Cochrane as Chief Admiral of Greece and on April 11th Kapodistrias, at that time in Paris, was appointed as President of Greece for a period of seven years. To await his arrival a Committee of three Chiefs was appointed to act for him and another Committee was formed with Mavrokordatos as its senior member to work out a new constitution. The members of the Assembly were in a strange situation and gave themselves political appointments without any real meaning or power. To counteract this they devised the most extraordinary titles for themselves and at least these honours were shared out under the Philhellenic supervision with reasonable fairness.

Sir Richard Church had been one of the few not willing to make a hasty judgement on the post of Generalissimo which was urged upon him mainly by his old comrade at arms, Kolokotronis and supported nominally by the other factions of Mavrokordatos and Koundriotis. Hamilton advised him against taking the post on the grounds that, unlike Cochrane, he had no funds immediately at his disposal and this could put him into an intolerable and even dangerous position. As always the advice preferred by Hamilton was probably the soundest available but Church's love of Greece, of adventure and possibly the promise of fortune to come when the war was won persuaded him against accepting this wise counsel. On Easter Sunday, April 15th 1827, General Sir Richard Church, son of a Quaker merchant in Cork, Ireland, stood before the National Assembly of Greece in the presence of the Archbishop of Arta. Resplendent in his dress uniform and bedecked with his medals and battle honours, he took the oath over sword and an ancient Byzantine crucifix and became the Supreme Commander of the Greek Army.

Wisely examining all the available reports, and having many lengthy discussions with General Gordon, Church decided that the action undertaken by Heideck on land, from the ships of Hastings and Miaoulis, at Oropos had been the correct one even if it had ended in such dishonourable failure. The warnings of Hamilton, however, came true within hours of Church's appointment when he was informed by Cochrane that the main effort must come again from a frontal attack upon Athens rather than the more protracted process of cutting off the Turkish supply lines. Church indeed had little or no finance and Cochrane had retained some £20,000 which he kept securely locked and guarded on his private yacht, a lavishly appointed schooner which for safety was still under an English flag. This was the first of many bad decisions by Cochrane who used his wealth acquired from the Greek Committees to overrule those who were not only more expert in Greek warfare, but were in the country for reasons of honour rather than finance.

The Turkish supply route to Athens was from Negrepont (Halkida) to Oropos and thence to Athens but the plan agreed by Gordon, Church and Hastings was to attack higher up in Thessaly where the supply vessels gathered prior to their journey to Evia. The main port of departure was Volos. Despite the opposition of Lord Cochrane to cutting off land supply, Hastings and the *'Karteria'* were chosen to lead a squadron to Volos. This consisted of the corvette *'Thermistocles'* under Captain Raphael, the brig *'Ares'* under Captain Kriezes and two schooners, the *'Panaghia'* and *'Aspasia'*. They left Poros to undertake the daunting task of cutting the supply lines at Volos without the back-up of land forces.

The harbour of Volos had been selected by the Turks as one of the safest in the area, being enclosed by a horseshoe bay defended on one side from the near ruins of an old fortress containing guns and from the other entrance by shore batteries. The bay itself is at the northern part of yet another bay some thirty miles long and a maximum of around the same in width but with a narrow entrance at the southern extremity of only five miles. The entrance is guarded by the town of Trikeri and at that time the Turks had a twelve gun battery protecting the harbour.

During the night of April 19th and 20th the engine of the *'Karteria'* was stopped whilst a leak was repaired but at two in the morning it was restarted and the little fleet moved to an anchorage just to the south of the Gulf of Volos and dropped anchor at four-thirty.

After a couple of hours of well earned rest the Captains of the other vessels came aboard the *'Karteria'* for a conference with their new Fleet Commander, and he gave them the news that not only could they expect to be fired upon from Trikeri and later from the Turkish defences at Volos, but that the Pasha's finest man-of-war in the area mounting sixteen heavy guns and two mortars which had been constructed for the siege at Messolongi, was reputedly at Volos. Perhaps for the first time in modern Greek naval history there was no recorded suggestion that any resistance was shown to the clearly risky expedition ahead of them. None thought to argue with the authority or calmness of Captain Hastings.

At ten in the morning the squadron was ordered to weigh anchor, but the other vessels had to wait for the *'Karteria'* whose capstan machinery broke and she therefore had to rig up a block and tackle and pull up the starboard anchor from fifteen fathoms by hand. Within half an hour the fleet had rounded the point and came abeam of Trikeri where they observed a brig-of-war and four schooners anchored close in to the houses. A few badly aimed shots were fired from the batteries and several soldiers opened fire with muskets as the ships passed close to the eastern edge of the narrow entrance to the Gulf of Volos.

By eleven that morning the fleet was out of range of the defences at Trikeri and with light and variable winds barely ruffling the sea they were ordered to hoist all sail and steer north for the town of Volos. The day was beautifully bright and clear and their target soon came into view. Hastings, knowing from his experience on the *'Thermistocles'*, the Greek habit of becoming separated and thus vulnerable, herded his little fleet together like a mother hen with her chicks. With the defences of Volos clearly in view, at four in the afternoon, Hastings ordered the *'Thermistocles'* and the *'Ares'* to anchor just out of musket range of the shore batteries and once they had established their positions, not before, to open fire on the batteries and fort.

At four-twenty firing commenced and was returned. Under the cover of the noise and smoke the *'Karteria'*, followed by the two small schooners, steamed through the heads and dropped anchor in range of the town and inner batteries. Having dropped his starboard anchor in five fathoms, Hastings managed to fix a spring from the starboard quarter to bring the port broadside to the town. The first rounds of shells soon quietened the firing from the shore guns and attention was turned onto the eight transport brigs in the harbour. The object of the adventure was to capture supplies rather than a military victory, therefore Hastings decided to use grape shot on the transports to attempt to clear them of the many troops on board guarding the valuable victuals. Each gun was loaded with three hundred two-ounce balls which inflicted the most horrible damage to any person remaining within range and quickly the Turks fled the terrible bombardment.

The boats from the '*Karteria*' and the two schooners were dropped speedily into the water and under covering fire from the anchored vessels pulled alongside the transports and took warps back out to tow them off. The three nearest were quickly taken off shore as prizes. The fourth was caught up with the anchor and collided with the '*Karteria*', tearing off the anchor-board and also damaging the bowsprit. Having taken the first four ships, the boats returned to attack two more brigs anchored near to the shore batteries and were met with severe resistance. The boatswain from the '*Karteria*', Ralph Hall, led the boarding party to the first, but was wounded as he scrambled aboard. With great bravery Hall pulled himself over the bulwarks and hauled down the Turkish flag, only to find that one of the Turks was in hiding with a loaded pistol, and as he jumped out a ball from the handgun grazed Hall on the forehead.

The Turk jumped over the side of the brig and started to swim for the shore but an English sailor, fearing that the popular Northumbrian boatswain had been killed, dived after him carrying only his pocket knife. The unfortunate Turk was the weaker swimmer and paid for his deficiency by having his throat cut by the Englishman who also paid the penalty of his Captain's tongue for such unprofessional conduct. As the two brigs were found to be unladen and without sails the attackers set fire to them and returned to the fleet.

The '*Karteria*' continued to be fired upon by the batteries and at six in the evening she was struck by several shots, one of which carried away the main gaff. Hastings decided to heat some shot to bring the action to a close. Several of these took effect and within an hour there were fires throughout the town. Once again the ship's boats were sent out to set fire to two other transport brigs and at nine in the evening the final transport, loaded with ammunition, was taken in tow and the order given to leave the harbour. The '*Thermistocles*' and the '*Ares*' had done their task well, and the '*Karteria*' and her accompanying schooners plus the prizes were able to quit the port without sustaining any further damage, although the Turks were hurriedly preparing two guns on a point as a "send off", but these were destroyed by the accurate artillery of John Hane.

Dr Howe recorded the sight of the departure in darkness as quite spectacular, with the burning transports reflecting from the water, and fires all around the area of the town with the most dramatic coming from the powder magazines and stores which had been so completely destroyed. The Turkish name for the '*Karteria*', of the "fire-frigate" or "fire-ship", could not have been bettered at that particular time. The fleet sailed south towards Trikeri and in the early hours of the morning anchored in a bay about half way down the Gulf of Volos. During the day of that Saturday, 21st April 1827, the crew worked at full pace to repair as much of the damage to the '*Karteria*' and her rigging as possible whilst Hastings took stock of the action the previous day which had only lasted from four-thirty in the afternoon to nine in the evening.

The prizes which now sailed with them were four brigs laden with provisions and a further one with ammunition. Three other ships had been destroyed by fire as had a large part of the town and garrison of Volos. Some damage had been sustained but the overall result was far beyond the wildest expectations of any other than her Captain. There remained only one part of his theories to be proved—that of going around in circles and using his guns in succession—and this he vowed to try the following evening.

Commander of the Karteria

A Greek fishing boat had come alongside the '*Karteria*' and had reported that the Turkish brig-of-war with the mortar guns from Messolongi was in fact the one they had seen anchored at Trikeri when they had sailed into the Gulf on the previous Friday morning. Under cover of darkness the '*Karteria*' and her entourage sailed for Trikeri with the intention of taking the Turks by surprise and attempting to capture the brig and possibly the three schooners reported to be with her. Their arrival was greeted by a strong barrage from the battery of twelve 12-pounders, along with musket fire from so many troops that it was clear that their arrival had been awaited. It was then quite clear that there was no chance of snatching the Turkish ships as prizes and Hastings ordered the fleet to withdraw to safety until the following day when the object of their actions would be to destroy the enemy.

The '*Karteria*', her boilers steamed up and shot heated, moved on her own to about half a mile off the Turkish brig and proceeded to go around in circles firing each of her long guns loaded with hot shot in turn. After about half an hour of this action she moved back to rejoin the others in the fleet who were out of range. At first nothing was apparently happening aboard the enemy vessel but after a time more smoke appeared from her decks and hundreds of Turks poured onto the ship to put out the fires. Hastings now loaded the long guns with heavy grape and the carronades with shells. At eleven in the morning he ordered the '*Thermistocles*' and the '*Ares*' to follow him in to open fire on the Turks again to prevent the crews from extinguishing the flames licking up at the spars from the decks. At the same time the three schooners took a considerable pounding from the three ships, and whilst they did not sink they were rendered quite unserviceable without major repairs.

The shore batteries kept up their fire of twelve-pound shot and one of these achieved a direct hit upon the fluke of the port anchor. It rebounded into the stomach of the boatswain, Ralph Hall, who had already been so badly injured three days earlier. On this occasion he was killed instantly. Another shot hit the bowsprit, and several more went into the hull.

Aboard the Turkish brig the fires were becoming unmanageable, the rigging was aflame, and even the starboard guns which were pointed towards the shore batteries and loaded ready for use, went off causing quite some damage to their own troops on shore. Her topsides caught fire and eventually the bollards holding her to her anchor and moorings parted and the ship drifted towards the rocky coast. The magazine caught fire before the ship ran aground and with a mighty explosion the topsides parted from the hull and, carrying all her important guns, the Turkish brig sank into deep water. Captain Frank Abney Hastings must have experienced great satisfaction as at noon he ordered his squadron to leave Trikeri, for he had completely vindicated his naval theories. In practice he had established a revolution in naval warfare which was to survive him by many decades and additionally he had shown that the Greek crew could heat sixty-eight pound shots below, carry it on deck and load it even whilst the ship was moving.

Shortly after the fleet left the Gulf of Volos, the mood of excitement was turned to one of great sorrow as Captain Hastings conducted the funeral service for Ralph Hall, and he was buried at sea with full naval honours. It took all the discipline of the Captain to restrain the English crew members from murdering the several Turkish prisoners cramped into the small cabins at either end of the paddle wheel housing. The men maintained that both Turk and Greek victors had the right to kill their captives and indeed one very experienced old English sailor threatened to quit Greece if he could not slit the throats of the prisoners. By a combination of argument and threat, Hastings averted any ugly scenes, although his crew man did leave the service and return to England at the first possible opportunity.

The damage to the '*Karteria*' necessitated the return of the fleet to Poros, but during the voyage, Hastings observed that it was not only through Volos that the Turkish supplies were being sent to Athens. Passing close to the eastern seaboard of Evia the fleet observed a number of vessels either at anchor or pulled up on the beach of a small harbour some two miles from the town of Kimi. As the vessels approached the shore they saw Turkish inhabitants leaving the stationary ships and running off towards the safety of the town, and boats from the '*Karteria*' and '*Thermistocles*' were launched to ascertain the nature of the commercial trade that was so evidently taking place.

One of the vessels was flying under Russian colours and to their absolute horror another, which had just started to unload its cargo of wheat, was a Greek schooner from Psara. It became clear that while Greek troops had spent the winter fighting for the very life of Athens, other Greeks had been supplying the Turks through the port of Kimi. About one third of the wheat from the well stocked grain store was transferred to the transports captured at Volos. The Russian ship was left alone, another two ships were taken by Hastings and presented to the Greek Admiralty Court at Poros along with the other prizes. While Hastings protested most vehemently about the treachery of the Greeks trading with the Turks in the supplies for which he was risking his ship and his men, it became obvious that some members of the Government knew of the trade and indeed profited from it.

Very little interest was shown in the complaints of Captain Hastings, or even in the fact that his squadron had left with a total of five vessels and returned with twelve. The interest of all Greeks was centred on the campaign ordered by Cochrane to carry out a full frontal attack upon Athens to relieve Fabvier and the other troops who had been under siege for so long at the Acropolis. On April 20th, the very day that the '*Karteria*' had led the remarkable attack upon Volos, the Greek troops had assembled for what Cochrane considered to be the final battle for Athens. Despite the opposite advice from Church, Gordon, Karaiskakis and Kolokotronis, it was seen by the mercenary Lord as an opportunity to cover himself once more in international glory and a method of subduing the complaints about the amount of money he had acquired from the Greek loans.

The estimates of the number of troops available to him varied considerably but in reality the figure was somewhere around seventeen thousand. Karaiskakis had some five thousand on the plains to the west of Athens. Gordon had four thousand in the hills at Munchya. Kolokotronis, having been given the military command of Morea, had supplied three thousand under the command of his son and Major Urquhart, a relative of Cochrane, had raised one thousand Hydriotes who annoyed the veteran Romeliot troops by strutting round in fancy uniforms and arms, and were being paid more money! For several days letters went back and forth with reasons that the frontal attack should be cancelled or delayed. Cochrane would accept none of the pleas and whilst most of the arguments used the fact that the Muslim Albanian troops still occupied the Monastery of St Spyridon, Cochrane countered this by saying that it was no more in the way than the church on the island of Poros.

On April 25th the action started when Cochrane was looking at two enemy lines and a skirmish broke out. Seeing an opportunity of defeating these lines he waved his telescope, the only item he was carrying, and urged the troops of Kolokotronis to follow him. This successful, but comparatively minor action was probably the only one in which Cochrane conducted himself to the level of his reputation. The following day Karaiskakis advanced his own troops to Piraeus and the Monastery was shelled from the '*Hellas*' by Miaoulis, but with much less accuracy that the previous bombardment by the 'Karteria'.

Despite the attempts by Cochrane to negotiate a surrender by the occupants, the Albanians were resolute in their determination to fight to the death, probably on the assumption that they would be killed even if they did capitulate. For this reason General Church handed over command of the forces in Attica on April 28th to Karaiskakis, and told him to use his influence to obtain the surrender. The only way in which Karaiskakis could convince the Muslims that they would not be murdered was to offer himself, Blaquiere and his officers as hostages to guarantee their safe conduct. Urquhart removed his unruly Hydriote troops to safety. Church's men were on the other side of the harbour. Cochrane was safely back aboard his yacht and Miaoulis, Gordon and Finlay watched the scene from aboard the '*Hellas*'.

The two hundred Albanians, accompanied by their hostages walked out of the battle scarred, once holy, building. One of the Greek troops moved forward to grab a pistol held by a prisoner and it went off into the man signalling the other Greek troops to attack. The bloody carnage was watched in horror by those powerless to intervene and by the time that Karaiskakis had brought the men back under control only seventy of the two hundred were alive.

For the second time during the Greek Wars of Independence, Thomas Gordon found the behaviour of the forces totally abhorrent and once more he resigned his post and decided to quit the country with all speed. Church too, although both Finlay and Gordon blamed him for allowing the murders by negligence, tried to resign. However Karaiskakis talked him out of any precipitous actions by promising both to punish the men involved in the killings and that he would raise no further objections to attacking Athens.

Cochrane, who neither accepted any responsibility for the massacre, nor appeared to understand why Gordon should have felt so strongly, still pushed for a landing on the main part of the troops and a push to the Acropolis. The order went out that the landings would be made on May 5th under cover of darkness to enable the main attack to be made the following day, with the troops still being under the command of Karaiskakis. However, the evening before the scheduled date for the invasion the Hydriote soldiers under Urquhart indulged in a drunken orgy and fighting broke out between them and the forces under Karaiskakis. The chieftain was badly wounded during the brawl and died in the company of Richard Church the following day.

The effect upon the morale of the Greeks and Philhellenes was very traumatic and they all assumed that Cochrane would rescind his orders for the landings in the light of Karaiskakis' great personal popularity and the fact that of all the Greek commanders, he was certainly the most honourable and truly patriotic. The order stood and Cochrane insisted that nothing had changed. Amid scenes of most appalling confusion the forces were landed at points around Piraeus only to find at daybreak that Reshid had taken advantage of the delays and disagreements to position his regiments in readiness. The Greeks were completely routed, and the survivors were evacuated less than twenty-four hours after Cochrane's glorious landings.

Many who did not survive were brutally murdered in revenge for the treatment of the prisoners of St Spyridon.

Cochrane, perhaps wisely, fled on his yacht, but Church opted to stay with his troops back in the hills of Munchya and only retreated three weeks later when he learned that there was little chance of relieving the Acropolis. The men under siege had decided they would not leave even if the Greeks arrived to escort them out. They had made a decision to fight for the ancient ruins to their very death.

The Chief Admiral retreated from the devastation for which he had been responsible and landed at Poros where Hastings had just finished the repairs to the *'Karteria'*. In fact, while Cochrane had been overseeing the shambles at Piraeus, Hastings had written to him tendering his resignation largely due to what he saw as the misappropriation of money by Cochrane and the differences of finance for various ships. He complained that he was still paying for the *'Karteria'* out of his own pocket and that he had to use the last of his cash for the repairs after Volos and Trikeri. Cochrane convinced him, knowing Hastings' innate sense of duty, that the time would be altogether wrong for such an action with the recent debacle at Piraeus, and the departure of so many good Philhellenes.

They set off together in the *'Karteria'* and the *'Hellas'* on one of Cochrane's wild goose chases. He decided to attack and sack a minor stronghold of the Turks in north-west Morea, the Castel Tornese and also to attempt to capture Ibrahim Pasha who was reported to be on his flagship in the same area. Hastings became even more disillusioned with Cochrane when they found the fortress had been taken some time previously. He was more than pleased when engine failure on the *'Karteria'* left the *'Hellas'* and Cochrane alone to chase Ibrahim. In the event, Ibrahim had long since departed. Struggling back to Hydra, the *'Karteria'* was dismasted in a gale off Cape Malea and also lost two men overboard. Once more she returned to Poros to repair the damage.

Cochrane landed on Kythera and decided that the next action that might cover him in glory was to attack the main Egyptian fleet in their home port of Alexandria. On June 6th he gathered around him a squadron under the '*Sauveur*' with ten brigs and eight fire-ships, and the following day sent an incomplete message to Hastings at Poros.

The same day that this message was written, June 7th, the Acropolis of Athens capitulated to the Turks. Fabvier, learning of the departure of Gordon, the failure of Church to make provision for prisoners at St Spyridon, the killings of Karaiskakis and the actions of Cochrane, had appealed to his relative, the French Admiral de Rigny, for assistance. Having heard the brave words that the besieged would fight to the death, it was a considerable surprise when French marines led the Greek troops under Fabvier to the safety of the French warships anchored off Phaleron. Athens had completely fallen into Turkish hands again.

The news could not have reached Cochrane as he sailed from Kythera. His message, sent to Hastings at Poros, was:

"*Memo.—*

If the Perseverance is fit for service, please join the squadron without delay.

Cochrane.

Hellas, 7th June 1827.
Captain Hastings, Perserverance".

The ridiculous part of the memo was that it did not tell Hastings where to meet the fleet! All he knew was that Cochrane had some scheme to attack the Egyptians at Alexandria. The '*Karteria*' left Poros to search for Cochrane, but by the time it approached the North African coast it was obvious that the fleet had left without doing any damage. In fact the Greek vessels refused to follow Cochrane into the harbour and the two fire-ships which they had lit were too far away from the enemy and merely burnt themselves out in the Mediterranean. The fleet was pursued by the Egyptians back to Rhodes and then to Poros. As Ali's sailors were returning to Alexandria, they saw the '*Karteria*' in the distance. Knowing the fearsome reputation of Hastings' ship they retreated from view, but in fact missed the perfect opportunity to sink their most dangerous opponent. The '*Karteria*'s engines had again broken down and would have been no match for twenty or more enemy ships.

Chapter 10

1827: July to December

The involvement of the international powers accelerated during 1827, particularly by the election of George Canning as Prime Minister of Britain in April. Russia, Britain and France produced a treaty more or less acceptable to them all. In its broad outline the Treaty of London, which was signed on July 6th, was quite ambiguous. It offered a friendly mediation between Greece and Turkey guaranteeing a free Greek state within boundaries to be agreed by both parties.

The ambiguity arose from the course of action to be taken by the allied naval forces in the likely event of the Ottomans not agreeing to an armistice. On the one hand the Supreme Allied Naval Commander, Admiral Codrington, was ordered to take every step to avoid direct hostilities with the Turks. On the other hand, the allied forces were to treat the Greeks as a friendly nation and stop further supplies reaching their enemy from Egypt or Greece. The predictions that Constantinople would not accept the terms of the Treaty were correct but the fact that Russia was one of the signatories forced the Sultan to avoid any precipitation of hostilities likely to produce a state of war between Turkey and the Tsar.

The free state offered in the treaty meant that Greece would remain under the Ottoman umbrella It was not entirely satisfactory for the Christian Greeks. Nor, with the degree of autonomy allowed the Greeks, did it please the Turks. Envoys sent from the Powers to Egypt to encourage Mehemet Ali to withdraw Ibrahim's forces from

Greece, met with an equal lack of success. He merely played for time until it became obvious which way his master, the Sultan, was going to react. In any case Ibrahim at that time had control of large sections of Morea, and in particular the main coastal forts including Navarin.

Admiral Codrington arrived in Nauplio in anticipation of the Treaty and witnessed yet another civil war starting between the various Greek chieftains. Two separate factions, each holding a mountain stronghold behind Nauplio, started firing upon each other, as on previous outbreaks of that nature, Kolokotronis supported one of the parties. In desperation, Codrington, from his ship the '*Asia*' evacuated the Greek Executive and Legislative Commissions to the island fort of Bourdzi. He then sent messages back to Britain informing the British Government that the Greek Government was still in active existence.

It was again left to Richard Church to settle the partisan differences and he was badly criticised for acting in favour of his old friend, Kolokotronis. There was an uneasy peace and the despatch of troops to the more useful task of containing Ibrahim Pasha in the Morea helped the situation. They were to prove highly successful during the following two months and by September Ibrahim was in a totally defensive position at Modon, Navarin and Koron. His supply lines had largely been cut off from Alexandria by Admiral Miaoulis and a naval blockade.

News of the Treaty of London had reached Greece very quickly but its ambiguous text did not reach Admirals Codrington and de Rigny until mid August. The Greek Government speedily agreed to the terms and the armistice. However, as the Turks had not agreed, hostilities did not cease. Whilst the Russians were the co-signatories of the Treaty, their Admiral had not arrived in the Levant. Agents in Constantinople encouraged the Turks not to sign, in the hopes that this could lead to an excuse for Russia to declare war independently.

The Greek Government, anxious to acquire as much territory as possible before the European Powers forced Turkey to the negotiating table, ordered an increase in hostilities and Cochrane agreed to meet Church and his troops at Cape Papas in north-west Morea to transport them to the western mainland of Epirus. The fleet consisted of the 'Hellas', the 'Karteria', the 'Sauveur' and some twenty or more other ships, and they headed north past Navarin where the Egyptian and Turkish fleets were at anchor.

By September 18th the fleet had reached the Gulf of Patras, and a Turkish squadron of ten vessels were observed sailing through the narrows between Morea and Rumelia and into the Gulf of Corinth, then known as the Gulf of Lepanto. The straits were well defended by a castle on each side of the passage referred to as the Dardanelles of Lepanto, and any journey through was considered to be extremely dangerous. Lord Cochrane was fully aware of the risky nature of making the passage but also realised the danger to Church's troops of making any landings under fire from the Turkish ships and he decided to detach Hastings and ordered him in pursuit. The decision had already been pre-empted by the Captain of the 'Karteria'. To save Cochrane, whom he had so publicly denounced, the embarrassment of giving such a potentially fatal order, Hastings volunteered to sail through the narrows. Cochrane's reply was suitably worded:

"Off Messolonghi, 18th Sept. 1827.

"You have been good enough to volunteer to proceed into the Gulf of Lepanto, into which, under existing circumstances, I should not have ordered the 'Karteria'. I therefore leave all the proceedings to your judgement, intimating only, that the transporting of General Church's troops to the north of the Gulf, and the destruction or capture of the enemy's vessels, will be services of high importance to the service of Greece".

Cochrane and the remainder of the fleet sailed north to Kalomnos to carry out negotiations with the local Chieftains, leaving the 'Karteria', the 'Sauveur', the gunboats 'Bavaria' and 'Philhellene' and two armed schooners to transport troops to the north shore of Morea in the Gulf. In darkness, the little fleet made passage through the Dardanelles of Lepanto without incident and four days later landed Church's men to join up with the Chieftains who had been upholding the Greek cause alone for so long. Hastings then turned his attention to the other aspects of his expedition, chasing and capturing or destroying the Turkish flotilla.

The reports received from the land forces suggested that the enemy vessels were in the Gulf of Salona to the north east, and they immediately set sail. Once again the engines of the *'Karteria'*, which would be so important in any action, failed them and the *'Karteria'* was left behind whilst the gallant Captain Thomas led the remaining ships into the Gulf of Salona. The bay is roughly the shape of the traditional diagrammatic heart with the bottom tip cut away to become the narrow entrance. Captain Thomas found the Turks at anchor close to the shore in the top right, north-easterly curve. Although the brig *'Sauveur'* carried some eighteen guns, it became impossible for the ship to sail close enough to be in range without endangering herself from the two batteries on the eastern shore. He wisely decided to wait until he could join up with the *'Karteria'*, and this happened on the evening of September 27th.

Whilst at anchor the crew of the gunboat *'Baveria'* had in fear of the action to come, deserted the ship, and Lieut. Darby from the *'Karteria'* was sent to man her with crews from the *'Sauveur'* and *'Karteria'*. On the following day, preparations were made to launch the attack on the 29th to allow time to stop the leaks in the engine room of the steamship. By midnight of September 28th, the crew changes were complete and the repairs had been executed. The squadron was on station off the point of the Gulf of Salona.

Neither Hastings nor the Turkish Commodore were aware at that time of the diplomatic activities which had taken place at Navarin only three days before the eve of battle at Salona. Having seen the joint agreements of the Treaty of London, Admiral de Rigny sailed to Navarin where the combined Turkish and Egyptian fleets under Ibrahim Pasha lay at anchor, to convince him that the allies had the real power in the Levant, and that he and Codrington were of one accord. On September 25th the two allied Admirals had a conference with Ibrahim Pasha; by then the once glamorous young man was described as *"a fat butcher-like creature with a heavy, pock-marked face"*. He persuaded Ibrahim to cease hostilities until he received further orders from either his own Government or that in Constantinople.

The allied commanders assumed the agreement to mean that Ibrahim would carry out no further battle for the time being, whereas it appeared that the Egyptian's understanding was that he had only promised to delay his plan to attack Hydra. In return Codrington agreed to issue an order to Cochrane and Church to the effect that they should terminate their actions in the seizure of new territories. Accordingly he left for the Gulf of Patras, foolishly leaving only two ships to hold the mighty Armada in the Bay of Navarin. At about the same time as Codrington's departure, an Austrian ship entered Navarin carrying messages to Ibrahim that the Treaty of London had not been agreed by Turkey. It also carried the news that Cochrane had been with a strong force at Cape Papas and that part of his fleet, led by the feared Hastings in his dreaded fire-frigate, the '*Karteria*', had chased the Turkish fleet through the Dardanelles of Lepanto. The very night that the '*Karteria*' stood off Salona, Ibrahim Pasha decided that the agreements with the Admirals were void.

The fine morning of Saturday 29th September started early aboard the '*Karteria*'. With a moderate easterly breeze to hold them on station, the crew of the steamship was called at three in the morning to light the engine fires and by eight were ordered to start the process of heating shells. A near disaster took place when two of the shells exploded in the fire-box, probably caused by water in the shells, but, apart from damaging the bar on the box, little damage was done.

Daybreak had shown that the Turks had prepared for action following the attempts of the previous days by the Greek fleet. They had moved their vessels from the shore to a line across the narrowest point of the north eastern bay. As the '*Karteria*' moved closer, a formidable line-up was encountered. To the west of the line were three Austrian transports, packed with troops from the shore, close to the northern end of the line, a small gun boat and the main blockade from north to south being a magnificent Algerine schooner carrying twenty long brass guns, an armed transport brig, the Admiral's brig, two schooners and a gun boat, with the stern of the Admiral's brig being protected by a further brig. The southernmost vessel was within yards of the shore, and a battery with two guns, and the second single gun battery was two hundred yards further round to the north east.

The Turks clearly thought with their level of fire power, five hundred experienced troops ashore backing them up and the protection from the batteries, that they had the opportunity of destroying the two most successful and powerful ships of the Greek Navy. Rather than risk the attack being called off, they held their fire until Hastings gave the order to anchor. Incredibly the *Karteria* moved to a position only 250 to 300 yards from the nearest Turk and at eleven thirty gave the order to drop anchor to his fleet some 500 yards astern. The *Karteria* hove to, starboard broadside to the brig carrying the Turkish Admiral's ensign and the crew were ordered to bring two hot shells for the long guns. The signal for battle to commence was given by the roar of one of the *Karteria's* 68-pounders flying cold shot to obtain the correct range. The amazing coolness of this action by the Captain and John Hane, the Artillery Officer, to preserve the hot shells for more effective use after sighting, showed their absolute faith in the methods of warfare they had developed with such meticulous planning.

At the sound of the *Karteria's* gun the Turks opened fire from all sides, aiming only at the one target and, whilst they did create some damage, the well trained crew of the *Karteria* were able to fire two hot shells from the long guns and two carcase shells from the carronades. At eleven forty-five the devastation of the vastly superior fleet had started. The Admiral's brig was hit in the powder magazine by a carcase shell and an explosion soon created panic as she began to sink. The schooner lying adjacent to the south of her was hit in the bow. The brig on the other side received a carcase shell in the bow and hot shell in the stern causing her to disappear beneath the sea.

Captain Thomas of the 'Sauveur' was at the same time undertaking the task of silencing the shore batteries with grape shot and successfully drove back the troops from the water's edge to less vulnerable positions behind rocks. Having completed this action the *'Sauveur'* and the other vessels pulled into a closer position astern of the *'Karteria'* and fire was directed by all vessels upon the Algerine schooner. A shell from the *'Karteria'* exploded between her decks and some of the crew, in panic, jumped over the sides and swam for shore. Hastings gave the order for the boats of his fleet to be lowered and to take the abandoned schooner as a prize. Lieutenant Scanlan from the *'Sauveur'* led the boarding parties but the troops who had been driven behind the rocks re-emerged and opened fire on the decks of the schooner which were well within their vision and range. The fire from the *'Sauveur'* had been halted to allow the boarding parties access but Hastings ordered Thomas to open up again with grape shot.

While this drove the Turkish soldiers back to cover, they had successfully driven off the first boarding party and Lieutenant Scanlan had been killed in the action. Thomas kept the troops subdued but not totally silent by his sustained firing of grape shot, whilst Hastings took the *'Karteria'* to within a cable's length of the Algerine schooner. At the same time several small craft were occupied in taking the Austrian transports, and the first Lieutenant of the *'Karteria'*, Lieutenant Phalanger, was sent to destroy an armed transport brig which was not on fire.

Still under spasmodic fire from the muskets of the troops ashore, the stern cable of the *'Karteria'* was attached to the schooner and the engines gradually took up the slack. The tide was falling and the schooner lay in about a fathom of water. The attempt to tow her off failed when the heavy rope parted. Perhaps if he had been a few minutes earlier, Hastings may have captured the fine ship. With some sadness he ordered his crew aboard and helped by men from the *'Sauveur'*, the Master-at-Arms and several others were taken prisoner. The heavy guns and several other items were taken aboard the Greek fleet and the task of lighting fire to destroy the ship commenced. It had become clear that after one rope had parted and a second larger rope belonging to the schooner had no effect, that she was firmly aground. At five in the afternoon after several struggles the rope between the two was cut. The flames gradually engulfed the vessel as the 'Karteria' pulled away from the shore.

The shore batteries which had re-formed after the early pounding from the 'Sauveur' had again opened fire upon the 'Karteria'. A number of shots were accurate doing some damage to the steamer's paddle wheels. Hastings signalled to Captain Thomas and the fleet left the picturesque little bay. By nine in the evening they were all anchored safely out of range along with the three captured Austrian vessels, two brigs and a tribaculo and they had time to survey the results. Their own losses were six men, including Lieutenant Scanlan and around thirty wounded, two of whom, Darby and Freitson, were officers on the 'Bavaria'. Of the nine Turkish ships at Salona that morning, only two, a small boat and a schooner, had not been set alight or sunk.

The Algerine schooner, almost in a last act of defiance, nearly took revenge upon the 'Karteria'. At around eleven at night the tide and wind caused the blazing hulk to refloat and drift out of the bay on a direct course for the 'Karteria'. A boat had to be sent to take her in tow and divert her around the headland. At midnight she went aground on a tiny island around the point of the bay and continued to burn for most of the night.

The following morning Hastings sent for the Captains of the Austrian prizes and explained to them that if they had placed themselves under his protection and not allowed the Turkish troops to use them as bases, then they would not have been taken. As it was he was obliged to capture their craft, send their papers to the Greek Government and await instructions as to what should happen to the prisoners.

During the afternoon of Sunday 30th September, Hastings had the pleasurable job of writing his report for Lord Cochrane. Having reported the unembellished facts of the action he turned to the individual efforts of the men involved:

"It is a pleasure for me to be able to inform your Lordship of the meritorious conduct of all the officers and men employed in this

service. *The exertions of Captain Thomas were very great, and his first Lieutenant Mr Scanlan distinguished himself in trying to float the schooner until disabled by two wounds. The commanders of the gunboats, Mr Freitson and Mr Darby, both distinguished themselves by their exertions and gallantry and are both wounded. The services of Captain Hane of the Artillery serving on board this vessel are too well known on every former affair to make it necessary for me to say more than that I am equally indebted to him now as on other occasions. The meritorious conduct of Mr Phalanger I have already mentioned, and Captain Thomas speaks highly in praise of Mr Urquhart".*

By the time the *'Karteria'* reached General Church's camp the next morning, October 1st, the Greek troops had already received the news of his remarkable victory and great celebrations were prepared for Hastings, Thomas and their crews. As the news had spread through Morea, hundreds of Greeks sped to join Church but they brought news with them that Ibrahim had become wild with rage when he learned of the battle of Salona and had vowed to avenge himself upon the two English Captains. On the very day that the news reached the Armada at Navarin, Ibrahim had already sent some ships out of the bay to investigate the actions of Cochrane to the north. His first ships had instructions to defend Patras from Church and ensure that the entrance to the Gulf of Corinth was not blocked to them. However, in his rage at the news of Salona, he led out a second flotilla to join up with the original thirty-eight vessels to hunt out and destroy the *'Karteria'* and Hastings. In total over fifty craft were employed with this one vengeful aim.

Hastings and Church decided that their first task must be to protect the *'Karteria'* and *'Sauveur'* at all costs. They had proved too valuable to be put at risk and the little port of Stava was chosen as the best defensive point for the ships to guard themselves from the might of the combined Turkish and Egyptian fleets. The port was in a bay in the western end of the Gulf of Corinth which was protected by two rocky islands. The steep sides of Mount Geranion came down to the sea, making it virtually impossible to land troops in any numbers. Church provided extra troops to accompany the fleet and assist with their protection. They were stationed on the rocky slopes, whilst the islands were turned into defensive fortresses with a ship's gun on each and with another two, covering the entrance, placed on shore. Hastings was ready to greet Ibrahim. The son of Mehemet Ali never arrived to do battle with his hated, but much admired, adversary which almost undoubtedly displeased both of them.

The first wave of Egyptian ships had arrived off Cape Papas on 2nd October, only to be intercepted by Admiral Sir Edward Codrington with a mere four vessels. He rather bravely fired a few shots across the bows of the Muslim force and their Captains, still unsure of their attitude towards the British and French allies, turned south, trailed by the four English craft. The following morning the two flotillas under Ibrahim met up and they headed north together for a while. However the effects of a strong gale soon sent them back towards Navarin and, seeing this, Codrington ran for Zante to obtain supplies. Despite the terrible weather conditions, the Muslims again turned north to attempt to reach the Gulf of Patras before the British Admiral. Then the wind veered, making a passage into the Gulf too dangerous and forcing the fifty-six ships to take refuge under the lee of Cape Papas.

Once more Codrington set off in pursuit but like Ibrahim, was unable to round the Cape in safety and he had to shelter in close company with the large fleet. The combination of foul weather, which was to last for several more days, and the constant harassment by Codrington's four ships forced the Muslim fleet to return to Navarin. It was, however, quite clear that if weather had allowed, Ibrahim would have continued into the Gulf of Corinth to pursue Hastings and probably Church's troops at the same time.

A combination of events culminating in the news of Salona had cancelled any thoughts of an armistice and Ibrahim's rage with Hastings had broken down any trust between the allied Admirals and the Muslims. Codrington had taken an immense risk by snapping at the heels of the inflamed Egyptian Commander. Four ships against fifty-six was hardly good odds but he had succeeded in sending them back to Navarin.

News of the assembly of the fleets at Cape Papas had reached Lord Cochrane who had been sheltering off Messolongi and he realised that the squadron led by the *'Karteria'* was in great potential danger. On 12th October 1827 he sent what was to be his last official communication to Frank Hastings before he left Greece:

"You have done so much good, and so much is anticipated from your keeping open the communications between the shores of the gulf, that I think you would do well to remain for a while where you are. You occupy, however, a position of risk, if the reports are true regarding the fleet being off Patras; and therefore I leave you to act in all things as you judge best for the public service".

For the second time Frank received a flattering order from Cochrane and the latter certainly suggested that the Admiral was happy to shelve responsibility of the *'Karteria'* to her Captain.

To the south, the allied Admirals, Codrington and de Rigny, had been joined by the Russian, Heydon. All agreed that it was vital to keep the Turkish and Egyptian fleets inside the bay to prevent them from breaking out in bad weather and taking Hydra. If such a situation was allowed, then the allied total of 27 ships carrying around 1,300 guns would have been no match for the Muslim total of 82 vessels mounting over 2,000 guns. In addition there was a small Tunisian squadron in the bay of three frigates and a brig which may have joined any action but never did.

The bay of Navarin is a little over four miles in length and protected to the west by the long thin island of Sfaktiria, giving a breadth of about two and a half miles at the maximum point. During the early afternoon of October 20th, the allies moved into the protection of the bay where they could watch the Muslim fleet without the risk of being blown off station. At its very best this situation could only have been considered as highly provocative.

The sight that greeted them as they entered the bay was of the armada spread out in a horseshoe shape in three rows. The first row was of twenty-two of the heavier ships, and covering the gaps between them in the second row, twenty-six smaller frigates and corvettes. Three fire ships were placed at the extremities of the front rows and the third consisted of the corvettes, brigs and schooners held in reserve to aid any larger vessel requiring assistance. The total fleet was: 3 line-of-battle ships; 5 twin-decked, sixty gun frigates; 22 frigates; 33 corvettes,; 13 brigs and schooners and 6 fire ships.

The intention of the allies as they were led in by Codrington on the *'Asia'*, was for the English to anchor at the centre with the French on their right and the Russians on their left and leaving the *'Dartmouth'*, under a Captain Fellowes, watching the fire ships on the northern flank. There was no state of war between the allies and the Egyptians or the Turks. Indeed some allied Commanders, in retrospect, tried to defend the incident by claiming it was a genuine attempt to maintain the armistice. The arrival of twenty-seven heavily armed warships in the bay could not have appeared as anything other than distinctly hostile to the Muslims.

The fire ships near the *'Dartmouth'* prepared for action and the English vessel sent a pinnace out to stop them. This was fired upon and Fellowes sent a larger cutter to board the fire ship which also came under attack. As the Turks understandably assumed that action was about to take place, the brulot was lighted and both the *'Dartmouth'* and the French Flagship *'Sirene'* opened fire. This was the signal for a four hour battle which although horrifically bloody and devastating, was little more than a shooting competition. At such short range the larger—calibred guns of the allies, and the superior trained gun crews had a great advantage in the inglorious action. Although several allied ships were damaged and around two hundred officers and men killed, none were sunk.

The Muslims lost sixty vessels during that four hour slogging match and some eight thousand men were butchered by allied guns. The Battle of Navarino, as it has become known, is often thought of as a brave and gallant naval action however the author believes it was nothing of the sort. Despite his agreements with Ibrahim, Codrington had allowed the Battle of Salona to take place and thus lost all honour to a man whose religion ordered that his word alone was a binding contract. Nor had Codrington sent any word to Ibrahim that the entry into Navarin was supposedly peaceful. Perhaps worst of all, he had not taken instructions from a higher level before precipitating an action which could well have resulted in an all out European war. Admiral Codrington was subsequently recalled to London and punished for a neglect of duty—perhaps the charge should have been higher.

To the Greeks and their Philhellenic supporters it did not matter that the events of Navarin were rather less than honourable, nor necessary. The greatest threat to their potential independence had been annihilated for them by foreign powers each with differing motives but all with the common ground of wanting to assert their influence upon a new state. During the battle, Hastings and Church had been aboard the '*Karteria*' studying the coast of the northern part of the Gulf of Corinth. It was there that the news reached them about the Battle of Navarino. Their source of information was a Greek fishing boat and it was only on their return to Church's camp that they accepted its truth. The celebrations during that night of October 27th were considerable; fires were lit on mountain tops, the men in the camp drank and danced throughout the night. Even the reserved Frank Abney Hastings joined in the celebrations and allowed the guns of the '*Karteria*' to be fired for several hours.

Cochrane's reaction upon hearing the news of Navarin was one of any person paid handsomely to do a job only to find outsiders had already done it. He now needed a glorious victory to justify his position. He readily agreed to accompany Fabvier and his two thousand troops on a mission to relieve the island of Scio. On October 28th he sailed to Scio on the '*Hellas*' in company with the '*Hydra*', under Captain Crosbie, and ten other Greek brigs. They arrived off the scene of the bloody massacre some five and a half years earlier. The initial landings and bombardments were successful and the Turkish troops were obliged to take refuge in the citadel.

Only two days after the landings, Cochrane's opportunity to achieve any form of greatness in the Greek campaign was brought to a close by the receipt of orders from the allied Admirals forbidding further naval action. They also forbade any other hostile action between the Gulf of Corinth in the west and the Gulf of Volos in the east. It had clearly been decided that the new state would be restricted to the Peloponnese and Attica. Cochrane had little alternative but to retreat, although he protested. Fabvier, knowing that his relative de Rigny neither agreed with the order nor would uphold it, opted to remain with his troops on the island. At Codrington's suggestion, Cochrane returned to station off Navarin to prevent any break-out by the remains of the Muslim fleets.

The position of Hastings in the Gulf of Corinth had not been improved by the battle of Navarin. The defences at the Castles of Morea and Rumelia, on either side of the Gulf near Patras, had been considerably strengthened to prevent the *'Karteria'* from leaving the Gulf of Corinth in safety. Ibrahim, who had survived the action at Navarin, still vowed to destroy Hastings and his ship which he held responsible for the allies' actions. Shortage of money and supplies became an even worse problem for Hastings. The Greek Government had lost interest in their forces in the north after the destruction of the Muslim armada and Lord Cochrane held onto his purse in the hope of engaging himself in some future action. On November 17th Hastings wrote of his plight to Cochrane, although he never received an answer:

"I am now seven thousand pounds out of pocket by my service in Greece, and I am daily expending my own money for the public service. Our prizes are serving as transports for the army, and we must shortly either abandon this position or be paid. Without money I can no longer maintain this vessel. I will do all I can; but I must repeat, that it is not quite fair that I should end a beggar, after all the labour, vexation, and disappointment I have experienced for so many years".

The relationship between Hastings and Church also was under a great strain. Both men were short of supplies and Hastings considered at times that Church's demands upon his vessel were unreasonable. The flamboyant Irishman often considered that the rigid attitude of Hastings was unacceptable in Greece. In return the ship's Captain felt that if Church acted with a more ordered pattern then the demands on and risks to the *'Karteria'* would be less.

During the evening of the day on which Hastings had written of his financial difficulties to Cochrane, an order was received from Church to proceed immediately back to Cape Papas to transport the main bulk of the troops over the estuary from Morea to the north. The order involved the '*Karteria*' making the passage through the Dardanelles of Lepanto during the day and consequently running the gauntlet of the heavy armaments. If Church had thought about the matter he could either have issued the order a day earlier or delayed the crossing until night time.

The southern side of the straits was protected by fifty guns, of which at least twenty were large calibre. To the north there were twenty-seven guns giving between them a firing range which covered the whole passage. The little fleet consisting of the '*Karteria*', three prize ships and two Greek misticos, hoping to clear the straits under the protection of the '*Karteria*', sailed along the coastline on a clear, sunny morning with a moderate following breeze. As the ships approached the point around which they would turn fifty degrees to port onto a broad reach to enter the channel, the '*Karteria*' hoisted all sail onto the four masts and set the paddles in action.

The other craft followed suit but it was accepted that the steam ship would be the prime target and it was a case of each man for himself. Under perfect conditions the '*Karteria*' came into range of the shore batteries at the fastest speed she had ever done. At first it seemed she could again run the gauntlet with little damage. The Turks abandoned their normal practice of firing at random and settled down to a slow and methodical pattern of fire from both sides of the channel.

Several cannon balls penetrated the sails and rigging of the '*Karteria*'. Two from the northern shore hit the paddle wheel on the starboard side, tearing away the wooden blades. The patent windlass on the foredeck received a direct hit, splattering pieces of the metal workings dangerously around the decks. Two of Hastings' most reliable gunners were killed when a shot destroyed the quarter-deck carronade. A boy seaman had his hand torn off by another shot which hit the tall, black funnel of the ship. All this damage had been sustained before the '*Karteria*' had reached the halfway point of the straits and there was considerable concern that the destruction would be complete before she sailed out of range.

Even with the pounding she was taking, the ship, under the cool and professional handling of the Captain and crew, maintained her exceptional speed of over six knots. This did not allow time for the Turkish gunners to reload and re-aim their guns with the accuracy they had achieved for their initial passage. The '*Karteria*' escaped without further damage. The other vessels which had been ignored were now fired upon but with little effect. Despite his great sadness at the loss of two crew men and the wounding of the boy, Hastings was more worried that the Turkish gunners would exaggerate their partial success to Ibrahim and thus spur him to take further action.

Knowing Ibrahim's vow to destroy him, Frank decided to put on a display of power by steaming to the Egyptian camp at Patras. As he approached the shore, a large, well laden brig came into sight just out of range of the batteries. As she saw the '*Karteria*', men prepared to move her nearer to the protective guns in the harbour. A longboat approached her carrying an impressive ensign and a gentleman who, it transpired, was the Austrian Consul carrying the Austrian flag.

The '*Karteria*' positioned herself between the Consul and the brig and Hastings informed the Austrian that the Greek Government was blockading Patras. Firstly the Consul pointed out that the Austrian Government did not recognise Greece and that any such blockade was illegal. Hastings ignored him and demanded that the Consul go to the brig and send back the master with the ship's papers. The Consul then unwisely angered Frank Hastings:

"I believe I am speaking to an Englishman; and neither Austrian nor Turkey being at war with England, you are bound to respect the Austrian flag".

The retort came sharply back:

"You are speaking, sir, to an officer in the Greek service, commanding the blockade of Patras; and if the Austrian brig does not place itself under my protection in five minutes, I shall fire into the Turkish camp and it will be destroyed".

With that, Hastings looked at his watch and walked away across the deck. The Consul, instead of going to the brig with the order, went for the shore, signalling for the brig to move quickly under the shore batteries. True to his word, Hastings allowed the Consul exactly five minutes before taking the *'Karteria'* closer to the brig and opening fire. A few shells went into the camp and one went into the hull of the Austrian brig which, tearing away a great section of the beam, sank her immediately. The *'Karteria'* turned and pulled away from the shore. Frank Abney Hastings had, under the very nose of Ibrahim Pasha, shown that even if the *'Karteria'* had been damaged, she was still in business.

Hastings was furious to find that after all the risks he had encountered, coming through the Dardanelles in daylight and the injuries to his crew, General Church had not arrived. They had in fact been held up by torrential rains and hail in the mountains and did not arrive until a week later. This was an understandable delay but not one which engendered any more confidence in Church's leadership with Frank Hastings. It took two journeys to transport the depleted army of only fourteen hundred men across to Astakos, north-west of Messolongi. By December 4th they were safely landed and joined by chieftains from Western Greece. The numbers joining them were disappointing and many Greeks continued to serve the Ottomans as they had since the days of Ali Pasha.

Hastings put forward his next plan to Church, who despite their disagreements continued to admire the seaman. They agreed that Church should move his troops down to the area of Messolongi while, at the same time, the *'Karteria'* would attack the island fortress of Vasiladhi which guarded the entrance to the shallow lagoons in which lay the town where Byron had died. The fort was considered to be virtually unassailable, being on an island no more than a hundred yards in circumference and only rising six feet above the water. The depth of water around Vasiladhi was little more than three feet to well over a mile off shore, preventing a successful naval attack, or so it was thought. Hastings and Hane had other ideas.

To some extent the confidence of the defenders was well founded. Even with the skills and armaments of the *'Karteria'*, to hope to achieve any degree of accuracy over such a range, a day would be required with little or no wind, current or movement of the sea. Two attempts on December 22nd and 24th failed, even though the conditions had seemed acceptable and it was not until December 29th that the winds subsided enough to make a further sortie.

At four in the morning it was noticed that the winds were dropping rapidly and Hastings ordered the fires lit to heat the boilers. Four hours later the *'Karteria'* weighed anchor and steamed to within three thousand yards of Vasiladhi, dropping anchor in only ten feet of water. The first Lieutenant, Mr Phalanger, took charge of the wheel and Hastings and Hane busied themselves with the sights of the long guns. At nine o'clock they opened fire with the barrels at an elevation of twenty-three degrees and soon found the range and trajectory. The fortress was struck several times and at nine thirty a shell from the gun aimed by Hastings landed in the powder magazine which exploded violently. The ship's boats were immediately manned and the little island invaded.

Little resistance was met with and at ten-fifteen the Turks surrendered. Nine were dead and thirty-one taken prisoner on board the *'Karteria'*. There was some disagreement amongst the Greek members of the crew when it became apparent that several of the prisoners, including one wounded soldier, were their fellow countrymen and they were refused permission to put them to death. Having little enough money to feed his own crew, Hastings also did not wish to keep the prisoners aboard.

Through a Greek translator, Hastings informed the Commander of the Fort that he was sending the prisoners safely to Messolongi and that he should go there in one of the lagoon's flat-bottomed punts, a monoxylon, and send others back the following day for his men.

On the assumption that the prisoners were to be dealt with in the traditional manner of having their throats slit, the Turk thought that Hastings was merely taking him aside to allow him, as one officer to another, a more honourable death. With genuine gratitude, and very considerable honour he thanked Hastings and said that he was now prepared to accept his death in any manner the victor decided. It seems that Hastings and the Turkish Commander were the last people to perceive the misunderstanding and neither could understand why some merriment had broken out on the quarter-deck. It was only when a monoxylon with one of the Turkish soldiers appeared alongside that they both understood what had happened.

With great dignity the Turk again thanked his conqueror and set off for Messolongi. The following morning several craft arrived to take off the rest of the prisoners, except the Greek soldier who was kept for medical attention. They brought with them a letter from the Commander thanking Hastings for his actions and regretting that the Commander-in-Chief of Messolongi had forbidden him to come in person but sending gifts of a live sheep and his sabre. Hastings returned the prisoners with presents of sugar and coffee.

The news of this hitherto unseen generosity spread rapidly throughout Greece and Turkey. By his actions, Frank Hastings had shown both nations that it was both necessary and possible to show mercy even in victory. He had demonstrated that his personal attitudes of humanity were possible even for a proven warrior of great power.

Once again Church had not reached Messolongi at the stated time. His troops had been delayed by actions and successes on their route south. Hastings decided that the best place to meet would be off the Fort of Anatoliko but when he attacked on January 4th he found the defences were much stronger than had been anticipated.

This caused him to become so irate at the lack of support from Church that this time he wrote to Cochrane complaining of the inefficiency which he was meeting. On this occasion it was not entirely fair as Church had not been informed of the *'Karteria's'* movements and the proposed attack. In any case, Church was more than willing to put up with the tantrums of the Captain, knowing that whatever happened between them, Hastings would always be the best and most reliable officer in the Levant. Indeed he and Finlay had on many occasions talked Hastings out of any thoughts of resignation and both hoped that he would succeed Cochrane as the Supreme Admiral at the soonest possible opportunity.

Chapter 11

1828: January to April

Although the *'Karteria'* and the skill of her crew was regarded by Church, Gordon and many of those who had for so long been involved in the struggle as the key to a successful conclusion of the war, it was not seen in that light by the Government and some foreigners who had more recently arrived. The arrival of a second steam ship, the *'Epicheirisis'* originally the *'Enterprise'*, had in the eyes of many heralded the flood of the six promised vessels of a similar nature and also diminished the stature of the *'Karteria'*.

In practice the second and smaller of the steam vessels was even more faulty than the *'Karteria'*. Without the total commitment and perseverance of Frank Hastings, she never did achieve any measure of success. Her Captain, whose real name was Downing but used the alias of Kirkwood, was an employed seaman who did not have either the personal or financial involvement necessary to strive to put the *'Epicheirisis'* into a seamanlike order. The engines, again built by the untrustworthy engineer Galloway, never performed to the standards achieved by the engineers of the *'Karteria'*.

The money and supplies, promised by so many for such a long time, still had not been sent to the *'Karteria'*. Having been on such a high plain of excitement after the successful sacking of Vasiladhi, Hastings looked forward to the financial promises being kept. By 7th January 1828, hope was diminishing and he had become quite despondent. He wrote on that day to Finlay in Egina:

"I am full of misery. I have not a dollar. I owe my people three months pay, and five dollars a man gratuity for Vasiladhi. I have no provisions. I have lost an anchor and chain. If I can get out of my present difficulties I may perhaps go into the gulf".

Hastings had always gone against the normal convention in Greece, and in the past had paid for sheep and cattle when the ship called anywhere for supplies. In January he was obliged to send his men into the fields and hills to search for food, and in effect they became rustlers, an action he had always strongly criticised in others.

His earlier complaints to Lord Cochrane remained unanswered and that great man, seeing that there was little hope of achieving further glories, had washed his hands of any problems of financing the '*Karteria*'. In fact Cochrane, having failed to keep the Egyptian fleet in Navarin Bay, had sailed aboard his yacht, back to Poros. He reputedly spent his time after Christmas shooting game birds rather than the Turks. On 10th January, 1828, he made the decision anticipated by so many and handed over command of the Greek Navy to Admiral Miaoulis. Accompanied by his Flag Captain, Hutchings, he left Greece immediately and after a fast passage of just thirty-one days, he sailed through Spithead in the Solent and came to anchor in Cowes Road, appropriately opposite the point now occupied by the Royal Yacht Squadron.

Few believed that Cochrane would ever return to Greece but there is evidence to suggest that whilst he did not wish, or was not able, to repay the money advanced to him, he seemed prepared to return if called. He praised the actions of Navarin, and blamed any of his failures on the vessels at his disposal and he did give the appearance of still working for the good of Greece. Despite the hollow words which he sent to Greece, the new Government there were not being taken in by Cochrane for a second time and after one message from Paris to Egina, the only response was that Cochrane should sell the '*Unicorn*' and send the money straight back to Greece.

It was left to the Deputy, Louriottes, to suggest that as Cochrane had broken his contract, it would be honourable to return the advance of

£37,000. This met with little response other than a further complaint about the standard of Greek seamanship and vessels. Cochrane also claimed that it was his, rather than Hastings', actions in the Gulf of Lepanto which led to the situation of Navarin. Cochrane did return to Greece in autumn of 1828, and was met with a very cool reception.

After many arguments with the new Government and President about the advance and loans, Cochrane officially resigned his post and relinquished his claim to his second payment of £20,000 due when the war was over. Two months of bad feeling came to an end when Cochrane finally left aboard a Russian ship. The Government of Greece had inflicted their final indignity upon the man who had taken so much and given so little by failing to provide transport for his departure.

The interest in Cochrane's departure was overshadowed by the man appointed on April 11th the previous year to be the President of Greece for seven years, Count Kapodistrias. He first received news of his election whilst in Geneva and had returned to St. Petersburg to discuss his resignation with Tsar Nicholas. The fear of all other European countries about Kapodistrias was that his long relationship with Russia would lead to some form of Russian domination through his Presidency. To allay these fears, Kapodistrias set off on a tour of England, Belgium, France and Italy and made a particular point of avoiding meetings which pointed to Russian influence.

His reception was very mixed. In England, King George IV was rude and unreceptive. The Prince of Orange was over-friendly with an eye to the Greek throne. Charles X of France regarded him as a charlatan and the Italians treated him with great suspicion. The new British Foreign Secretary, Lord Downing, was far more receptive than either his King or the Duke of Wellington and agreed to provide a ship to take Kapodistrias to Greece when the time came.

The vessel provided was the '*Warspite*'. She left Ancona just after Christmas in 1827, arriving in Malta on 9th January 1828 and Kapodistrias was met with civility but no public honour by the British Resident, Mr Ponsonby. Kapodistrias requested that he should be allowed to carry on to Greece via Corfu to see his family but permission was refused on the grounds that ulterior motives would be read into such a visit. Ponsonby, in his intelligence report back to England describing his discussions with Kapodistrias, indicated that he was quite convinced that the Count was looking only at the interests of Greece and would not be influenced by Russia unless she were acting in accord with the other allied powers.

The main reported intentions of Kapodistrias were to unite the country, use the Navy to suppress piracy and rid Greece of Cochrane, whom he considered to be only a source of dispute and expenditure. On 15th January the '*Warspite*' left Malta in company with two other British ships, psychologically important as a counter to those who worried about the Russian connection and they arrived at Nauplio four days later. His first action in Greece was to order the cessation of hostilities between two Greek factions in the hills behind the town—somewhat surprisingly the commanders obeyed.

Kapodistrias arrived at the seat of Government in Egina on 24th January, 1828, to face an almost impossible task. The country was near destitute after years of civil war and conflict with the Turks. Many of the Philhellenes had left the cause in desperation and national unity was largely a sacred cow to which most paid lip-service but few regarded as a practical possibility. To add to the troubles, it was clear to Kapodistrias that the allies only held their alliance together in Greece to attain the maximum possible advantage to themselves as individual nations. These aims were better served by not allowing the Greeks any monies other than those raised privately by various committees.

The three-man committee which had been appointed to act in his absence immediately resigned upon his arrival and the task of governing the country began. Whilst the President accepted in principal the three constitutions for Greece which had been agreed by the national Assemblies, the last of which had been at Damala, he in practice superseded these with an assumption of almost dictatorial powers. He appointed his own Council consisting of thirty-one members and cleverly gave the key posts not only to those most able but also to any who may have caused him trouble. Koundriotis,

Kolokotronis, Petrobey, Mavrokordatos, Ipsilantis and even the Tombazis brothers were involved.

He even decided to use the Philhellenes where possible. For example, Dr Samuel Gridley Howe for some inexplicable reason was given the task of forming an agricultural colony. He had reports from Hastings on the formation of a Greek Navy at his disposal but during his first month chose to ignore them and rather accept the advice bombarding him on all sides from the Greeks. To his credit, much of his attention was turned to such matters as education, medicine and agriculture. The recalcitrant nation was having imposed upon it a genuinely centralised Government and bureaucracy. A form of benevolent dictatorship was probably the only type of administration which could possibly have worked under the circumstances.

The departure of Cochrane, although wished for by Kapodistrias, was the main cause for the delay in coming to grips with the formation of a Navy. The lack of funds available to the Government combined with the bad feeling left over from the payments to Cochrane created the situation whereby Frank's letter to the Government was ignored. The letter, which had been sent on 16th January to be with the President on his arrival, was in a similar vein to that he had sent two weeks earlier to Finlay, with a copy to Cochrane, and again complained of his being left without money or supplies:

"It has become an established maxim to leave this vessel without any supplies. Dr Goss has just been at Zante, and has left three hundred dollars for the 'Helvetia', now serving under my orders—but not one farthing, no provisions, and not even a single word for me".

Dr Goss was the agent for the Swiss Greek Committee, and the money was from amounts raised in that country. The letter continued:

"Five months ago I was promised eight thousand dollars in advance for the pay of my crew; and since that time I have only received one thousand dollars from the Naval chest of Lord Cochrane, and six hundred from the Military of General Church. This last sum is not sufficient to pay the expenses incurred by the detention of our prizes

in order to serve as transports for the Army. I have, in addition to the ordinary expenses of this vessel, been obliged to purchase wood for our steam-engine, and provisions for the gun-boat 'Helvetia'—to which I have also furnished two hundred dollars in money to pay the crew. The capture of Vasiladhi has cost me two thousand dollars; yet I have not taken the brass canon in that fort, and replaced them with the iron guns in our prizes, in order to assist me in paying our expenses".

That letter was an open letter to the Greek Government but in a more private letter to Kapodistrias, Hastings explained that the main problems which arose from the crews of the ships were created by the systems of payments:

"From the hour of my receiving the command of the 'Karteria', I determined to break down the system existing in the Navy of paying the sailors in advance, as such a practice is destructive of all discipline. The Greek Government and Lord Cochrane, however, did not adopt this rule. They paid their own equipages in advance, and they left mine unpaid".

It is certain that the President was taking note of the complaints and suggestions from Frank Hastings far more than the previous members of Government. News reached Egina of maritime activities in the Eastern islands adding to the need to maintain the '*Karteria*' and keep the support of her Captain.

Shortly before Cochrane had received and obeyed the order from the allied Admirals to cease hostilities in the east, Fabvier had successfully established some 2,000 troops on the island of Scio. He and his men had refused to leave when Cochrane's order arrived, on the correct assumption that de Rigny did not support the order but the withdrawal of sea support left them in a perilous position. Not only was there no maritime back-up but the uprising by the Sciotes who had either survived the massacre five years earlier, or subsequently returned to their homeland, did not come about. The French fleet, under Fabvier's relative, Admiral de Rigny, came to the assistance of the Greek troops by driving the Turkish ships away from the area and Greek ships undertook the blockade of the island.

Reports reached Egina that the Sultan had ordered the assembly of a fleet in the Dardanelles to reassert his total control of the land made important tactically by its proximity to the Turkish mainland. In early January, the Greek Government sent three powerful vessels to the area to counter the expected attack by the Muslims; the ships were the '*Sauveur*', still commanded by Captain Thomas, the '*Hydra*', under Captain Crosbie and the second steam-ship, the '*Epicheirisis*' with Captain Kirkwood alias Downing. The latter again failed to make any contribution and the ship's boilers burst, preventing her from reaching her destination.

On the night of 18th January a gale blew up and winds of near hurricane force were recorded driving before them hail and blizzard from the Asian hills to the north-west. The '*Sauveur*' dragged her anchors as she was driven towards the shore and the lines eventually parted causing her to founder before the wind. Thomas stayed with his ship until the last possible moment. Then realising that she was about to go down, he jumped into the icy maelstrom and swam for the shore. A lesser man could not have survived the conditions for more than a few minutes but Thomas did reach safety. The rest of the fleet had been blown all over the eastern Mediterranean by the brutal storm and the Turks who still held the fortress decided at daybreak to leave their stronghold and attack Fabvier's troops.

Whilst the Frenchman managed gallantly to hold them back, the action was bloody and took its toll which included the brother of George Finlay, Kirkman. Fabvier still refused to leave Scio, and held on for another three months until the Turks landed an army which drove his troops off the island to be rescued by de Rigny.

The '*Sauveur*' was one of the finest ships to sail in Greece at the time and Thomas was undoubtedly one of the most professional Captains. In consequence the news of the failure, had a great affect upon the new Kapodistrian Government. Whilst the Government was worried and saddened by the loss of the '*Sauveur*' this was not reflected by a speedy decision to assist Hastings. The personality of the new President, coupled with his many years of involvement with the intricate bureaucracy of the Tsar's court, made him one who would not reach a quick answer to any problems.

Hastings, still off the west coast, was becoming more and more desperate with his financial plight and was experiencing great frustrations from the orders, often conflicting, which he received from General Church. In the early days of February, plagued by weather, money and Church, his depression fell to match the short days and the barometer. He finally reached the conclusion that his Greek adventure was over. It was only his overdeveloped sense of duty that kept him motivated. His ambivalent feelings clearly showed in a letter he wrote to his friend Finlay on 11th February 1828:

"However, I think under existing circumstances my absence is desirable until recalled. Were I to return at this moment it would be said, and perhaps justly, I abandoned my station to look after my private interests. I am by no means particularly anxious to command the Greek Navy and would not accept of it but on condition such as would enable me to really make a Navy of it. If the Greek Government wants such a person, I think that both the length and importance of my services should entitle me to it—if they think differently I am ready to resign the command of this vessel to anybody they may name without a moment's regret".

All his senses said "leave"; his arrogance and duty said "plead with me—give in to my demands, and I won't leave".

It was poor Richard Church who actually received the anger of Frank, although his own position was only marginally better than that of the Captain:

"*Karteria—Karbousta,
14th Feb., 1828*

"Sir

"*It is painful for me to recur to the oft repeated subject of your interference with naval affairs. I am particularly desirous of quitting this station, that I may no longer be subjected either to this interference or to the disagreeable alternative of addressing you in a strain similar to the present, which has (to my regret) been rendered so frequently necessary. Our duties are so distinct that I cannot conceive how anybody can mistake them, even not having been brought up in the British service.*

I met at this place a 'bracciera' having your permission to carry grain. Had this grain been on board I certainly should have captured her. I will capture any loaded boats I meet with your passports. Your Excellency will recollect that the blockade of this part of the Morea was not undertaken by me without your sanction. I represented to you the scandalous traffic carrying on to Patras by land, and you concurred in the blockade as the only method to remedy it. If you had any exceptions to make, it would have been proper for you (I should think) to state the same to me, that I might give such passports, if the case should appear to me to require it, which I certainly think it does not. But what do you do? You give a monopoly of grain (without my knowledge or approbation) to a person here, and when the Helvetia' gun-boat, sent away a boat licensed by you, you then inform me and request me to permit the traffic. My reply is justly, I cannot, now that I am asked, and would not, had I been asked in the first instance in the proper manner, admit a monopoly near Patras at the moment I have seen endeavouring to suppress the commerce much further off. It would be such a glaring injustice, that I should be subject to the suspicion of profiting by the monopoly I was creating.

I hope that this is the last time I shall be obliged to refer to this disagreeable topic, for I shall very quickly now quit this station. The length of time I have been upon it without receiving any order from my Commander-in-Chief, his temporary absence from Greece, the silence of the Government, and the discretionary orders with which I was left by Lord Cochrane, all sanction my taking a step rendered necessary alone by your disapprobation of the manner in which I have conducted the naval affairs since I have been on this station".

The letter, over a minor infringement of normal procedures, was one of a man who was certainly tired, cold, wet, hungry and very touchy. It was to Church's great credit that even then he continued to be one of the greatest supporters and admirers of Frank Hastings.

Six days later, Hastings wrote a letter of resignation to Kapodistrias and informed him that he was taking the '*Karteria*' to Loutraki where he hoped to hand over his command to a new Captain appointed by the Government. On the morning of March 4th, the '*Karteria*' sailed into Loutraki. To Hastings' complete disgust, there was no acknowledgement of his letter nor did the local Commander know anything about a replacement master for the steam-ship. Frank dashed off another irate letter to George Finlay:

"Here I am arrived this morning, heartily disgusted with all the proceedings of the new Government towards me, and quite resolved not to stay in Greece an instant longer than is absolutely necessary to finish my affairs".

He went on to ask Finlay to join him in Loutraki to say farewell before he left Greece. He also wrote again to the President restating his problems and discussing the question of the new Captain of the '*Karteria*'. It is not clear what his intentions were but he indicated that he planned to go either to the Ionian Islands or to Italy.

At last the reaction, which Hastings had so long awaited, arrived from the President of the Republic of Greece. Kapodistrias ordered, in friendly terms, that the Englishman should go to Poros to meet him so that they might discuss naval matters. Hastings, after handing over command to Phalanger, his First Lieutenant, left immediately.

The meeting between the two men on 18th March, 1828, was most cordial and the President went through all the reports from Hastings with his usual attention to detail. He could find very little with which he did not agree. The general terms of reference for the Greek navy were laid down, including finance, dock yard repair facilities and a training programme for a regular national service. To carry out the programme under Hastings' guidance, it was intended that a Navy Board be established. Hastings wrote to Finlay on nearby Egina:

"I am trying to get things going for a Naval Organisation. I have found no difficulty on the part of the President; of course the usual difficulties in the detail. I am trying hard to get a Navy Board and Dock Yard established, and want you, as one of the Commissioners of the Navy Board. Emanuel Tombazis must be the President, he is a rogue but he had the direction of the Navy before I came, and must have a sop in the pan—we can get rid of him afterwards perhaps—I do not know where to look for a third".

A couple of days later he wrote again to Finlay regarding the accounts of a T. Darby which he had been asked to investigate and, in that letter, referred to the President as 'King John'. Such was the euphoria at the time that many assumed that Kapodistrias would at some time become the Monarch of the new Greece. Hastings' use of the royal title was more sarcastic and, although used in an amicable style, probably had more regard to the President's pedantic attention to detail. Although the Government had over the years received a considerable amount of paperwork from Frank, only some of this had been sent on to the new President and the first days in the post were mostly occupied by bringing together all the notes and proposals from the past.

Alexander Ross, Hastings' secretary, copied vast amounts of documents of every sort and little more than a week after arriving in Poros, Hastings had the proposals ready for a Navy modelled on that in Britain. These included the duties of all officer and seaman grades, the organisation of the Navy, staffing and pay, uniforms, messes, discipline, salutes, training, use of weapons and even his plans to overcome the problem of pirates in Greek waters. Even today the visitor to Greece is surprised to see how similar the men of the Navy appear to our own and to walk into a Greek naval establishment is almost uncanny in its likeness to walking into H.M. Dockyard at

Portsmouth or Plymouth. The guidelines laid down by Frank Abney Hastings in 1828 remain today as a fine memorial.

His original ideas were typically over-ambitious. Hastings soon wrote again to Finlay admitting that some of them were impractical in view of the lack of funds available to Greece. Rather than try immediately to have a whole fleet professionally manned and centrally administered and financed, he had modified his opinions. The maximum number of vessels he perceived as being possible to bring under the Navy Board in the first instance was two steam ships, a corvette and three gun boats. He based this theory of pay on the expenditure that he had made on the '*Karteria*'; which had a permanent crew of 59 men (although this number varied depending on circumstances).

In addition to the pay for the Officers and men, Hastings gave his opinions on the rations. Each individual should receive 1 ½ oz Cocoa; 1 ½ oz Sugar; 1 lb Bread per day. Also they would have 1 ½ lbs each of Beef and Pork per week. Adding to this the cost of fuel, maintenance and repairs, plus the traditional bonus for a victorious battle, it is quite easy to see how Frank Hastings had spent over £8,000 in a year out of his own pocket and still have been left in debt to Banff of Zante.

Commander of the Karteria

	Pay per month
Captain	£12
Captain's Secretary	£7
Chief Officer	£9
Lieutenants, x 3 @ £7	21
Chief Surgeon	£8
Surgeons, x 3 @ £5	£15
Marine Officer	£8
Carpenter	£6
Boatswain	£4.10.0
Quartermasters, x 3 @ £3	£9
Engineers, x 2 @ £10	£20
Stokers x 4 @ £5	£20
Captain's Steward	£3.10.0
Gunner's Mate	£3
Carpenter's Mates, x 2 @ £3	£6
Officer's Cook	£3
Ship's Cook	£3
Seaman, x 30 @ £2.10.0	£75
Armourer	£3
Total Monthly Pay	£193.00.0

The first two ships to be brought into the first official Greek Navy were the *'Hydra'* and the *'Karteria'*. Captain Crosbie of the *'Hydra'* was called to a meeting by Hastings and had explained to him the new way in which the crew of the ships was to be organised and, especially, paid. To settle any arguments on the question of the English-style naval ranks, they together produced a memorandum showing the equivalent naval and military ranks.

Some of his rank equivalents were disliked by many Philhellenes. The temptation of entering Greek service had been heightened by the prospect of being able to decide upon their own rank and title and to use this upon their return to their homelands.

Many, however, rejoiced at the sight of undisciplined Greek sailors given Petty Officer rank and being taught the basics of drill to pass on to their countrymen of lower status. Perhaps the trainee of today being drilled on the parade ground at Poros would not be quite as grateful to Captain Frank!

Men were brought in from many islands to lend their varied shipbuilding and repair skills to the new naval Dockyard. The '*Karteria*', battered and patched after so many skirmishes, was in a matter of ten days virtually stripped down and refurbished. Two new and longer masts were made and fitted and the stern was almost completely replaced along with many of the timbers on the starboard quarter. The ship's engineers spent their time taking the engine and boilers apart and were assisted by local craftsmen, mostly masons, whom they were training in modern engineering practice. Thus the navy of a new nation was founded, modelled on English lines, in such a short time, but with such attention to detail that it appeared to have been in existence for generations.

Whilst Kapodistrias supported, seemingly wholeheartedly, the new national maritime force, his ideas were less organised as far as the land forces were concerned. Church, who welcomed the arrival of the new President, expected to be recalled to form a properly trained army, as did Fabvier, who at that point was the only person to have trained regular troops. Kapodistrias, however, preferred to keep many local and almost autonomous brigades, fearing that a central army fashioned to a European style could too easily rise against him. Given the past record of so many of the indigenous combatants, this fear was very well founded and the army was left in its normal state of disarray and disorganisation. This caused even the faithful Richard Church to resign his command in early May, although he had no intention of leaving his position which had been building up for two months.

It was still accepted that Anatoliko, the gateway to Messolongi, had to be taken if supremacy was to be achieved in Epirus. From March onwards bodies of men had been joining Church in Dioni. In April a considerable army had moved south to the island of Agios Sostis near to Vasiladhi, which had remained in Greek hands since its capture by Hastings. Church had obtained some hundred or more of the flat bottomed monoxyla and armed them in preparation for the final attack which, it was hoped, would clear the whole region of Messolongi of Turkish troops.

Kapodistrias realised that there was a need for further support from the sea and implored Hastings to resume command of the *'Karteria'*. Seeing his ship in such pristine condition and also having left sufficient instruction for the continuity of the Naval Commission, he readily agreed. Probably two months of office—bound work did not appeal greatly to Frank who would have been anxious to return to more active service in the cause in which he so deeply believed. There still remained the question of the employment of George Finlay.

The President had refused to appoint Finlay to the Naval Commission on the grounds that it should be comprised of professional seamen. More probably the true motive was that he did not wish to place too much control in non-Greek hands. He put forward the proposal to Hastings that Finlay would be of greater service to Greece in a legal capacity for which he was qualified. However both men knew that Finlay, perhaps emulating Byron to whom he had become so close, had the dream of leading troops into battle as a warrior chieftain. They also both knew, that in reality, Finlay was an incurable romantic rather than a practical man and that in truth, Kapodistrias' suggestion was right.

It was left to Hastings, the closest friend of the Scot, to convince him that battle was not for him and to do it in such a manner that did not create too great a disappointment. On 20th April 1828 Hastings wrote from Poros to Finlay who was still at Egina:

"I sail tomorrow with the ship in high order. I wish you could see her, she is so smart now, and the thousand little improvements we have made answer so well. Enough, however, about the 'Karteria'. Now about yourself. Do let me recommend you not to go soldiering or sailoring; take a civil employment. I do not mean that you want

military talents—on the contrary, you would have made either a good sailor or soldier had you served an apprenticeship—but without this it is loss of time. When you reflect, I am sure you must be convinced that talent has less to do with the success in the military profession than being conversant with all the details of the trade. I do not hesitate to say that you would plan a battle better than Lord Nelson and on shore better probably than many Generals. But you would be beaten nevertheless, because if you commanded, all the details would have been so overlooked that your better disposition would not compensate for the defect of detail. It is by a scrupulous attention to trifles that the British Navy has often won battles which certainly they never owed to the plan of attack chosen by the Admiral.

Enough of this; when I come again on your side of the world I hope to find you in civil employment.

Yours very sincerely
F.A. HASTINGS"

There is no record anywhere to suggest that Finlay took any umbrage at the letter and in his own writings there is not the smallest hint of any diminution in his admiration for, or friendship towards, Hastings. Dr Samuel Gridley Howe wrote of George Finlay:

"He is a fine fellow, and conceals under the air of a man of the world, and partly of a misanthrope, a kind heart and delicate feelings. Most people think him cold blooded, sarcastic and selfish, and I once thought so, but he is not. He despises affectation or parade of feeling, but possesses it in reality".

Clearly the efforts of Frank Hastings did not wound the 'delicate feelings' of Finlay. The matter being settled to the best of his abilities at a distance, the master of the '*Karteria*' made preparations to sail from the narrow channel that divides Poros from the mainland of the Peloponnese. On a beautiful, warm spring morning, the '*Karteria*' slipped her lines to sail south-east, around the point of Hydra and to Anatoliko to support the army of General Sir Richard Church.

The previous voyage of the '*Karteria*' had seen her Captain depressed with the state of his ship and his finances. On 21st April, 1828, his mood once again was one of great elation. He was back at sea again and his ship looked and behaved better than she had ever done.

Chapter 12

1828: May to June and the Aftermath

Church, even with his great disappointment at the reorganisations imposed upon the army, had moved his troops to the area of Anatoliko and had been joined by considerable reinforcements from both land and sea. The '*Karteria*' arrived on 9th May and Church and Hastings, their recent disagreements seemingly put to one side, went together to a high point on the mainland held by the Greeks to reconnoitre the overall situation in the Messolongi lagoon.

The main enemy troops were based on the tiny, low island of Agios Thanasi. They also held a stronghold on the hills ashore guarding the island and protecting a route of supply and communication from the mainland. The Greek troops had their main camp at the monastery of St. Nicholas and were firmly in possession of the coastline along the entrance to the islands in front of Anatoliko. At sea they had an armed tambour guarding the right flank of Anatoliko. On station, to prevent any general attack or counter-attack from the Turks, and further out in the bay were an additional nine armed Greek vessels. The main problem had not changed since the attempt on the town the previous December. The lagoons and shallows only had enough depth for the flat-bottomed misticos and the well armed warships could not sail close enough to bring their targets within range.

Hastings and Church both agreed that the only way to attack the town was by the use of misticos armed with mortars. This involved building launching frames of timber onto each rocket carrier and

Mr Ryan, the Rocket Engineer aboard the '*Karteria*', was entrusted with the task. A delay arose when the first misticos to have the work completed refused to enter the lagoon without being paid in advance in both money and food. Church wrote a letter to the official Government representative, based with Greek troops on Agios Sostis, and after much deliberation they were provided with money and bread for ten days. Gradually they entered the shallows, but the preparations were not completed until May 15th.

At seven in the evening some two hundred and fifty troops were loaded aboard the punts and they advanced upon the town to be greeted by heavy and accurate fire from the Muslim shore batteries. By eight thirty, Anatoliko was within range of the rockets and for over three hours, taking the most terrible pounding themselves, the little boats launched several hundred 6-and 12-pound rockets. Their aim was good but luck was not with them and none of the projectiles managed to make contact with combustible targets. Around midnight, Hastings called off the attack, realising that other tactics must be used if the toll was not to be too great.

He and Church, working in great unison, decided that they must bring heavier guns to bear and two 68-pounders were dismantled and taken ashore to the two miniscule islands held by the Greeks, Poros, not to be confused with the larger island of Poros, and Agios Nicholaos. From these, grape shot was used for two days with great effect, to 'soften up' the Turks prior to the main attack which was scheduled for 21st May although General Church, seeing a long battle ahead, wished to wait until entrenching tools arrived from Zante. On the following evening, Church and Hastings were again in the higher ground watching any movements and when they saw some thirty Turkish cavalrymen crossing the plains towards Agios Thanasi they realised that even though the trenching tools had not yet arrived from Zante, they should go for an all—out attack at the earliest opportunity.

The troops were ready to go in including many who had recently joined and were no more than pirates—only looking for the plunder that might be obtained from victory. Those men deliberately based themselves with the misticos to ensure that they would have the opportunity to be first in at the pillage. At daybreak many craft were predominantly manned by the robbers. The planned action was that during the morning the gunboats and the two land-based 68-pounders would inflict the maximum damage upon the Turks and this would be followed by a concerted effort by the misticos.

This plan did not suit the boats containing the pirates and against orders they pushed ahead on their own. They were spotted by the officers in command of the gunboats, who assumed that Captain Hastings had actually given the order to advance. The Misticos came under very heavy fire from the Turkish positions and soon their greed was superseded by fear and they remained out of range of the fire from Anatoliko. The gunboats, however, bravely continued under a murderous rain of musketry until the gallant Captain of the leading boat, Captain Andreas Papapanou, fell dead with many of his men being either killed or wounded.

Hastings realised that the scene was one of complete disorder and although he knew they were not yet ready to go into battle, he boarded his gig to lead the attack. It was a brave but foolish action and within minutes of coming within range of the Muslims he fell with a wound in the left arm. The scene around had changed to one of carnage and the fall of their Commander signalled the retreat. The action was the epitome of all human strengths and weaknesses from the heights of bravery to the depths of greed and the final toll was some eighty dead and nearly two hundred wounded.

Since her launching, the '*Karteria*' had always carried at least one or more, surgeons such as Doctors Bruno and Gridley Howe. Due to the speed with which she was ordered from Poros to support Church and the new Government appointment for Dr Samuel Gridley Howe, there was not one surgeon on board on 23rd May. Church insisted on sending the army surgeon, Dr Getty, aboard the '*Karteria*' to treat Frank Hastings. The wound was dressed and Getty felt that it was not too serious although the Captain was clearly in pain. Despite regular visits from the Doctor and the good offices of his servant and secretary, Alexander Ross, Hastings remained in great pain.

Hastings continued to command his ship on station off the lagoons and believed Dr Getty when he said that the wound was of a comparatively minor nature. After three days he was looking forward to a further attempt to take Anatoliko. He wrote a lengthy report in French to Mavrokordatos, the Minister for the Marine, to explain what had happened and how this could be avoided on the next occasion. Confident that his wound was healing without complication he added at the end of the letter:

"J'espére que d'en trois ou quatre jours ma blessure me permettra de reprendre mon poste dans le lac d'Anatolico, et d'y surveiller les operations maritimes".

Two days after this display of confidence Dr Getty and the crew aboard the 'Karteria' became convinced by the regular fits and convulsions of the Captain that all was not well. A decision was made that the arm should be amputated and that the operation should take place in the hospital at Zante, where there were better surgical conditions and superior medical attention to that available from the army. The 'Karteria' rushed across to the island arriving during the afternoon of 1st June, 1828, and was met by two British residents, Hancock and Robinson, who immediately transferred Hastings to the hospital.

The actions are best described by Hancock himself in a letter to George Finlay the following day:

"I dare say you have already heard that poor Hastings received a wound in his wrist sone ten days ago in an affair before Anatoliko which was not considered serious; it appears, however, that about a week after it happened, spasmodic symptoms attacked the whole system and he was brought over here for further surgical advice and assistance: he arrived here yesterday afternoon and was got into the Lazaretto with as little loss of time as possible, but it was already too late, he was too much exhausted for amputation; the convulsive attacks were repeated and he died at half past eight in the evening. Robinson and I are just returned from rendering the last service in consigning him to the steamer's cutter. I need not tell you who knew him so intimately that Greece has lost one of the best and most efficient friends her cause has ever had."

The two men, along with Ross and Phalanger, who had been with them, returned to the '*Karteria*' that evening, to discuss the very considerable implications of the death. The men on board were heartbroken at the news of the loss of their Captain, whom many had been with through dangerous and bloody battles during the previous months. The Captain who rarely displayed signs of emotion or affection to those around him, had been unable to transmit this reserve to others, and many hardened seamen wept openly at the news. The following morning the Captain's cutter was taken to the shore and Hancock and Robinson returned to the hospital:

"Robinson and I are just returned from rendering him the last service in consigning him to the steamer's cutter. I need not tell you who knew him so intimately that Greece has lost one of the best and most efficient friends her cause has ever had. We have taken no decision as to the place of interment for his remains, further than to approve the body being taken aboard the steam vessel to Egina. The Officers seem to wish and think that it is likely that the Greek Government may send the body to England. We are of the opinion that the country he has been defending should be his grave.

The case appears to be widely different from Byron's, whose fame as a poet formed a strong argument for his being buried in England. Possibly you may know what were his own wishes on the subject; at any rate the Government will be able to do what they think right, therefore the plan adopted cannot but be so far right. We have furnished a quantity of spirits and everything necessary to preserve the corpse. None of his effects have been delivered".

In the lagoons Church had continued his vain attempt to take Anatoliko after the departure of the '*Karteria*'. However, with mounting casualties and no reinforcements in sight, he was forced to withdraw during the night of June 6th to the stronghold on Agios Sostis. The following morning he learnt of the death of Frank Abney Hastings. Although they had often quarrelled over military and naval matters, the two men had worked closely together for a long period. There was a great bond between them, both on a personal and a military level, General Sir Richard Church suffered a great sense of loss with the news.

It was a remarkable tribute to an English Naval Officer that it was left to ordinary Greek sailors to arrange the first of many funeral services for Hastings. The effect upon the whole population when the news spread was devastating. Kapodistrias, with typical efficiency, announced that the Greek National Tribute and Service would be held, appropriately, at Poros one year from the date of Frank's death and appointed a commission consisting of the Minister of the Marine and two of Hastings' closest friends, Finlay and Kalergy, to carry out the arrangements. To the many sailors who had served under the Captain, and were now at Egina, a delay of twelve months was not satisfactory and they took up a collection to employ the services of the clergy of Egina and the use of the largest Church on the island. A huge crowd, much larger than could ever have been contemplated for an unofficial service, thronged the Church. The congregation of piratical looking Greek seamen was pushed to the front by dozens of foreigners from a great number of nations as they participated in a solemn Greek Orthodox Requiem service for an Englishman.

A year after Hastings' death, the Government of Greece held the official burial ceremony at Poros. The body, preserved in brandy, was transported from Egina to Poros aboard the '*Karteria*'. For his last journey aboard the ship which had been so much a part of his life, Frank was escorted by the second and third steam vessels, the '*Epicheirisis*' and the '*Hermes*' and they were met by a thirty-seven gun salute. The reason for this was that although Hastings was only thirty-four years old on his death, it was felt that as a tribute, he should receive the same salute as Byron six years previously. As with many Greek heroes, the heart of Frank Abney Hastings was removed before the actual interment and placed in an urn which was given into the custody of Finlay, Hane and Kalergy.

Many hundreds of people turned out to see the funeral procession in Poros and the Church was packed with the ministers of the Greek Government, representatives of other nations, dozens of Philhellenes and many ordinary seamen who had served aboard the '*Karteria*'.

Finlay read the lesson in English during the service which was conducted by the senior Bishop. The Secretary of State, Tricoupi, pronounced the oration on behalf of Greece. The lengthy eulogy ended with the words:

"O Lord, in thy heavenly kingdom remember Frank Abney Hastings who died in defence of his suffering fellow creatures".

Any hope that the death of Hastings may have solved the financial disagreements which bedevilled the last year of his life were quickly dashed. It was left to George Finlay to act on his behalf in death as he had done in life. The executors of Hastings' Will in England, Rev. Macdowell of Ashby and Sir Edmund Antrobus of London, both readily agreed that Finlay should act on their behalf in Greece. Finlay wrote to the President to obtain a ruling on whether the Will should be administered under English or Greek law and also asking for the sums due to Hastings from the Government to be paid to allow the cash legacies to be distributed.

Confusion was added by the fact that Hastings had left debts in many places and also had sums of money in numerous banks. His belongings were largely aboard the '*Karteria*' and Finlay asked Ross to store these in safety at the Lazaretto Hospital on Zante, and to remain with them until further instructions. One item was missing. For some inexplicable reason, Hastings' sword, which he had willed to Captain Edward Hinton Scott RN, had been taken back to Scotland by Thomas Gordon. The sword, along with his Midshipman's Dirk, did get to Captain Edward Scott, who in 1840 donated them to the newly formed United Services Museum in London. This presentation was well recorded. To their great shame by the time of the 1924 catalogue the items were not listed by RUSI and the current whereabouts of the sword is unknown. Hastings' pistols in their original case, also bequeathed to Scott, are now in a private collection.

Finlay had learnt of the death of his closest friend at Egina on June 15th in letters from Hancock and also from Gibbon Fitzgibbon, and he replied on the same day:

"I received your melancholy letter of the 2 June this morning and immediately addressed myself to the Phronesterion her to ascertain where the 'Karteria' was to be found, that I might hire a vessel and join you to take such measures as the last wishes of my departed friend seemed to direct".

He went on to explain that he had received word from the Ministry of the Marine that they were awaiting a decision from the President regarding the body, and the appointment of Phalanger as Captain of the 'Karteria'. Finlay continued:

"If I have been left by my friend his executor, and there is any means of knowing his wishes, all I can do is fulfil them shall be done. Are you aware if I am his executor? If I am so I wish all his plate and property to be deposited in the Lazaretto under the care of Ross; if he desires to return to England that he may take them himself to Lady Hastings or to Sir Charles as the testament may direct. Tell Ross, I beg of you, not to be alarmed for his money in the bank, I will take charge of that and if he desires it, see that the sum is repaid him at Zante on his assigning his share to me. I authorise you as executor to act with me, and wish you to send the body, all the papers, and such of the books as are not disposed of by testament and not of value enough to be sent to England (I mean naval)—here".

It was interesting that Finlay, who knew perfectly well that he was not the executor, had assumed the role and he continued still with the assumption that the English Trustees would immediately appoint him as the executor in Greece.

"The body I think my friend would have wished interred in Greece; he at least expressed that wish to me more than once. The papers must be sent to his family ultimately, but I am authorised by him to arrange some which may be of use to Greece, and you may observe some in my handwriting, the naval books I think should be given to the Naval School—if this arrangement is not agreed by the heirs I will repay the price of anything thus given.

Could you come round yourself with these? In the meantime any expenses, you may find it necessary to go to Mr Robinson, who will furnish you with them on showing this order. I think it is worthwhile hiring a small vessel and proceeding immediately, but much must depend on the order of the President to Mr Phalanger which accompanies this letter".

During the year in which the preserved body of Frank Hastings awaited burial, the arguments raged over his remaining monies and various possessions. The English executors wished the Will to be dealt with under the laws of that country but the Greek Government had decreed that the Codicil, which had been written whilst in Greek service, should come under Greek law. Much of Finlay's time and energy was spent in trying to locate all the sums and items bequeathed by Hastings. He had considerable battles with the Government to obtain the money due to his friend that had not been forthcoming during his lifetime. The main problems came with the opposing interests of Hane and Kalergy, who had been left money in the Will and were both Greek residents and of Captain Edward Hinton Scott R.N who had been left £1,000 in the first Will but only the sword and arms in the Codicil.

Having no reply to early letters to General Thomas Gordon, Finlay was obliged to write a rather strong letter demanding the return of Hastings' sword, so that at least that part of the bequest could be sent to Scott. He wrote:

"Having been appointed acting executor of Captain Frank Abney Hastings' Will in Greece by a Power of Attorney from the Rev. Wm. Macdowell the executor in England, I have to inform you that you are requested to return a sword belonging to the late Captain Hastings in your possession, either to me or to the executor in England.

The sword is disposed of by Will to a highly regarded friend of the deceased, and I have frequently heard Captain Hastings during his lifetime express dissatisfaction at your carrying it away with you from Greece. I hope you will excuse my troubling you with the request to answer this letter".

The problem was exacerbated by the fact that Scott did not receive several letters written to him and had formed the strong opinion that the three legatees in Greece, Finlay, Kalergy and Hane, were deliberately withholding both information and the legacy from him, and indeed Scott instructed his solicitors to attempt to have the Will in total placed under the jurisdiction of the English Courts. Finlay wrote to Scott at his home in St. George's Street, Croydon, pointing out that previous letters had been written, if not received.

"This delay gives me the greatest uneasiness as I am mixed up in the affairs in a manner I by no means wish, and yet I really think it is my duty not to throw obstacles in the way of the execution of the last Will of my poor friend, which I know both Hane and Kalergy have at heart, tho' they have been placed by circumstances in a situation in which it was difficult to avoid delay".

Finlay explained to Scott that he had certified copies of the Codicil to the Will with a Mr Dakin, and that he had spent much of his time collecting many small sums which no other person knew were in existence and he went on:

"Hane and Kalergy both opposed the funds in Greece quitting this country, and I have all along wished that they would instantly take the administration of affairs in this country on themselves, but their absence (Hane being Governor of Candia, and Kalergy being absent as Governor of Argos and latterly of Syra) has hindered any steps being taken. The reason on which Hane and Kalergy oppose transmitting any money in this country to England is this—they claim the right to administer in Greece by the Civil Law as residuary legatees, and they do not see any reason for risking the results of a Chancery Suit which they have no means of carrying on. The second testament as being executed in Greece, and disposing of property in this country, they consider by no means as placing the funds in this country under the power of the English courts. They therefore resolved to take one letter of administration in this country, and then send the original Will to England by the authority of the Greek courts to take such measures as the law of England requires for the administration of the Estate, and the distribution of the funds in England. I have a good deal of contact

with Hane and Kalergy, and have shown them your letters. They both disclaim any hostile proceedings and are anxious to carry into effect poor Hastings' Will according to its letter and intent".

The letter went on to discuss part of the arms and the watch which had been left by Ross at Zante with Banff's for safe keeping but there was no mention of the sword which had been so specifically bequeathed to Captain Edward Scott R.N in Hastings' Will. By December 1829, Finlay was able to produce the final statement, and in that he referred to the proceeds from the sale of maps and arms, but still no reference was made to the sword. Several searches have been made over the years to locate the weapon, but without avail. Somewhere there exists a sword inscribed upon the blade '*This sword was bequeathed by Frank Abney Hastings to his friend Captain Edward Scott R.N*'.

It was certainly with great relief that Finlay was able to wind up the affairs of his friend eighteen months after his death, and on 21st December 1829 he issued the statement of the finances in Eginan Drachmas:

Balance in Mr Finlay's hands	3336 11 36
Due by Greek Government	5902 13 12
Due by D. Kalergy 100	486 10 00
Due by E. Kanos 152	739 11 00
Sums due:	10363 45 48

Proceeds of books, instruments, Charts,
maps and arms sold at sale.

Due to Captain Scott	466.13.33
To A. Ross—balance of clothes,	43.13.09
Wine and plate	4832.10.00
Legacy to Captain Scott 1000	2416.50.00
Legacy to Finlay 800	7757.86.42

The balance of around 700 ED was due to be shared by Hane and Kalergy, which equated to around three years pay to a Ship's Captain or a senior Army Officer, and would in modern terms be approximately £40,000 each. The sums to Edward Scott would certainly have left him a wealthy man.

One hundred years after the death of Captain Frank Abney Hastings, the Ministry of the Marine in Greece decreed that the nation should pay full honour to the man who had played such an important role in the formation of the nation. The Historical and National Museums of Athens produced an exhibition and booklet of Hastings' souvenirs. The Government struck commemorative medals bearing a representation of the Captain and the name Frank Abney Hastings on one side, and the words 'Greece grateful 1828-1928' on the other. The people of Messolongi and Etolica erected monuments to his memory. There are streets in Athens and Piraeus bearing his name to this day, and for many years a famous soap factory in Messolongi bore his name!

The Greek Navy were put in charge of the official Hastings' Centenary Programme and the details of this give an indication of the great importance of one Englishman to a whole nation:

Thursday 31st May 1928

14.00	Destroyers leave Phaleron for Patras.
22.00	Arrive Patras. Sleep in local hotel.

MESALONGHI CEREMONY—Friday 1st June 1928

08.00 Leave for Mesalonghi
Arrive Kryoneri
Proceed to Anotoliko and place wreaths on water where Hastings was wounded.

11.30 Unveiling of memorial erected by the Municipality of Mesalonghi, speeches and placing of wreaths.
13.0 Destroyers leave for Phaleron.

POROS CEREMONY—Saturday 2nd June 1928

09.00 Destroyers leave for Poros
11.00 Requiem at the grave of Hastings, placing of wreaths. Parade of Central Training Establishment personnel Before Minister of Marine. Speech by Professor Koughea.
13.00 Official lunch by Captain Inspector of Naval Training.
16.00 Boat Races. Seaplane display. Distribution of Commemorative medals.
18.0 Destroyers leave for Phaleron.

ATHENS CEREMONY—Sunday 3rd June 1928

10.15 Memorial Service in English Church. Placing of wreaths by the Government, the Navy, and the Mayor of Athens.
11.00 Opening of the Exhibition of Hastings relics at the Historical Museum
13.00 Official Lunch by Head of British Navel Mission.
16.30 Fete at Stadium
21.00 Dinner by Ministry of Foreign Affairs.

The participants in the Centenary Celebrations also received a copy of a special edition of the Naval Review containing a commemorative article written by Professor Constantine Rados describing the life of Frank Abney Hastings and his value to Greece.

The whole of Greece celebrated. Models of the *'Karteria'* were built and sold. Three models have been traced by the author; one is in the Hellenic Maritime Museum, Piraeus; one in the National Historical Museum, Athens; the final model is in the possession of the Baltic Exchange, London. Badges were produced as reproductions of the Medals and many tiny ports where the *'Karteria'* had visited put on their own displays and services to honour the man called Astiggas. The subject of such ceremony would have been duly proud of the interest and admiration in his ship, the *'Karteria'*, the ceremonies at Poros in the Naval School with which he had been so involved at its inception, and the fact that the Royal Navy representatives from Britain played their part in giving him such honour. Captain Frank Abney Hastings had truly become a part of Greek history.

Chapter 13

Legacy

The tiny Greek State experienced immense problems without the naval skills of Hastings but Richard Church, despite his disagreements with the Kapodistrians, continued to strengthen the army's gains in the north. The super-powers continued to bicker over the Greek/Turkish borders and always the Greeks fought between themselves for their war losses and power within the new state.

In fairness to Kapodistrias he had a near impossible task and even the troops, other than those under Kalergy and Kanaris, turned against him. Mavromichalis was imprisoned for a time and the great Admiral Miaoulis was in revolt. It was inevitable that the family of Petrobey Mavromichalis should seek revenge and this took the form of the assassination of Kapodistrias by them on October 9th, 1831. Again the infant state was in a state of civil war with the Russians supporting Kolokotronis and Agostino Kapodistrias, the brother of the dead leader. The French threw in their strength with Kolettis and once more Greece had two rival Governments.

It was left to foreigners again to find a solution, and this was done by the selection of Prince Otto, the seventeen-year-old son of Ludwig I of Bavaria as the King of a new Greece. He ruled over a small nation while even the majority of the islands remained in the hands of the Turks as did Epirus and Thessaloniki. Otto's strength lay largely in the 3,500 Bavarian troops who landed with him in January 1833. The power was vested in the three Regents appointed by France,

Bavaria and Russia. They became immensely unpopular during the first ten years of monarchy and it was only a temporary respite in the internecine quarrels of the old wartime leaders, Kolettis, Kolokotronis, Mavrokardatos, Koundriotis and others that allowed an assembly to replace the Regents.

Many genuine attempts by Otto failed due to the strengths of the old warriors but he reigned until 1862 when a revolution led by Admiral Kanaris removed him from the throne. Otto maintained his claim to the Greek throne until his death in 1867 although King George I of the Hellenes, the son of the King of Denmark, was elected by the Greeks in 1863.

Gradually the territories which are modern Greece were acquired, won by battle or revolt. Greece learned to live, as today, with a constant threat of civil war. Kings came and went as did dictators. As part of the E.U. and N.A.T.O. and one of the most popular tourist areas of the world, Greece looks as stable today as it ever has in its short history.

The Greeks of rank and learning still remember the Philhellenes who helped them so much—Hastings, Finlay, Church, Gordon, Hane, Byron, and many others. Several of them remained in Greece after the Wars of Independence to add their skills and proven loyalty to the new state.

General Sir Richard Church moved his family to Greece and played a major part in the election of King George and his home was the political salon of Athens for many years. When his death came in his ninetieth year, such was the importance of the old man that King George I and many of his court were waiting sadly in an adjoining room for the news. It was indeed appropriate that Church and Hastings today both have memorials in St Paul's Anglican Church in Athens.

Thomas Gordon returned to Athens in 1828 and bought a home, which he loaned to Church in 1831 when he returned to Scotland to write his "History of the Greek Revolution". This work complete, he again returned at Church's request to assist with the work of quelling the bands of brigands who roamed the rural areas freely. In 1835 the Scottish labourer was promoted to Major-General and Acting Chief-of-Staff and the following year to Governor of the Peloponnese. As so often in his earlier life, he found himself in disagreement with the authorities and in February 1839, left Greece and only returned once more on a private visit to see old friends. The historical work of Thomas Gordon was his greatest memorial.

Perhaps the most badly treated man by history was John Hane, whose great disadvantage was spending most of the wars so close to Frank Hastings and certainly being eclipsed by him. The Greek Government did honour him with the Military Medal and Cross of the Redeemer after the war. In April, 1829, he succeeded Colonel Urquhart as Commandant of Grabeasa. Under King Otto, he was promoted to Colonel and married the niece of Mavrokordatos. He was only removed from office by the ascendancy of the numerous Bavarian officials in 1842 which left him in considerable financial difficulty. Finlay, Dr Gridley Howe and Charles Holte Bracebridge pleaded his cause through Prime Minister Mavrokordatos, though none of his dues were ever paid, despite assurances, during his life. John Hane tried to cover his poverty but it was left to his friends to tactfully try and provide for his wife and three children. Despite this help he died destitute and heart-broken on September 18th, 1844. It is to be hoped that one day more will be uncovered about this brave and loyal man and that he will take his rightful place in modern Greek history.

George Finlay, the great historian and closest friend of Frank Abney Hastings, lived on in Greece until his death in 1875. He involved himself greatly in politics in the early years and as a member of the Provincial Council of Attica was involved with the plans for modern Athens, foundation of the Bank of Greece and agricultural reform of the land. He also held the unofficial post of Public Relations Offices to the new nation and wrote prolifically to the newspapers of the world. For ten years he was the Athens correspondent of the Times and he was on the management committee to build the Anglican

Church of St Paul where he eventually immured the heart of Frank Hastings.

His place in any history on Greece must come from the many volumes published on all aspects of Greece and Professor Felton of Harvard once wrote to Finlay, *"I would rather be author of your histories than Prime Minister of England"*.

One of the two great modern British historians of the period, Douglas Dakin, goes almost as far:

"Finlay's history ranks in magnitude with Gibbon's 'Decline and Fall'; it has, moreover, qualities which Gibbon's work does not possess, a great insight into the importance of economic factors, a thorough grasp of administrative history, and a great subtlety of treatment between ideas, social changes and the actions of individuals. Even the literary quality of Finlay's work, his graceful constructions and power of language, compares favourably with that of Gibbon".

To any study of Frank Abney Hastings must be closely linked the name George Finlay—for the warrior, a great advantage that his closest friend and confidant became the historian to the nation for whom he fought and died; for the historian, to travel with the warrior provided the perfect base from which to view the emergence of Greece.

If the life and death of Frank Abney Hastings had little effect upon his family and fellow Englishmen, it certainly did upon a foreign state, and the friendship between he and Finlay has been the basis upon which this life story is recorded. Hitherto an unknown man even in his home town of Ashby de la Zouch, Leicestershire, Captain Frank Abney Hastings will live forever in the hearts and minds of the Greeks.

Appendix 1

MEMOIR

ON THE USE OF

SHELLS, HOT SHOT

AND

CARCASS SHELLS

FROM

SHIP ARTILLERY

By

FRANK ABNEY HASTINGS
CAPTAIN OF THE GREEK STEAM VESSEL OF WAR,
KARTERIA

LONDON

JAMES RIDGEWAY, PICADILLY.

MDCCC.XXVIII

Preface

There are few men who have visited Greece, and who can write, who have not been delivered of a book on their return to Europe, as it is called (and justly so) in this part of the world. I have hitherto resisted the temptation of writing about myself, Author; and as I had half-pledged myself not to give my enemies (if I have any) such an advantage over me as they will now possess, I will simply relate how I have come to take this rash step. I was before the fort of Vasiladhi, bombarding it; a friend who came from England with me, and to whom I have great obligations, and was a visitor with me, left for Egina (via the Gulf of Lepanto) rather despairing of our success; at length, hearing of it, he wrote me the following letter.

Egina, January 4th 1828
"My Dear Hastings

I had a good passage through the enemy's Castles, and the day after, in a strong Paleo Castro: they sent a ship, a Vampori, to defend Trisognia, and would not listen to my proposition of fortifying it, which I told them would not cost one eighth of a vessel for two months, and would be surer defence: they have written to Lord Cochrane on the subject, etc.
"January 5. I have just received your letter, and you can imagine hoe delighted I was. Well, fortune has certainly played you one or two tricks with old Bampori (Note 1); but now she has balanced matters. Human ingenuity is sadly at fault with these pudding-headed Turks, as was proved by our sage conjectures on the letter(2) In spite of your success, I am sure you are in sad difficulties with provisions, etc. But I

hope God will give you some assistance. I hope Hane is Commandant of Vasiladhi; and if he will give me a house, I may come and see his city. I suppose you will unable to do any thing at Anatolico, etc.etc.

"The English new twenty-eights are frigates; the Columbine, an eighteen gun corvette, beats them all, but is crank; the frigates are stiff, and can use their guns when the corvettes cannot. The George the Fourth is launched; she is pierced for one hundred and thirty-six guns, and has thirty-two pounders on her lower and middle decks; twenty-four on her main deck; on her quarter deck, and forecastle, thirty-two pound carronades, and long twelves. What a vessel she would be with your sixty-eights on her three decks; and what castles of Lepanto would stand her rattling shells at them. She might have gone into Navarino alone, and done the business, more effectually. You really ought, and I hope you will, when you have leisure, write a pamphlet, if not more, on your views concerning Marine Artillery. I see Lord C— is quite of your opinion about large guns, and good firing, and thinks one gun, if big enough, quite sufficient. You may imagine I am in high spirits at your success, etc.

"The Irresistible Greek steam vessel, you have perhaps heard, took fire in the river, and was burnt to the water's edge. There has been the most extraordinary degree of folly, roguery, and bad fortune, in these Greek Officers, which were, we suspect, accumulated in one mass.

"Yours, ever sincerely,—"

Shortly after receiving this friendly epistle, as I had little to do, I occupied myself in writing the following pages. I have not shown them to my friend, because I know he would disapprove of the general style and tone of the work, whilst he might consider the matter less objectionable: but as I hate writing, and if I was to make another attempt, should not succeed better, this must even go to the press as it is.

Memoir

The Science of Artillery has been studied in the British Navy much more generally, of late years, than formerly. The importance of attaining the most perfect Artillery practice from Ships, seems now to be duly appreciated. There was a time, when, to know that the cartridge ought to be put into the gun before the shot, was considered all the Artillery knowledge requisite to form a British Naval Officer; even at this day, I believe gunnery does not form part of the examination to qualify a Midshipman to be promoted to the rank of Lieutenant; therefore any knowledge acquired by Officers of the Navy in the art of gunnery, is obtained gratuitously. When we consider the Naval battles are always fought, and ninety-nine times out of a hundred decided by Artillery, is it not strange that a knowledge of the principles of the art should not be considered essential to the forming of a Naval Officer? The Officers of the British Navy used to be (and, I still believe, are still) the best Men of War Seaman in the world; but all the Seaman's help in the world will avail little, if your Artillery practice is inferior to that of your enemy. It has been a good deal the fashion, (I suspect, however, more out of the Navy than in it) to attribute the success of the British Navy to advantages obtained by Manoeuvering. For my part, I feel convinced that in nine Naval battles out of ten, the superior Artillery must win, even though coupled with inferior seamanship to that possessed by the enemy. Manoeuvring is a very indefinite word, and that is why I dislike it. There are fashions in manoeuvring as in the cut of a coat;—formerly, the weather gage was the desideratum;—that has, however, lost its value; and raking is now the enviable position. There are circumstances, it is true, where a raking position may be decisive of a victory; as, for instance, at anchor, or even at sea, passing under the stern of an enemy in discharging the first broadside; but at sea, in single actions, (to which I chiefly allude) manoeuvring for a raking position will usually be attended with risk, not at all compensated for by the position, if you gain it. In attempting it, a few ropes shot away may lose you the battle; when attained, this raking position being but momentary, does not admit of the guns being relaid, which is rendered necessary by th change in the inclination of the Ship, and, probably some have not yet been reloaded after discharge: thus it is more than probable, that two or three shots are the utmost that take effect in a whole raking broadside. Sir Howard Douglas, in his valuable work on Naval Gunnery, makes the same remark, I think, upon broadsides given in yawing: now raking broadsides in manoeuvring, are, literally yawing broadsides. The less the inclination and direction is altered whilst firing, the more correct is the fire likely to prove. Far be it from me to undervalue the merit of the seamanship of the Officers of the British Navy; for, to this, British Naval superiority is principally due. A battle is not all gained on the day of the battle; it is alone by being conversant in all the details of a Ship, and by daily assiduity in preparing precautions against accidents and proper attention to the health and discipline of the crew, that British Men of War can keep the sea for several months, not only without suffering, but with such advantage as to be in better condition to encounter an enemy at the end, than at the commencement of their cruise.

As a proof how little gunnery was studied in the British Navy, I had served seven years and been in two Naval Battles, without knowing that the line of metal was not parallel to the cylinder of the gun. I shall, probably, be laughed at for this acknowledgement; but let those who laugh prove they were better informed. I heard old sailors say, that shot rose at sea on quitting the gun, and took for granted their explanation of the shot going above where aimed at. The first attempt which I saw, of giving the line parallel to the cylinder, (it was a clumsy one enough for sea, God knows) was by painting three white lines along the gun, viz. One from each quarter sight and one along the top sight. In the act of exercising, some bothered old gunner, half drunk, or wholly stupid from previous habits of drunkenness, mumbled out, "Look along your side sights for your elevation;—look along your top sights for your direction;—cock your locks—fire." During which operations, the ship had lurched to leeward, rolled to windward, pitched forward, sended aft half a dozen times, altering the elevation a dozen degrees at each movement, and the direction some points. I have no doubt but that this quarter-sight system, produced worse firing than the less scientific one of the old seamen, who, upon the received maxim that the shot rose on quitting the gun, looked along the line of metal, and at point blank ranges pointed under the object by guess. The new system, however, had the merit of showing the principle (and owing to its clumsiness) of exercising the ingenuity of these men not altogether stultified by love of routine, *(Note 3)* and produced the top-sight parallel to the bore, than which nothing can be better for point blank ranges; ultimately, some Officers placed raised sights on the guns for firing at angles of elevation, arranged in various ways, according to their taste, or the capacity of workmen they had to execute them. *(Note 4)* Sir W. Congreve has since, I understand, introduced a sight, of which the principle is the same as of all other sights of elevation, but has the objection of being more costly and more complicated. Since it is but recently that any tolerable precision has been obtained in ship firing, or that Naval Officers have become acquainted with the first principles of the art, it is not astonishing that the old system of round shot and full charges should be invariably used, whatever the distance, or the nature of the object fired at. People, little conversant with Naval matters, are not aware how much hammering a ship may take without sinking; or even how difficult it is to sink a ship at all by firing at her with round shot. Witness all the Naval battles of the last war. Almost the only way a shot can penetrate under water, is by the movement of the ship; which, at one moment exposes above water a part afterwards emersed. A shot fired from a ship, perhaps, two degrees depression, to five or six degrees elevation, *(Note 5)* will ricochet on the water, and therefore cannot, by possibility, strike the ship under water, but by the movement of the ship: such shots as do not ricochet, will, usually, be too much deadened to penetrate a ship under water, should they come into contact with her bottom, which is improbable, from the angle a ship's bottom makes with the horizon. In fact, the object in a naval battle always was to kill the crew, as the readiest way of getting possession of the ship; and thus naval actions have lasted much longer than one conversant with naval affairs would imagine possible, when fighting so close.

(Note 6) Being engaged in a naval warfare, where our matériel was so excessively inferior to that of our enemy, as to leave no hope of success, whilst using the same mode of war, I turned my thoughts to some projectile more destructive than ordinary round shot, and I at first proposed hot shot; there is nothing new in this; it is a what coast batteries usually employed against shipping; it is what destroyed the floating batteries of the Spaniards at Gibraltar; it is what has been used already by shipping; and if this latter case, without any important result, the failure may, perhaps, be ascribed to an injudicious manner of using them. The chief objection to the use of hot shot on board a ship, is, that the gun, after being loaded, has to be run out, to be pointed, etc. During which operation, if the fire should communicate to the cartridge, the people working the gun would be endangered. However, I imagined that, with a wet clay wad between the yarn wad and the shot, it was next to impossible any accident should occur. I made the experiment. And found that, although the exterior of the gun about the shot became very hot, and remained so for a length of time, nevertheless the shot became cold in the gun, without any accident. I have since continually used hot shot, and with perfect safety; my people having become familiar with them, employ them with as little apprehension as if using cold shot. The clay wad, however, has the inconvenience of fouling the gun; and there are these objections to hot shot; namely, the length of time required to heat them, and the small quantity there is a possibility of heating on board a ship; consequently, hot shot can only be used in limited numbers, and for particular occasions. A French officer, M. Jourdan, arrived in Greece, with a project of incendiary balls, which he cast, in fact, as carcasses, and proposed to fire from guns at shipping; and. According to his calculation, they were to burn the whole Turkish fleet. However, he only succeeded in burning an hydriote, and his own hat; his incendiary balls went off in smoke, as they should have done. The absurdity of this project, and its failure, occasioned the neglect of a proposition of his, which merited a better fate; namely the use of carcass shells. I relate this because it was what first directed my attention to the use of shells from guns. I reflected upon it alone, and I conversed upon it with artillery officers, until I was satisfied within myself of its practicability and utility; yet I could not convince any body else; but, on the contrary, got heartily laughed at for my pains, (so I have been told, by Lord Byron), and some other genius's *(Note 7)*. When half ashamed of my project, and sadly in want of some countenance, I had the good fortune to see the work of M. Pauchans, and resolved, not only to prosecute my project of shells, but to adopt his ideas on the canon à bombes; and I take this opportunity of returning my grateful thanks to M. Pauchans for the essential service his book has rendered me, and to assure him, I have no pretension to be thought the original projector of an aim, the merit of the introduction, and the success of which, is entirely due to him.

Having obtained the command of a steam vessel, destined for Greece, *(Note 8)* I prepared for her armament eight sixty-eight pounders; four of these carronades, Government pattern, thirty-six hundred weight, five feet two inches, and four long shorts, after drawings I gave; these were seven feet four inches long, and fifty-eight hundred weight, with the form of a carronade in all, but having trumicons to mount them, the same as long guns; but these trumicons are not placed, as is usual in long guns, below the line of the quarter sight, / (to admit of which sight is the only reason I could ever imagine for placing them thus low,) but so as to intersect the gun horizontally. On my arrival in Greece, the guns were there, but without carriages: I then proceeded to mount them on four ten inch howitzer carriages, which have answered the purpose admirably; these had originally dumb trucks in the rear of cast iron, which I changed for wood; these dumb trucks deadened the recoil very advantageously; at the expense, however, of more labour in running them out; but I thought the decrease of recoil on these terms desirable; I ultimately fitted an iron lever, with two rollers, which hooking on to the rear of the carriage, lifted the dumb trucks off the deck in running out the guns, thus facilitating running ot the guns and diminishing their recoil. The carronades had the usual carriages and slides. I had prepared in ~England six hundred eight inch shells, strapped to wooden bottoms; the object of the wooden bottoms was to preserve the shell in the proper direction; viz. With the fuzee towards the muzzle of the gun; these not having arrived, I substituted two giummets of rope or salvegee, frapped together by yarns, and found to answer the purpose; but as it consumed much rope and yarns, I tried one giummet, frapped to the fuzee head, and found it to answer even better than the two giummets, and. Ultimately, I fired without any giummets or wooden bottom at all, taking particular care to place the fuzee in the proper direction; this of course, will not succeed if there is much motion; but in moderate weather, not more than one shell out of thirty will break its fuzee, and this will never be attended with any danger, the shell always bursting outside the gun, and all the pieces going like grape or langrage, in the direction the gun was pointed. You may place your fuzee next to your cartridge without doing any further injury than bursting the shell in going out of the gun; you will neither injure the gun nor yourself; I have tried it.

At the Island of Samos, I made experiments on the different ranges with different charges, and found, to my surprise, that. Fired with more than four pound charges, the shells usually lost their fuzees; the extreme ranges, from the long guns, was particularly satisfactory; I calculated about two thousand five hundred yards, with four pounds, at point blank; the carronades were by no means so true, or did they give equal ranges. Anxious to increase the charges, if necessary, I tried a variety of methods of driving the fuzees, so as to prevent their falling out, and have at length succeeded by tying a piece of leather around that part of the fuzee which is inside the shell, and diminishing the fuzee, so as to allow the leather to go with some difficulty into the fuzee hole; when driven in, the leather naturally expands, and prevents the fuzee from coming out again; thus a wooden spring would be still better, I found that, with this contrivance, a shell will retain its fuzee, fired with ten pounds of powder; to my surprise, saw more than nine out of ten burnt under water.

An objection which I have frequently heard made to the use of shells on board of a ship is, the danger of having a quantity of loaded shells continually on board; to me, loaded shells have always appeared less dangerous than powder in cartridges, or in any other form. I placed each loaded shell in a box; these were stowed in the shell room in rows, retained by stancheons and shifting battens; and on the lid of each box was written the length of each fuzee, and the nature of the shell; each shell was handed up in its box, and only taken out of it at the moment of being placed in the gun; how there can be any danger in using shells thus, sufficient to justify an objection to their use, I am at a loss to conceive; certainly there is danger in using gunpowder at all, but there is less liability to accident from a shell, than from a cartridge; and I am prepared to prove, however paradoxical it may appear at first sight, that the liability to accidents from explosion on board a ship, is much diminished by the use of shells. I have fired about eighteen thousand shells from this ship, and have never had the slightest accident from explosion; the guns have never broken a breeching, drawn a bolt or injured a carriage. I was in but two naval actions in the British service, in each of which we had accidents. In the Neptune, in the battle of Trafalgar, an explosion on the lower deck killed and wounded sixteen men. In the Seahorse, with the Badra Zaffar, a gun going off while loading, killed one or two men.

I went with the Karteria into the Piraeus, to batter a Monastery possessed by the Turks; our shells did infinite mischief: there was a storehouse to the right of the Monastery, in which it was remarked there were some Turks; I ordered our fire to be directed upon it; two shells, bursting at the same moment inside, brought the whole fabric to the ground, leaving but a heap of stones, out of which walked, to our surprise, five Turks, proving (what I have remarked on other occasions,) how much less destructive to life Artillery is than people usually imagine. Upon another day I went into Piraeus, to support Colonel Gordon, who was attacked by Kutayi Pashaw: the Turks had several pieces of Artillery, and fired chiefly grenades from howitzers at us: several of these struck us without exploding; but one, from an eighteen pounder, exploded in the counter, and tore out the planking of two streaks for a length of six feet, and started out the planking from the two adjacent streaks; in a sea way, a ship, built in the usual manner, *(Note 9)* would have been sunk by the explosion of nine ounces of powder; what then might not be expected from the explosion of two and a half pounds of powder, which a sixty-eight pound shell contains, even with space for some incendiary composition.

I was engaged with some fascine batteries at Oropos; a shell set fire to one, and burnt it entirely, blowing up the powder they had in it. I was engaged in the harbour of Volos with the batteries; our shells did great execution, and some hot shot set a part of the town on fire, which was, however, soon extinguished. I was engaged in endeavouring to destroy a Turkish brig at Tricheri. I fired hot shot, and burnt her; one shell exploded on board of her; but this was after she was on fire.

Perceiving that the weight of our shot broke frequently through both sides of small vessels, and required long to heat, I imagined at Salona to heat empty shells, for which purpose I plugged up the fuzee hole; whilst heating them, the air expanding inside, forced out the plugs with a considerable explosion: I afterwards fired them with the fuzee hole open. If I were to use them again, I should stop up the fuzee hole, all but a very small vent to carry off the rarefied air. On this occasion I fired hot shells from a short long forward; carcass shells, with five orifices, from a short long aft, and shells from two carronades: but by the time we had fired twice, a brig of war blew up, owing to a shell exploding in her magazine; an armed transport brig sunk forward, owing to a shell exploding in her bow, and was set on fire aft by a hot shell. A schooner of war was set on fire by a carcass, at least I imagine so; although, in contradiction to the statement to his Consul at Patras, of an Austrian serving on board another Turkish schooner at Salona; who says, the Turks set fire to her; in all else his statement and mine agree. My reason for thinking we burnt her, is, that as she continued firing after all the other vessels were abandoned, I ordered the after gun to fire a few carcass shells into her; and as I saw one strike her, I have reason to think the Austrian mistaken. Another schooner, of sixteen brass twelves, had received two of our shells; one burnt on board, toe up the deck, and killed three men; the other was found in the hold, and had not burnt; she was abandoned *(Note 10.)* We were distant about five hundred yards from the enemy, and fired with four pounds of powder at point blank, to obtain the lowest ricochets. I always prefer ricochet against shipping in smooth water; at a similar distance I should fire, another time, at three pounds. With four pounds our short longs only recoiled about two feet; we had previously ascertained this, and, therefore, only ran the muzzles just outside the ports, when firing with low charges.

Previous to entering the Gulf of Lepanto, I had fired at the fortress of Vasiladhi, without success. A previous knowledge of the position of Vasiladhi is requisite to understand this account of our operations; I will, therefore, describe it for the advantage of such as know nothing about the place. It is a miserable little fort, built on a small island in the middle of the canal to Missolongi, and, therefore, commands the passage by sea to that town; for one mile outside there is no more than three feet of water, and frequently but one foot; and at about three thousand yards is found quarter less two, where I used to anchor when bombarding it; add to the great distance, the object being about four feet above the surface of the water, renders it a mark extremely difficult to hit. There is a passage for boats of three or four feet water close to the walls of Vasiladhi; but it is very intricate and winding. At first I tried firing en ricochet, but made wretched practice of it; all our shells and shot turning off from the fort to the right and left on striking the water, and I do not think we put one, out of a hundred, into the place; they almost all exploded in the water. The fuzees of the shells may be supposed to have occasioned this deviation on striking the water; yet this was never remarked to such an extent on any other occasion; and, as the shot were not more correct than the shells, and as they invariably turned from the fortress, I am inclined to attribute this deviation to the shallowness of the water, and to the mud receding round the fort.

On another occasion I bombarded Vasiladhi, and fired at high angles elevation, with eight pounds of powder; the weather appeared favourable, the water smooth, and but little wind; yet our practice was not good; the shells all varied greatly to the right which was in a contrary direction to the little wind there was; this makes me believe there was a strong contrary current of air aloft. I also found that some error in the ranges was occasioned by a mistake in filling (during the absence of the officer charged with the ammunition *(Note 11)*, some eighteen pound cartridges with fine powder. Some days afterwards, I again bombarded Vasiladhi; I fired at the full elevation which our ports admit of with five pounds of powder, the distance about three thousand yards; the direction was correct, and after the third discharge we threw a shell into the magazine, which occasioned the capture of the place. I have now related all the examples respecting the use of shells from guns which have fallen under my observation, and they appear to me conclusive of the amazing superiority they give to the ship using them, over any vessel firing cold shot.

Let us retrace in our minds, for an instant, what has been said, and I think it will be admitted, that hot shot, shells and carcasses, may be used from a ship with that degree of security to the party using them, which is consistent with prudence. Hot shot cannot be a projectile generally used from shipping, nor can it ever be the one exclusively used on board of any vessel, owing to the length of time required to heat them, and the limited number it is possible to heat; they may be used in small quantities from steam vessels in the way I used them. Shells can be generally employed with less danger than ordinary cold shot; because to render shells effective, you must, or ought to increase the calibres of your guns very much, and therefore, to diminish the number of your guns, a few being all that are necessary with shells; thus a vessel, carrying eighteen guns on the present system, might carry eight sixty-eights for the use of shells; so that, in action, instead of having nine cartridges in circulation at once, and nine guns firing, you would only have four cartridges in circulation, and four explosions; you have also (which adds materially to the safety of the thing) so much more room between your guns, and so much less jostling and confusion, and so many more officers to superintend the service of each gun. To this I ascribe the universal absence of accidents on board the Karteria; certainly, not to any superior order or discipline, which was impossible, situated as I was. Of carcass shells it is scarcely necessary to remark, that they are an excellent substitute for hot shot; but I suspect, that after being filled a short time their effort is very uncertain. The only precaution necessary to be taken in using shells, are to leave them placed properly in the guns, and not ram them hard. I had a cavity in my runners to receive the fuzee head; wooden battens are certainly desirable, and fuzees to screw into the orifice of the shells, so as not to protrude; this would increase the precision of fire. The shells should be filled as full as possible, so as to leave the least possible movement for the powder inside during its flight; and some roche, a few, or ant other kind of incendiary composition might be put in also. At close quarters, say two hundred yards, oblong shells might be used with tremendous effect: they would not require wooden battens, and made to contain double the quantity of powder contained in a spherical shell, say five pounds for a sixty-eight pounder, their effect on an adversary would be immense.

It is necessary, in using shells, to pay great attention to the charges of powder, and to adopt it to the ranges, so as to avoid going through both sides of an enemy. I had cartridges of 2, 3, 4, 5, 6,7, 8, 9, and 10 pounds; I used them without any difficulty—any body else can do the same. I should always lay down as a maxim, that any charge, above what will penetrate the enemy's side, is not only a waste of powder, but a mischievous waste of powder; it exposes you to go through both sides of your adversary, and thus lose the effect of the explosion; it diminishes the effect of splinters, it makes a hole more easily plugged up, it renders the fuzee taking fire less certain, it exposes you to break breechings, bolts, carriages, slides, etc.; and it occasions a loss of time in running the guns all the way out, instead of a part. The system of high charges cannot be too much reprobated, *(Note 12.)*.

Every person in the habit of practising with pistols or rifles, knows this; and the same principle not only holds good, but is increased with the size of the gun. It may perhaps be thought that the use of shells would occasion a double expense in the article of powder; this, if true, is not an objection which ought to be allowed to weigh; because it would be literally a saving, if by doubling the expense of powder in a brig, you could make her perform the service of a frigate; but I suspect there would be a saving of powder; because by diminishing the charges, your average charge of gun and shell would surpass by little the now ordinary charge of a gun in the same sized vessel; whereas, in an eighteen gun brig, for example, you would fire nine with shot, and only four with shells; besides which, one broadside of shells would settle the affair with an adversary of equal size, and it would require thirty or forty, or even a hundred discharges, from each gun to decide it with shot. I think I now hear somebody exclaiming, that this may be all very true, but it is unfair.

If nations will settle by treaty what arms it is fair to fight with, I will then content myself with telling you, not to be the first to break the agreement, but to be at all times prepared to encounter with equal arms, whoever does do so; for certain it is, the first nation you beat by sea, will adopt the method which she considers the most likely to beat you in turn.

This objection of unfair is so ridiculous, and so childish, that I should consider I was insulting the understanding of the public by mentioning it, had I not heard it reiterated so often, and by people whose opinions go for something in the world. The fact is, war is the art of killing one's adversary, or taking him, the most speedy way possible; or else why not prohibit all arms but those nature has given us, viz. Our fists? I have heard pretenders to humanity talk of the cruelty of hot shot, shells, etc.; it really appears to me the superlative of cant to talk of the art of war (or, in other words, the method of killing men most expeditiously) and humanity in the same breath. However, even this plea will fail, as it is evident, that fewer lives will be lost when the object is to destroy the ship, than where it is to kill the crew. At Tricheri, I believe there were but two Turks killed in the brig we burnt. At Salona, as nearly as I could learn, nine in the brig were blown up; three in the schooner abandoned; say in all, fifteen or twenty, out of six armed vessels; which with the brig at Tricheri, might mount, in all, sixty-two guns and two mortars, which cost the vanquished twenty-two men at most; not an exorbitant expenditure of lives; and the victors had six killed and a dozen wounded; certainly not an increased expenditure of life. I shall be told, perhaps, that all these vessels were either aground or lashed along side the shore, or, otherwise, their loss would have been greater. Not at all so. Had they been at sea, they would only have been obliged to surrender, (which even Turks will do under similar circumstances,) and the loss is the same.

At Vasiladhi, the Turks lost, I believe, about twelve men out of fifty-one; a much less slaughter than if carried by assault.

M. Paichans exults in the expectation of beating the English by sea with shells; for my part, I cannot see any thing upon which he can found his hopes of superiority, unless the English neglect to use shells also, *(Note 13)* of which there is little likelihood; as even, if they were to allow the French the initiative, they would soon be beaten into an imitation of their enemy. Whist the English use arms similar to those of their enemies, their success will depend on the same causes as heretofore, namely, weapons, and ships of superior workmanship—superior skill in the administration and conducting of such ships and weapons, and superior discipline and courage. The question will not be altered; the real propositions will be changed, but not the relative ones; it will be merely A-4, opposed to B-4, instead of A-1, opposed to B-1. The change which this system would make in the art of war, would probably be to reduce the size, and augment the number of ships of war; and to force combatants to keep that respectable distance formerly observed by our good old forefathers, and thus play skill or luck against one another. It is true, that the use of shells, and the probable perfectioning of steam or some other motive power for impelling vessels, will necessitate an improved system of education for our naval officers; and if the instruction of British naval officers is neglected, and those of the French or any other nation is paid particular attention to, we shall probably be beaten, not because shells are used, or stem is used, but because we use them less skilfully than our adversaries. If, on the contrary, the British naval officers stand, as they should do, a pattern to all the world for theoretical and practical knowledge, British arms will be as successful by sea as they have hitherto ever been *(Note 14)*.

Notes

1. The Greeks, in their endeavour to imitate the Italian word, Vapori, were in the habit of calling the *Karteria* 'Bampori', Pampori' and 'Vampori'.

2. The officer commanding the blockade between Missolongi and Vasiladhi, intercepted a letter from the Governor of Missalongi to the Commandant of Vasiladhi, in which the former exhorts the latter to defend himself courageously, which he has no doubt will be successful, as Vasiladhi contains provisions for six months, and water in greater plenty than salt: he informs him he has sent to Lepanto for sailors, and that, in a few days, he will have fifty large boats, with guns, carrying five hundred men, to raise the blockade between Missolongi and Vasiladhi. As we knew the impossibility of the latter assertion, and as we were satisfied the Commandant of Vasiladhi must know it also, we concluded the whole story to have been arranged on purpose to fall into our hands, and that Vasiladhi, on the contrary, had but little provisions or water; the chances were always in favour of this state of things in a Turkish fort. On capitulating it, we found they really had provisions for six months.

3. Let it not be supposed I depreciate that kind of routine which teaches every body to do the same thing the same way, which preserves a strict uniformity in whatever relates to the service; this is the soul of a military system; and, so far from thinking it carried too far in the British Navy, I imagine, in some instances, it might be extended with advantage: I

only allude to that species of routine which makes the mind reject every improvement, without weighing their merits; which has some such answer as the following ready for every proposition; viz. We have gone on very well till now on the old system, and therefore it is superfluous to change it.

Too strict an uniformity cannot be preserved on all the minutiae of service, on board every ship; the system, of course, should emanate from the Admiralty, each captain, or even every officer, being at liberty to propose, for the consideration of the Admiralty, what might strike him as an improvement, but not to make the slightest change in his ship until the Admiralty should have thought proper to order such change to be generally adopted throughout the Navy. There is, alone, one point of service on which an uniform system, emanating from headquarters, must be prejudicial; I mean the mode of giving battle: this, I believe, in the British service, has ever been left(and very properly so) to the officer commanding: the French, I believe, had some very silly regimens on this head. An officer is unfit for his command, if he cannot be intrusted with this discretionary power; and anyone who sets out with the determination to fight, in some particular way, on all occasions, (and I have known many profess this,) may, it is true, be successful, but he is just as likely to be beaten in all that depends upon him: if his crew bring him off, by their superior courage, under disadvantages his incapacity has placed them under, their's is the merit, his the disgrace.

4. The elevating or tangent sights I had on my guns, were perpendicular sights, of iron, fixed on the reinforcing ring, resembling the sights on a rifle, the top of which, and the sight on the muzzle, form an horizontal line, with the gun at all the elevation the port admits of. It must be admitted, that these sights have the disadvantage of being incorrect, when any motion of the ship throws them off their true perpendicular; but this is an objection common to all elevated sights. I am

certain, that without some such sights, we never could have attained the precision our practice displayed at Vasiladhi.

5. I do not pretend to any very great accuracy, the degrees of elevation or depression at which a gun may be fixed, with the advantage of its shot rising from the water. Must, of course, depend on the height of the gun above the water, the size of shot, and the charge used; shells ricochet better, of course, than shot. The surprising distance our shells went, en ricochet, when firing the first time at Vasiladhi, astonished all who saw it. I should think, that with high charges, and the gun near the level of the water, firing perfectly horizontally, shells would go quite as far, en ricochet, as fired at an angle, giving the greatest range.

6. This warfare was that of the Greeks against the Turks. The Greeks possessed nothing but merchant vessels, mounting from eight to twenty guns, and of these rarely four of the same calibre on board of the same vessel: the calibres varied from three to twelve pounds, and some had a twenty-four pound carronade or two. The Turks had fifty or sixty sail of men of war, from three decked ships, down to schooners, and could put to sea twenty or twenty-five ships of the line and frigates. Whoever knows any thing of naval warfare, will know that the whole of the Greek fleet could not, in twenty-four hours time, have sunk or dismantled a frigate, even supposing that frigate had nobody on board to resist; luckily for the Greeks, neither themselves nor the Turks knew this. The Turks thought (and justly so) that they had achieved an amazing undertaking, when they traversed the Archipelago, without running against a rock; considering how they were manned, it is really surprising they lost so few ships. To man their fleet, they one year pressed all the bakers they could catch: a Christian would suppose their reason to be, that they might be provided with a daily supply of fresh bread; not at all; their reason was, that as bakers were in the habit of sitting up at nights, they would not fail to keep an excellent watch. Another time, they pressed some masons

they found on high preparing a house; a bribe (without this nothing can be done in the East) released the alarmed sons of brick and mortar; but as this transaction was illegal, as well as profitable, the same unfortunate individuals found themselves seized upon a second time, but strenuously refused to use their former agreement for release; they were embarked, as luck would have it, on board the very ship of the Captain Pashaw, and seized the first favourable opportunity of imploring his clemency; he investigated the affair, and finding their complaint well founded, bastinadoed half to death the extortioner, and made him restore the money; not so the masons their liberty, as they had fondly imagined:no; Captain Pashaw was a man of more judgement; he knew how to detect merit; and, therefore, after ascertaining who among the individuals was master mason, ordered him to be made master of the main top, which promotion he was sure would be justified by his conduct, having been accustomed to climb so high. Enough of such anecdotes there are to fill a volume.

7. Lord Byron may have been the first poet of his time, but he knew nothing of Artillery, or even of War, otherwise he would have chosen better the people he had about him at Messolongi. I do not know whether I am more unfortunate in what I am about to complain of than other people, but I am usually cursed with having an authority quoted against me, instead of having a reason opposed to me; it always gives me a mean opinion of the intellect of the person quoting, and is frequently even more unjust towards the individual whose name is thus made use of, than towards him whose scheme is thus disingenuously opposed; there is usually some topic upon which any man, however talented, may make himself ridiculous.

8. The Admiralty is, I believe, in possession of a Report on that steam vessel, the Karteria, (Perseverance,) which is any thing but favourable. I am told she was the subject of the official criticism of a youngster, who had not long finished his course of education at Portsmouth. He declared the vessel

too weak to carry her guns, the engine weak and defective, and pronounced the employment of hot shot and shells as impossible, owing to there not being an artillery officer on board,—to sum up, she was totally unfit for the service she was built for.

This vessel, so far from being weak, was so unnecessarily strong, that I would engage to fire eight-inch mortars from the deck at forty-five degrees, without doing her any injury. As to the strictures on the engine, I would lay a wager this youth did not know the working cylinder from the air pump; he hit exactly on the defect (perhaps the only one,) which the engine had not; it has its faults, but want of strength is certainly not one. Respecting the employment of hot shot and shells; he is guilty of two absurdities in one sentence: 1st There was an artillery officer on board. 2nd I would qualify, in ten days, most naval officers to use shells and hot shot, quite as well as if there were any number of artillery officers on board. I beg, by the bye, to be understood, that I by no means engage myself to instruct the young gentleman in question.

9. The Karteria was built with her timbers close and caulked together; and would, therefore, have floated without planking. I had several opportunities of remarking the advantage of building thus, to resist shot; nothing less than an eighteen pounder ever came through us; this, 'tis true, might be partly attributed to Turkish bad powder; but those shot that did come through, always made a nice clean round hole without a splinter. However, against shells it would have a disadvantage, as they would be more likely to stick in it. Perhaps if shells become generally used, it will be proper to make the upper works of a ship as slight as is consistent with strength, and iron ribs might perhaps be good. The Karteria had another peculiarity in her build—two solid bulk heads inclosing the engine room, and caulked and lined, so as to be water tight; the intention of this was, in the event of one part of the ship being leaky from any cause whatever, the water could not flow into another part of the ship. This

arrangement, which is due to the ingenuity of Mr Brent, the builder, once saved this ship from fire, which broke out with great force in the after-part of the engine room, and would have communicated to the shell room very quickly, but for this bulk-head, which kept the fire forward, and gave us time to subdue it. I see no reason why all men of war should not be furnished with similar partitions. The same builder saved another ship (the Rising Star,) from sinking, by this contrivance.

10. If I were writing the history of the Greek Naval war, I should mention the names of the officers who distinguished themselves in taking possession of the abandoned schooner; as it is, I am only describing the employment of shells, hot shot and carcasses; and the effect was so rapid as to leave nothing to do for the artillery of the other vessel, unless it were to fire on the batteries. The two gun-boats mounted each a short long sixty-eight; and if any thing had been left for their guns to perform, I have no doubt they would have done as much as this vessel. These gun-boats were very formidable craft near the land; one I had with me at Vasiladhi, had beaten off, in the harbour of Katacule, a Turkish brig of twenty-four guns; she then mounted a long thirty-two; I changed it for a sixty-eight. If she had the latter gun when engaged with the brig, she would probably have destroyed her. With the sixty-eight, she would have taken Vasiladhi alone.

11. I had an artillery officer in charge of my ammunition. I always thought that the men called gunners on board a man of war were usually the persons on board the least conversant with artillery. An officer of marine artillery would, I should think, be the proper person to entrust the charge of the artillery stores to. In fact, that class of men, the marines, might be made the most useful men in every respect on board a ship. I could say a great deal on this subject, if it were not foreign to this present work, and sufficient to fill a pamphlet of itself.

12. In the action of the Sea Horse with the Badra Zaffar, all our carronades were rendered useless, by breaking either carriages or slides. I cannot take upon myself to say positively that this was caused by using too high charges, but I am internally convinced such was the cause. An Idriote merchant, a M. Tombrase, had a fine schooner, mounting, among other guns, a forty-eight pound carronade on a swivel; he complained to me that this gun could with difficulty be retained, owing to its excessive recoil. I enquired the charges used, and found he used five ocars, very nearly fifteen pounds, with a forty-eight pound shot from a gun, probably not more than twenty-eight hundred weight; luckily for him, his powder, I suppose, was bad.

13. It must be recollected that the superiority of materiel frequently gave the British Navy a decided superiority over her enemies. The British Navy was the first to place locks on the guns, to use carronades, and many other improvements. The first of these was so n enormous stride in naval gunnery, that I should think it is decisive of any battle fought with an enemy not mounting more than half as many more guns, and using the match. For my own part, I should as soon expect to strike my object from a ship when firing with my eyes shut as with a match.

I entered the British Navy too late, and was too young to judge when I did enter it, of the comparative correctness of British and other firing; but judging from what I can gather, our firing was always better than that of our enemy at very close quarters, because our discipline was better, (not to say any thing of superior courage): but, at great distances, I suspect we generally got the worst of it, because their practice was better. Perhaps carronades may sometimes have occasioned worse firing than long guns at short distances, say from fifty to one hundred yards. The sailor having got into his head the notion that shot rise on quitting the gun, was in the habit (at short distances) of pointing under the object, looking along thye line of metal sight; now if the looking along the line of metal sight of a carronade, he pointed as much below his object as he was in the habit of doing with a long gun, he would always go over his mark at the distance above quoted; because the carronade line of metal gives one degree more elevation than that of the long gun. I know that carronade are cast with disport sights, but these are clumsily imagined, and sailors knew not the intention of them;—that the officers did not, was proved by the white lines they painted along their quarter sights. There was a time, therefore, when the British Admiralty did not disdain using superior weapons to her enemies. I hope the same spirit still pervades it, and that percussion locks on guns, and all other improvements, whether relating to gunnery or any other part of the service of a ship, will be adopted in the British Navy before they find their way into those of other nations.

14. Is it not strange, that in a nation like England, so proud, and so jealous of its naval force, such pains should be taken with the education of officers of the army, whilst that of the officers of the navy is comparatively disregarded? Is it that people think less science requisite to form a military officer by sea, than by land? Do they imagine that the same education (except what gives the manners and feelings of a gentleman,) suffices indiscriminately to qualify a man to command a collier and a vessel of war? I could say much on the subject of the education, not only of boys destined to become officers, but of officers themselves, if it were not foreign to the object of the work, and I had not already trespassed by digressions too long on the patience of my readers.

Appendix 2

Graphology Report by the late Patricia Marne, Graphologist, Essex, England

Re: Frank Abney Hastings

Sex: Male
Specimen submitted: One page of handwriting.
Dated 19th August 1984: Patricia Marne, Graphologist.

This writer was an extremely active man preferring action rather than contemplation. Intelligent and quick witted, he was able to communicate well.

He enjoyed having people around him, wasn't always discreet or tactful but had a great deal of empathy for human weakness.

There are signs of a highly sensitive nature, quick to take offence but his short fuse and sharp temper were over rapidly.

He was a traditionalist and at the time of writing there are signs of considerable mental strain. Under pressure he could act rashly, and not always wisely as his objectivity could be lost in his haste to get things accomplished.

He possessed a dry sense of humour, was inclined to have changeable moods which would have resulted in irritability when thwarted, making him sometimes difficult to deal with.

He was an enterprising man with a sense of justice, and although he could handle authority and delegate when necessary, he was occasionally almost muddled in his thinking when his emotions were involved—and they frequently were. There were times when he was composed and calm, at other times almost lacking in mental discipline.

He could act rashly and perhaps at times not wisely, was a very human man with some aggression and slightly exaggerated self-esteem, but with a huge sense of honour.

His weakness was a tendency to get things done quickly and not always, perhaps, as thoroughly as they might be.

There is a conscientiousness indicated in his script plus a spontaneous curiosity about the world and a need to keep moving.

This writer was used to making decisions and taking the initiative in his sphere of influence, yet shows an underlying subjectivity.

He was impatient with detail and yet observant and had excellent powers of imagination, but was used to having his own way.

Appendix 3

Details of Personalities Mentioned in the Book

Abney—Hastings, Captain Frank—Read the Book!

Ali Pasha of Ioannina (sometimes of Tepelen) was an Albanian and lived from 1741-1822. Ruler (Pasha) of Western Rumelia on behalf of Ottoman Empire with his Court in Ioannina where he kept a vast harem of both girls and boys! Semi—independent despot who ruled much of western Greece and the Peloponnese. Lord Byron visited his court as early as 1809 and this was recorded in his great poem, Childe Harold.

Blaquiere, Edward Blaquiere was a former Irish sea captain and a founder member of the London Greek Committee. He is described by Prof Douglas Dakin as a "radical international busybody". He called upon Byron in Genova in 1823, later spending 2 months in Morea to provide his Report on the State of the Greek Federation to the LGC (London Greek Committee) in September. He was responsible for causing many funds to be raised, and for influencing Lord Byron. He remained in Greece as a Captain and worked closely with Church and Cochrane in the Wars.

Botsaris, Marcos (1788-1823) and **Botsaris,** Gen Kostas (1790-1853) were two sons of Captain Kitsos Botsaris who was murdered in 1809 on the orders of Ali Pasha. Marcos was a klepht (brigand or clan) leader who rose against the Ottomans with other Suliots in Western Greece. Marcos was distinguished in the first defence of Messolongi (1822-1823) and led the attack on Karpensi by 350 Suliots against 4,000 Albanians. He was shot in the head and died, but to this day is remembered as one of the great heroes. On the death of his elder brother, Marcos, Kostas took over and completed the victory at Karpensi. He lived to become a General and Senator in Greece. Whilst a great patriot, he was not regarded as quite such a hero as his elder sibling whose statue shares park space with Byron and Captain Frank in the Greek National Heroes Garden in Messolongi. Kostas' son, Dimitrios (1813-1870) was three time Minister of War under Otto of Greece and King George 1 of Greece.

Brown, J Hamilton. A British "civil servant" who was serving on the Ionian Islands at the outbreak of hostilities, but became instrumental in carrying messages, and more importantly, money, between the London Greek Committee, Byron and many of the revolutionary leaders. He was probably more important than previously acknowledged, in providing the structure which was to finance modern-day Greece

Canning, George (1770-1827). British Statesman and Foreign Secretary from 1822-1827. With Admiral Codrington, he came under fire in Parliament over his handling of the Battle of Navarino and in particular his seeming tacit approval to allow Hastings and Church to continue operations in the north despite a *de facto* armistice.

Canning, Sir Stratford (1786-1880). Nephew of George Canning. British Diplomat and Ambassador on three occasions to the Ottomans in Constantinople. On the first occasion he was forced to flee to London after the Battle of Navarino but the following year (1828) returned to Poros where he and other ambassadors signed the Poros Protocols granting Crete, Samos and Euboea to the new Greek State. He was so castigated by the British government that he was forced to resign.

Capo d'Istrias—See KAPODISTRIAS

Church, Richard (Later General Sir Richard, 1784-1873; 'liberator of Greece'; b. Cork, Quaker; British Army in Egypt, Italy, and Ionian Islands; pleaded for Greek Independence at Council of Vienna. Major in charge of small British force which took Zante in 1809 where he was joined by Kolokotris as a Captain. Served the Neapolitan Government, 1816; expelled by revolutionaries when commander-in-chief of Sicily in 1820. Knighted 1822; led Greek revolutionary campaign in Western Greece; settled in Greece; member of Council of State, inspector general of the Army; d. 30 March 1873, Athens.

Cochrane, Lord. Rear Admiral Lord Thomas, Tenth Earl of Dundonald (1775-1860). Had a remarkable naval career, later becoming an MP, being convicted of stock-exchange fraud in 1814 and imprisoned for a year. He escaped, but was recaptured. From 1817 he commanded the Chilean Navy and went on to command the Brazilian and Greek Navies. There is no doubt that he arrived in Greece as a hero, but by the time he left he was exposed as a fraud and a mercenary. Without Cochrane, the Greek cause would have terminated much earlier, and the monies he misappropriated spent more beneficially. It is also probable that Frank Abney Hastings may not have been wounded and died if Cochrane had not stolen monies donated to the Greek nation, and that these had been used to pay the crews of the Greek Navy ships.

Codrington, Admiral Sir Edward (April 1770-April 1851). In December 1826, Codrington was appointed to the Mediterranean command, and sailed on the 1 February 1827. From that date until his recall on the 21 June 1828 he was engaged in the arduous duties imposed on him by the Greek War of Independence. His orders were to enforce a peaceful solution on the situation in Greece, but Codrington was not known for his diplomacy, and on 20 October 1827 he destroyed the Turkish and Egyptian fleet at the Battle of Navarino while in command of a combined British, French and Russian fleet. He was subject to huge political criticism as a result of his handling of these events.

Ellice, Edward A banker appointed originally by the London Greek Committee, and later working on behalf of Lord Cochrane. Although it seems he realised his mistakes in the end, his support for the "naval hero" certainly caused disagreements with the Greek participants and the London Greek Committee.

Fabvier, Col C., a kinsman of the French Naval Commander, Admiral de Rigny, was a very early participant in the Greek Wars of Independence. He was a skilled, brave and meticulous Army Officer who worked tirelessly for the main Greek force to be comprised of regulars rather than the bands of brigands. He briefly took over as leader of the regular Greek forces in July 1825 and served alongside Karaiskakis, but still had problems with the irregulars under his command. Hastings, Gordon and Church supported him but, as so often, Cochrane did not release sufficient funds. After Navarino he attacked Chios with Cochrane, but was again let down and had to be rescued by de Rigny. This shortness of funds caused him to resign and return to France in August 1828. Fabvier was a character who is not well enough researched and applauded by the Greeks, but he, perhaps more than any other French participant, played a vital role.

Finlay, George (1799-1875), an historian of Scottish descent, was born in Faversham, Kent, where his father, an Army Officer was inspector of government powder mills. His initial training at the Universities of Glasgow and Edinburgh was in law, but as a young man he became an enthusiast for the Greek cause. This was exacerbated by his meetings with Byron and with Frank Abney Hastings. He and Hastings were to become very good friends and he spent many months at sea observing the course of the war at first hand—an ideal viewpoint for an historian. After the war, and Frank's death, he bought a property off Adrianou Street in the district of Athens now known as the Plaka. He was closely involved with the development of the country post war, but met with little success due probably to his involvement with many of the wartime leaders who were either dead or fallen out of favour under the new royalist regimes. His lasting legacy was his History of Greece which he wrote between 1843 and 1861.

Gordon, General Thomas 1788-1841. Born in Aberdeenshire, Scotland, Gordon was educated at Eton College and Brasenose College, Oxford. He first served with the Scots Greys from 1808-1810, but then left and went to meet Ali Pasha at Ioannina. Prior to serving for the Greek cause he spent a period as a Staff Captain with the Russian Army. He became the first British Philhellene to join the Greek forces with his appointment as Chief of Staff to Ipsilantis in the Morea in April 1821, but on seeing the murderous behaviour of the Moreot troops on taking Tripolitsa he resigned. Returning to London he became a founder member of the London Greek Committee in March 1823, but refused to return to Greece due to his mistrust of the Moreots in the Greek Government. Eventually he gave in and was to accompany Frank Abney Hastings as a land commander at the first action of the *Karteria* at Piraeus. He was in agreement with Hastings and Church against Cochrane on the need to attack Turkish supply routes by sea. Gordon's greatest achievement was the writing of his History of the Greek Revolution which was published in 2 Volumes in Edinburgh 1833. Although sometimes in seeming disagreement with the other two major contemporary historians, Finlay and Trikoupis, Gordon's work is certainly one of the great histories of the period.

Hane, Captain John, Arrived in Greece in 1821 and sailed with Frank Abney Hastings and Jarvis on Themistocles in 1822 during the attempts to retake Chios. Later that year the three men were together at Bourzi. Appointed by Frank as his gunnery officer commanding 1,200 men on Crete, and returned with him to England to discuss arrangements with the London Greek Committee and assist the supervision of the building of the ship. Served on the *Karteria* until the death of his friend and Captain. Remained in the Greek Army as Colonel, but as he had married a niece of Mavrokordatos he lost his post in 1842 and lived in near poverty. He only survived with the help of fellow residents of Athens, Finlay, Gordon and Church. He died, it is said, of a broken heart, in September 1844.

Howe, Dr Samuel Gridley Perhaps the most significant American philhellene, Howe was born in 1802, studied at Brown University and qualified in medicine at Harvard. He performed many acts of gallantry and was immortalised in the poem *The Hero* by Whittier where he saved a wounded Greek from a Turkish cavalryman. He joined the *Karteria* as Chief Surgeon to the Greek fleet in 1826. He wrote copious letters and reports to influential Americans and raised huge sums of money. Many of his reports were shared with Finlay. He left military service in 1827 to distribute American relief to Greek civilians.

Ibrahim Pasha (1789-10th November 1848). Perhaps the most well known Egyptian General of the period, he was certainly the main hope for the Ottomans to retain their empire in Greece and the Balkans. He was the eldest son of Muhammed (also written Mehemet) Ali, Governor of Egypt under the Ottomans, and later Governor of Morea, and had become a general at a very early age in successful campaigns against the Wahabi tribes in Arabia, but was called on by the Sultan to lead the Muslim forces from 1823 to quell the Greek independence cause. Captain Frank, and of course the *Karteria* were certainly his greatest single fear, and Frank Abney Hastings did hold his opponent in great awe. After Navarino his time was clearly limited in Greece, and eventually he was forced to leave in 1828 by the French. In 1846 he was received by Queen Victoria in London as one of the world's great military leaders, and when his father became insane he became Viceroy of Egypt for the last months of his life. His son went on to rule Egypt from 1863-1879.

Ipsilantes Prince Alexandros and Prince Constantine. Grandfather and father respectively of brothers Alexandros and Dimitrios. The family lived mostly in Constantinople and were leaders of the Fanariot community. They were wealthy and well connected on the international stage.

Ipsilantes Alexandros (1792-1828). The family moved to Russia in 1805 and Alexandros served very successfully with the Imperial Army becoming a Major General in the Hussars at the age of 25. He was elected as leader of the Filiki Eteria when Kolokotronis turned down the post, and as such led Greek/Russian troops into Greece in 1821. He was defeated by 10,000 Ottoman troops and fled to Austria where he was imprisoned until just before his death in 1828.

Ipsilantes Dimitrios (1793-1832). Like his elder brother he served in the Russian Army until turning to Greece. Appointed by his brother as military commander of the Morea in 1821, and appointed the first of the English Philhellenes, Thomas Gordon, as his Chief of Staff. Dimitrios briefly lead the Greek legislative assembly in 1822/23, and in 1828 was appointed by Kapodistrias as Commander of Eastern Greece. His notable military successes were the defence of Castro Larissa, and his defeat of the Turks at the Battle of Petra in 1829.

Kallergis, Col Dimitrios. (1803-1867) A Cretan military commander who led a force of 1,600 against 11,000 of Ibrahim Pasha's men at Methoni near to Navarino. Fortunately many of his troops were rescued by the late arrival of Mavrokordatos. Subsequently as a General he led the Kapodistrian troops especially in the revolt of 1831 on Poros. He remained as a senior officer much involved with politics, and was one of the leaders of a bloodless coup in 1843.

Kanaris, Admiral Konstantinos (1794-1877) He was born at Psara and headed the naval fleet of that island. He first achieved fame by his actions in 1822 when he destroyed the Turkish flagship and Frank Abney Hastings first attracted his attention. Later that year he was blockading the route between Tenedos and the Asian mainland, and sank one of the largest Turkish men-of-war. He played a significant part in maritime activities during the war, but in the revolt of 1831 he remained loyal to Kapodistrias and in July was arrested by Miaoulis and Mavrokordatos, and his flagship, the *Spetzai,* was seized. He was reunited by his fellow heroes of the wars, and by 1844 undertook the first of 6 separate terms of office as Prime Minister which lasted until his death in September 1877. He was, and is honoured as a Greek national hero.

Kapodistrias, Count Ioannis (1776-1831). A Greek diplomat of the Russian Empire and first head of state of independent Greece. He was born in Corfu (then Venetian), studied medicine in Padova in Italy, and returned to Corfu to establish a medical practice. France had made huge gains in the Ionian islands and fear caused the Russians and the Ottomans to drive out the French, who by then ruled seven islands, and declared an independent Septisinsular Republic appointing Kapodistrias as one of the two ministers of state, and he continued to work for the Russians as a diplomat. By

1822 he had retired to Switzerland but was informed that the new Greek National Assembly had appointed him as the first Governor of Greece. Sadly whilst he brought much sanity, modernity and even the potato to Greece he became hated by the Maniotes, the Rumeliotes and especially the rich ship owning families of Hydra, Spetses and Psara. Having declared revolution Admiral Miaoulis and Mavrocordatos sailed and took much of the Hellenic Navy at Poros in 1831. The *Karteria*, still with the most loyal and disciplined crew, was not taken. Things came to a head when Kapodistrias ordered the arrest of the Maniote leader, Petrobey Mavromichales, whose family took this as a great insult and the Petrobey's brother and son assassinated the first leader of Greece at the church of St Spyridon at Nauplio on October 9th 1831. Today Kapodistrias enjoys his rightful place as a hero of Greece.

Kolokotronis, Theodoros (1770-1843). Kolokotronis learned his military skills at a young age as leader of a group in an armed rebellion in Morea in the early 1800's, and in 1805 he served in the Russian Navy in the Russo-Turkish wars. In 1810 he joined a Greek brigade in the British army on Zakynthos becoming a Brigadier. He served with great honour and distinction through the Wars of Independence, but was imprisoned by Petrobey Mavromichalis astonishingly to be released by Ibrahim Pasha. He then was appointed as the leader of the Greek forces in the Morea, and was a great supporter of Kapodistrias. After the latter's assassination in 1831 he created his own administration in support of Prince Otto of Bavaria, but later fell out with the Bavarian faction. He was charged with treason and sentenced to death in 1834, but the following year was pardoned and lived in Athens until his death in 1843. The most famous monument to him is astride his horse in front of the Old Parliament Building on Stadiou Street in Athens, and his helmet, weapons and armour are on display at the National Historical Museum housed in the same building.

Mavrokordatos, Alexandros (1791-1865) was born of a wealthy Fanariot family in Constantinople and with so many others from the region was educated at Padova University. He became an early member of the Philiki Eteria and rushed to the Morea at the outbreak of the Wars of Independence in 1821. In 1822 he was elected as "President of the Executive" at the first National Assembly, and whilst not a professional soldier, he did lead the unsuccessful Greek assault of the Central Western Mainland in 1822, and more successfully the siege of Messolongi in 1822/3. He was an astute politician who survived various political factions, served three times as Prime Minister and in many other Ministerial and Envoy posts. Perhaps less "swash-buckling" than the naval and military heroes of the wars, Mavrokordatos and many other Phanariots brought an internationalism to the cause without which it would not have been recognised in the world at large.

Mavromichalis, Petros "Petrobey" (1765-1848) came from a Maniot family with a long history of resistance to the Ottomans in the Mani. Although granted the title of Bey (or Chief) by the Sultan in an effort to control him, Petros was a member of the Philiki Eteria and became involved in the early campaigns of 1821/22. He decided to concentrate on politics and left military efforts to two of his sons both of whom were killed. He joined a Senate under Kapodistrias, but they were soon in disagreement and Petrobey along with his brother, Tzanis were imprisoned. As a result, and despite disagreement from Petros, another brother, Konstantinos, murdered Kapodistrias in September 1831. He became Vice President of the State Council under King Otto, and later a Senator.

Miaoulis, Admiral Andreas (1768-1835) was a wealthy corn merchant and ship owner from Hydra and was chosen to lead the island's fleet as "navarch" or Admiral. Very involved and successful in the early years of the war, he commanded the fleet until the arrival of Lord Cochrane in 1827 which caused him to retire from the front line. An active member of the anti-Kapodistrian movement, he was responsible for sending in fire ships at Poros in 1831. Later, with the demise of Cochrane, he was appointed Rear Admiral and then Vice Admiral, by King Otto. He died in Athens in 1835, and today the urn containing his heart is on display at the museum at Hydra.

Tombazis Jakomaki (1782-1829) and Manolis (1784-1850?). Hydriote ship owners and captains who were to play a significant role in the naval wars of independence. They were the first to meet Hastings and Jarvis when they arrived on Hydra in 1822, and supported their applications to sail (along with Hane and other Philhellenes) on their two main warships, the *Themistocles* and the *Leonidas*. Of all the Greek maritime patriots, the brothers probably were the closest to Frank, and they certainly played a major part in the burial arrangements after his death. The Tombazis family were members of the Philiki Eteria and the two brothers worked with Frank Abney Hastings in the establishment of a Hellenic Navy at Poros. They had a great mistrust of Lord Cochrane,and provided a strong voice for his removal from Greece and repayment of the fortune he had accepted. Although early supporters of Kapodistrias, like their fellow Hydriote Admiral, Miaoulis, they later turned against him and were part of the plot to wreck the Hellenic fleet at Poros.

Index

A

Abney, Parnell 14, 15
Abney, Sir Thomas 14
Admiral Saumarez 7
Alexandria, Egypt 34, 108, 109, 116, 154, 155, 157
Ali Pasha 43, 44, 45, 48, 49, 50, 51, 52, 107, 172
Anatoliko 174, 189, 191, 193, 194, 195, 196, 197
Ares 144, 145, 147, 148
Argos 128, 202
Ashby de la Zouch 3, 13, 14, 18, 54, 127, 210
Astakos 172
Athens 60, 62, 111, 112, 128, 130, 136, 137, 138, 140, 141, 144, 149, 150, 152, 154, 204, 205, 208, 209, 246

B

Badra Zaffar 21, 221, 234
Battle of Navarino 167, 168, 241
Blaquiere, Edward 107, 109, 110, 111, 115, 134, 135, 141, 142, 151, 239
Botsaris 44, 45, 48, 50, 239
Bourdzi 129, 157
Brent, Daniel
, Shipbuilder 116
British School at Athens 4, 11
Brulots 66
Byzantium 34, 35, 36, 37, 38, 40, 52

C

Caen 32, 33, 126
Canning, George 156, 240

Cape Papas 158, 160, 165, 166, 170
Castel Tornese 153
Castles of Morea and Rumelia 169
Church, General Sir Richard 3, 34, 35, 36, 37, 38, 40, 42, 46, 47, 111, 134, 141, 142, 143, 144, 150, 151, 152, 153, 154, 157, 158, 160, 164, 165, 168, 169, 170, 172, 174, 176, 180, 183, 185, 189, 190, 191, 193, 194, 195, 197, 198, 205, 207, 208, 209, 210, 239, 240, 241, 242, 243
Clavell, Captain John 25, 31
Cochrane, Admiral Lord 9, 31, 110, 116, 117, 118, 122, 123, 124, 130, 131, 132, 134, 135, 141, 142, 143, 144, 150, 151, 152, 153, 154, 158, 160, 163, 164, 166, 168, 169, 170, 174, 175, 177, 178, 179, 180, 181, 185, 213, 239, 241, 242, 243, 247, 248
Codrington, Admiral Sir Edward 156, 157, 159, 160, 165, 166, 167, 168, 169, 240, 241
Constantinople 34, 35, 36, 38, 39, 40, 41, 42, 43, 45, 49, 50, 53, 137, 156, 157, 160, 244

D

Dardanelles of Lepanto 158, 160, 170

E

Egina 134, 135, 136, 139, 142, 176, 177, 179, 181, 182, 186, 190, 197, 198, 199, 213
Ellice, Edward 111, 113, 115, 131, 242
Epicheirisis 182

F

Fabvier, Colonel 136, 150, 154, 168, 169, 181, 182, 189, 242
Finlay, George 1, 2, 9, 11, 60, 107, 112, 113, 121, 122, 124, 125, 126, 127, 130, 134, 151, 152, 175, 176, 180, 182, 183, 185, 186, 187, 190, 191, 196, 198, 199, 200, 201, 202, 203, 204, 208, 209, 210, 242, 243, 244
Fireships 66
Freemantle Captain Thomas 7, 15, 17, 18, 19, 20, 21

G

Galloway, Alexander 116, 119, 123, 130, 176
Garden of Heroes 4
Gordon, General Thomas 1, 115, 128, 136, 137, 138, 139, 143, 144, 150, 151, 152, 154, 176, 199, 201, 208, 209, 221, 242, 243, 245
Graphology Report 237
Greek Navy 161, 177, 180, 183, 188, 204
Gulf of Corinth 164

H

Hamilton, Captain 109, 114, 132, 135, 141, 142, 143, 240
Hane, John 62, 63, 110, 111, 118, 126, 127, 129, 130, 132, 134, 139, 147, 161, 164, 173, 198, 201, 202, 203, 204, 208, 209, 213, 243, 248
Hasting, General Sir Charles 26, 30, 31, 55
Hastings, General Sir Charles 7, 15, 16, 18, 21
Hastings, General Sir Charlesl 14
Hastings, Warren 26
Heideck, General 140, 141
Hellas 130, 132, 133, 140, 142, 151, 153, 158, 168
Hellenic Maritime Museum 4
Hickey, Captain Fred 22
HMS Anaconda 7, 23, 24
HMS Atalante 7, 22, 23
HMS Elk 7, 25
HMS Iphizerea 8
HMS Kangaroo 8, 26, 27, 122
HMS Neptune 7, 15, 17, 18, 19, 20
HMS Orlando 25
HMS Pelican 7, 25
HMS San Domingo 7, 22
HMS Seahorse 7, 20, 21
HMS Victory 7, 16, 17, 19, 22
Hobhouse, John Cam 111, 113, 115, 125
Howe, Dr Samuel Gridley 114, 115, 133, 140, 147, 180, 191, 195, 209, 243
Hydra 53, 54, 56, 57, 58, 59, 62, 64, 65, 107, 108, 112, 130, 134, 137, 153, 160, 166, 168, 182, 188, 191

I

Ibrahim Pasha 108, 109, 110, 112, 114, 135, 153, 157, 159, 160, 172
Iphizerea HMS 27

J

Jackson, General Andrew 23, 24
Jarvis, George 8, 54, 56
Jourdain, Count Philippe 62, 63
Jourdan 218

K

Kanaris, Admiral Constantinos 64, 207, 208, 245
Kapodistrias, Ioannis 9, 45, 46, 48, 49, 50, 134, 135, 143, 178, 179, 180, 181, 185, 186, 189, 190, 198, 207, 245, 246, 247, 248
Kimi 149, 150

Kolokotronis, Theodoris 9, 41, 44, 45, 46, 48, 49, 50, 105, 107, 112, 134, 141, 142, 143, 150, 151, 157, 180, 207, 208, 244, 246

L

Lepanto, Gulf of 158, 178, 213, 223
London Greek Committee 65, 105, 106, 110, 111, 113, 115, 123, 242, 243
Loutraki 185

M

Marseilles 8, 34, 52, 54, 55
Maurice and Françoise Renee 32
Mavrokordatos, Alexandros 9, 41, 50, 58, 59, 61, 63, 104, 105, 107, 112, 114, 127, 135, 143, 180, 196, 209, 243, 245, 246, 247
Mavromichalis, Petros 48, 50, 52, 207, 246, 247
Messolongi 4, 104, 105, 106, 127, 128, 131, 145, 148, 166, 172, 173, 174, 189, 193, 204
Miaoulis, Admiral Andreas 64, 108, 114, 127, 132, 140, 141, 142, 143, 151, 157, 177, 207, 245, 246, 247, 248
Misticos 195
Monastery at St. Spyridon 137
Munchya 138, 140, 141, 150, 153

N

Napier, Colonel Charles 106, 107, 110, 111
National Historical Museum 4
Nauplio 105, 107, 109, 110, 112, 113, 118, 125, 128, 130, 132, 157, 179
Navarin 114, 157, 158, 159, 160, 164, 165, 166, 168, 169, 177, 178
Neptune, HMS 221
New Orleans 23, 24, 26, 31, 57
New Orleans, Battle of 7

O

Oropos 140, 141, 143, 144

P

Pakenham, Sir Edward 23, 24
Paris 8
Parker, Captain Hyde 8, 27, 28, 29, 30, 33
Patras
    Gulf of Patras 52, 158, 160, 164, 165, 166, 169, 171, 172, 184, 204, 222
Phaleron 137, 154, 204, 205
Piraeus 4, 10, 136, 137, 138, 139, 151, 152, 153, 204, 221
Popham, Rear-Admiral Sir Home 27

Popham, Sir Home 27, 30, 33
Poros 142, 144, 149, 150, 151, 153, 154, 177, 185, 186, 189, 190, 191, 194, 195, 198, 205, 206, 245
Port Royal 8, 27, 28, 31
Port Royal, Jamaica 27
Portsmouth 15, 16, 17, 19, 20, 187, 232
Psara 64, 108, 150, 245, 246

R

Rawden, Sir Francis 15

S

Salamina 136, 137
Salona 104, 105, 159, 160, 163, 164, 165, 167, 222, 226
Samathraki 68
Samos 220
Sauveur 142, 154, 158, 159, 161, 162, 163, 164, 182
Scio 64, 65, 66, 108, 168, 181, 182
Scott, Captain Edward, R.N. 127
Scott, Edward Hinton 11, 25, 54, 127, 199, 201, 202, 203, 204
Seahorse, HMS 221
Sea of Marmara 68
Spetses 108, 130, 134, 141, 246
SS Epicheirisis 176, 198
SS 176
Stewart
 ,Captain John 7
Stewart, Captain John 20, 21
St Pauls Anglican Church , Athens. 208

T

Thermistocles 58, 59, 62, 63, 64, 65, 66, 144, 145, 147, 148, 150
The Society for the Study of Hellenic History 4
Tombazis, Manolis 57, 58, 59, 62, 180, 186
Trafalgar 19, 20, 26, 33, 57, 221
Trafalgar, Battle of 7
Treaty of London 156, 157, 159, 160
Trelawny, Edward 104, 105, 107, 112, 114
Tricheri 222, 226
Trikeri 144, 145, 147, 148, 149, 153
Trontheim 53, 54, 55, 56

V

Vasiladhi 4, 172, 173, 176, 177, 181, 190, 213, 214, 223, 226, 229, 230, 231, 234
Victory, HMS 127
Villeneuve, Admiral 17, 18, 20
Volos 144, 145, 147, 149, 150, 153, 169

W

Willesley 11, 13, 14
  Willesley Hall 14, 16, 22, 24, 25, 32, 113

Z

Zante 44, 46, 47, 54, 105, 106, 165, 180, 187, 194, 196, 199, 200, 203